A SEAT FOR LIFE

by

Tony Paterson

Introduction by Lord George Thomson of Monifieth

© Tony Paterson 1980

DUNDEE
DAVID WINTER & SON LTD.
15 SHORE TERRACE

ISBN 0 902804 06 5

A SEAT FOR LIFE

the story of Winston S. Churchill when he was Liberal Member of Parliament for Dundee from 1908-1922.

Promoted from Under Secretary of the Colonies to the crucial post of Minister at the Board of Trade Winston stands outside 10 Downing Street. *(By permission of the Daily Mirror)*

To Norma

CONTENTS

A SEAT FOR LIFE

Chapters:

ACKNOWLEDGEMENTS

Lady Soames, for permission to reprint a number of Clementine Churchill's words quoted from "Winston S. Churchill".

Lord George Thomson who kindly read the proofs and wrote the Foreword.

D. C. Thomson & Co. Ltd., for permission to reprint photographs, cartoons, and for all the excellent and clearly reported material drawn on for this book; also those members of present day staff who have been so helpful with advice and information.

Miss A. M. Scrymgeour for information and memories of 'Neddy' Scrymgeour.

Miss Flora Scrymgeour for kindly lending me her autograph book.

The Glasgow Herald; The Sunday Times; The Observer; Miss Bradish of The Churchill Trust; Mrs Broome, The National Trust, Chartwell; The late Robin Richardson for his early encouragement; The late Sir Garnet Wilson; Mrs Janet Weatherhead; Fladgate & Co., London; Mr George Ritchie; Mr Peter Connors; Mr D. G. Simpson; Mr G. S. Henderson; Mr G. McGregor; Mr R. D. Johnston; Mr Stevenson; Mr Macdonald; D. C. Thomson & Co. Ltd.; Low and Bonar Textiles Ltd.; Mrs N. Davey, Barrack Street Museum, Dundee; Mrs Elma Gibson; Dundee Liberal Club; Dundee Labour Party; The Abertay Historical Society; The staff of The Library, University of Dundee; The staff of Dundee Public Libraries, Barrack Street, Dundee; The staff of Dundee Reference Library; Churchill College, Cambridge; Mr Roger Pennington.

And the following printed authorities:

"Winston Churchill" by Henry Pelling, Macmillan & Co. Ltd., London.

"Winston S. Churchill" Vols. 1 and 2, by Randolph S. Churchill, Wm. Heinemann Ltd., London.

"Winston S. Churchill" Vol. 3, by Martin Gilbert, Wm. Heinemann Ltd., London.

"Churchill: A Study in Failure" by Robert Rhodes James, Weidenfeld & Nicolson Ltd., London.

"Churchill's Complete Speeches" 8 Vols. Robert Rhodes James.

"Churchill, 4 Faces and the Man" Penguin Press.

"Winston Churchill As I Knew Him" by Violet Bonham Carter, Eyre & Spottiswoode Ltd., London.

"The Life of F. E. Smith, 1st Earl of Birkenhead, F.E." by his son the 2nd Earl of Birkenhead, Eyre & Spottiswoode Ltd., London.

"The World Crisis" by Winston S. Churchill, Thornton & Butterworth.

"Thoughts and Adventures" by Winston S. Churchill, Odhams.

"My Early Life" by Winston S. Churchill, Odhams.

"Great Contemporaries" by Winston S. Churchill, Thornton & Butterworth.

"The River War" by Winston S. Churchill, Longmans Green.

"Study of a Genius" by Hugh Martin, Victor Gollancz Ltd., London.

"E. D. Morel, The Man and His Work" by F. S. Cocks, Allen & Unwin Ltd., London.

"With Winston Churchill at the Front" by Captain A. D. Gibb, Gowans & Gray.

"Breaking the Fetters" by Robert Stewart.

"Memories and Reflections" by the Earl of Oxford and Asquith, Cassell & Co., London.

"Rolling of the Thunder" by William Gallacher, Lawrence & Wishart Ltd., London.

"Revolt on the Clyde" by William Gallacher, Lawrence & Wishart Ltd., London.

"Last Memoirs" by William Gallacher, Lawrence & Wishart Ltd., London.

"Making of a Lord Provost" by Garnet Wilson, David Winter & Son Ltd., Dundee.

ILLUSTRATIONS

PREFACE by the Rt. Hon. Lord Thomson of Monifieth, who as George Thomson was MP for East Dundee 1952-72

I would not have believed it possible to write something new about the life and times of Winston Churchill. Yet this is what Tony Paterson has succeeded in doing. He has provided a distinctive addition to the mountain of Churchilliana by concentrating on Churchill's relationship with one constituency which he represented for fourteen years. He was in fact Dundee's longest-serving MP since the Reform Act until I had the good fortune to outdistance him by half-a-dozen years. He called it "A seat for life" when he accepted the Dundee Liberals' invitation in 1908.

It was not quite that, but it turned out to be a seat for one of the several political lives which made up Churchill's historic career. His defeat in Dundee, so dramatically described here, was one of several watersheds in his life. When he left Dundee he is said to have remarked wryly that in the twinkling of an eye he had lost his seat, his party—and his appendix.

I recall the late Randolph Churchill, when he was beginning the mammoth task of his father's official biography, asking me about some of the background to his father's period as MP for Dundee. Randolph Churchill startled me by saying that in the 'thirties his father was depressed and became convinced that he was going to die a failure. My first reaction was that it seemed inconceivable to think of Churchill as a failure, but on reflection I realised that night might have been the verdict of history if the course of the Second World War had not thrust him into the role of an heroic Prime Minister, personifying the British people standing alone in the face of Fascism.

It would certainly have been the verdict of Dundee where old and bitter memories of the events described in this book died hard even as the war went on.

For me, Mr Paterson's book stirs many personal memories of a different kind. Like Churchill I became MP for Dundee at a by-election on which national attention was focused. It lacked, I am happy to say, the passion and turbulence of the campaigns described here. But it was in many ways the last pre-television election, when people flocked to meetings, when a Caird Hall meeting was not a matter of a few hundred huddled in the front rows, but was still judged, as in Churchill's day, by how many were turned away to form an overflow gathering outside. It was still the age of the heckler, whom Dundee produced in rich abundance.

It was the period of the Bevanite argument in the Labour Party.

The Tory hecklers were sent out primed with a supply of quotations from some of the more colourful rhetoric of Aneurin Bevan. I was asked whether I agreed with some of his famous attacks on the Tories. I had a good deal of fun quoting back some of the violent descriptions of the Conservative Party delivered by Churchill from the same platform on which I was standing. Aneurin Bevan, I said innocently, was much too moderate-minded a man to use such language about the Conservatives!

Winston Churchill had just become Prime Minister in 1952 and the political ghost of Dundee's former MP kept walking across my platforms. One of my chairmen, faced with a particularly rowdy meeting, told the story of a notorious Churchillian heckler, a lady with a dinner bell which she rang every time she disagreed with Winston, which was frequently. There was also a well-intentioned but inexperienced chairman who said that in accordance with the best democratic practice he would take a vote on whether the audience wished to hear Winston Churchill or the lady with the dinner bell. There was a big majority for the dinner bell, and the meeting came to an unruly end. My chairman warned my hecklers that he had no intention of allowing any democracy to rear its head from the floor at my meeting.

On the eve of poll an elderly voter wished me a victory as decisive as the one in which he had taken part in 1922, when he remembered the voters zig-zagging their way from the public house door to the polling booth door to vote against Churchill by voting for Neddy Scrymgeour and Total Prohibition!

But as far as I was concerned, Winston Churchill had the last word. In 1952 I enjoyed a famous victory, and due to national circumstances quite outside my control, the Labour majority had spectacularly increased. As I walked up the Floor of the House to be introduced, the Labour benches erupted. They shouted across at the Prime Minister—"Resign! Resign! It's the voice of Dundee." Winston, by this time a deaf old man but looking more cherubic than usual, listened to the clamour for a moment or two. Then he began an elaborate ritual of fumbling with his hearing aid, removing it, and tucking it in his waistcoat pocket. By the time he had finished, every eye was on the Prime Minister enjoying his little joke, and the victor of the East Dundee by-election was forced into second place. The voice of Dundee had been switched off.

CHAPTER I.

THE CARPET-BAGGER

POLLING DAY SATURDAY MAY 9th 1908 dawned bright and sunny and Dundee's dingy streets took on an unaccustomed gaiety. For the first time rosettes showing the party colours were worn, selling by their thousands. The Unionists sported blue, or alternatively red white and blue, the Liberals red and yellow, Labour red or tartan, the Prohibitionists white, and the Suffragettes white and green. Also for the first time motor cars were used on a large scale to carry voters to the poll and to advertise the candidates. Some bore placards saying "Vote for Churchill" and others "Baxter This Time" although the Labour candidate, with his flimsy resources, had to be content with a fleet of bicycles decorated with posters and red and white streamers. At every polling station the Suffragettes were on duty to waylay and whisper to each of the all-male electors as they came in to record their votes, "Keep the Liberal out Sir." The Dundee Irish, despite the strictures of their priests, cried "Keep in Churchill, Dundee's Churchill, Churchill boys, hooray!"

The excitement and interest generated nationwide by a contest which, not only presented a prominent politician fighting for his political career, but also a Liberal Government in difficulties faced with a second vote of no confidence, ensured a tremendous turnout, and long before the close of the poll it was known that the voting had been more than usually heavy. This fact may or may not have been a good thing as far as Winston was concerned; and as the votes were being counted amid the noisy echoing bustle of the Sheriff Court-house, cleared for the occasion, it seemed that the result would be very close. "There was," Winston recalled afterwards, "a wave of panic amongst friends and helpers from London and the large staff of Press correspondents who followed the contest. It was said I was out again, and that this would be final."

In his decision to fight Dundee, an industrial and predominantly working class constituency, when he could have had the pick of safer seats, Winston displayed his characteristic panache. But, as usual, choosing to dash gloriously towards the hottest fight in the battlefield he took a risk bordering on the reckless, for a great gulf lay between him and his prospective constituents.

Winston's early childhood had been dominated by aristocratic tradition. His father, Lord Randolph Spencer Churchill, was the third son of the seventh Duke of Marlborough and a successful young Tory politician. His mother, Jenny Jerome, was a beautiful American heiress famous in society circles; the high-spirited daughter of Leonard Jerome a New York journalist and dashing man of business.

Winston's father Randolph possessed wit, originality and daring and, proclaiming the new creed Tory democracy, had won not only popular acclaim for his flamboyant oratory but revitalised the tired conventionality of both the Tory and Liberal parties. As Winston observed in his biography of his father: "He warmed the heart of England and strangely stirred the imagination of her people."

Lord Randolph had met Jenny Jerome at a ball on board the cruiser "Ariadne" anchored off Cowes in August 1873 which was given in honour of the Czarevitch and Czarevna. He was then twenty-four and she was nineteen. On a tour of Europe with her mother and sister Claire, Jenny was perfectly at home in the circles of the international aristocracy. She had been born in Italy where her father was United States Consul at Trieste and had been educated in the Paris of Napoleon III and the Empress Eugenie. Her father, an adventurer aristocrat in the American mould, had won and lost several fortunes before settling down as owner and co-editor of the New York Times. He was the principal founder of the first two great race courses established in the States—Jerome Park and the Coney Island Jockey Club, and is regarded as the father of the American turf. Randolph and Jenny fell in love at first sight and after a whirlwind courtship, during which strenuous efforts were made by both families to break off the proposed match, they were finally married at the British Embassy in Paris on April 15th 1874.

Winston, born only seven months later at the end of November, 1874, was to be taunted later by envious rivals as being "a young man in a hurry."

Tenderly cared for by his nanny Mrs Everest, Winston saw little of his parents with their busy public lives, and could only love them from afar. He was not what everyone would have considered a loveable child. Red haired, freckled, snub-nosed, cheekily bright, with pale blue eyes and a precocious bubbling vitality, he was difficult to live with. "Not much yet, but a good un" Lord Randolph once apologised to Bram Stoker the Irish civil servant who later became famous as the author of 'Dracula'. Nevertheless Mrs Everest loved him.

At seven years of age Winston was sent away from home to endure the stern rigours of a preparatory school, which, unknown to his parents, was run by a sadistic headmaster. There, every week the little boys would be gathered together in the Great Hall to hear the cries of those of their companions who had committed misdemeanours being beaten on the bare buttocks until the blood ran. Winston lived in a state of fear and anxiety, though his letters to his parents stoically told them nothing. Hating the Headmaster, Winston brooded and plotted revenge. At last he kicked the Headmaster's hat to pieces but was caught and beaten like the others. Only after his health began to deteriorate was he taken away.

He recovered at his next Prep. school under the kindlier regime of two maiden ladies in Brighton. He must have tried their patience. He was cheeky in a particularly annoying way. Once when told to call out in class the number of good conduct marks he had received, and to say "No" if he had not lost any, Winston persisted in calling out "Nein"; and his blue eyes opened wide in innocent astonishment when the class mistress told him not to talk nonsense, he couldn't have lost nine. "But I was only talking German" he replied.

Games did not attract him, but he was fascinated by toy theatricals. When the holidays came he blew his pocket money and threw himself into a grandiose production of Aladdin – though it is not recorded if it ever got beyond rehearsals! When he was eight he took part in a school play, and although his slight impediment of speech might have inhibited an other child, Winston performed with verve, relying on his exceptional memory and his inbuilt sense of drama. It was at this time he founded and wrote The Critic, one of several competing school journals – there was only one issue!

Winston's health remained delicate, and on the Brighton seafront he caught a chill and nearly died of double pneumonia. Once again he recovered, but he was left with a weak chest, and when the time came for his entry to Eton, his father's old school, he was entered instead for Harrow, which stands on high ground clear of the Thames' damp fogs.

Despite, or perhaps because of, these brushes with mortality, Winston early on had a burning sense of his own destiny. In a birthday book at the date November 30th the signature Winston Spencer Churchill is followed by these lines from "Paradise Lost":

"To reign is worth ambition though in hell;
Better to reign in hell than serve in heaven."

Although his interest in the world around him had been awakened by the Brighton ladies, Winston's aptitude for academic studies remained minimal, and it was only due to his father's influence that he managed to scrape into Harrow.

"I did not do well in examinations." Winston recalled in later life, bringing hope to generations of poor scholars, "this was especially true of my entrance examination into Harrow. The Headmaster, Mr Welldon, however, took a broadminded view of my Latin prose: he showed discernment in judging my general ability. This was the more remarkable, because I was found unable to answer a single question in the Latin paper. I wrote my name at the top of the page. I wrote down the number of the question '1.' After much reflection I put a bracket round it thus '(1).' But thereafter I could not think of anything connected with it that was either relevant or true. Incidentally there arrived from nowhere in particular a blot and several smudges. I gazed for two whole hours at this sad spectacle: and then merciful ushers collected my piece of foolscap with all the others and carried it up to the Headmaster's table. It was from these slender indications of scholarship that Mr Welldon drew the conclusion that I was worthy to pass into Harrow. It is very much to his credit. It showed that he was a man capable of looking beneath the surface of things: a man not dependent upon paper manifestations. I have always had the greatest regard for him."

Accordingly, Winston was admitted into the lowest form, and for the next four and a half years, within the rigid confines of the public school curriculum, showed neither ability for work or games, with the sole exception of English language which was the only subject the Masters thought he could come to grips with. That, he learned thoroughly, if nothing else.

What he disliked most about games was that there was no romance in them. Winston's idea of football was to gallop round shouting "For St. George, St. Dunstans and the Devil!" Harrow did not take much to that sort of attitude. He once went so far as to organise a campaign against football during the examination period known as Trials Week, on the ground that it was contrary to an ancient statute of the school which laid down that it was injurious to serious study. Surprisingly, the school authorities conceded he had a point, but Winston's reputation was not enhanced by this victory in the eyes of his fellow pupils.

He never emerged from the Junior school because of his lack of academic attainment, but received instead the dubious glory of being appointed Head of the Fags when he grew too old to be a Fag himself. It was in this humiliating situation that Winston took to journalism.

The editor of the school magazine was Leopold Amery, a distinguished sixth former and head of his house. Some time earlier Winston, mistaking the diminutive Amery for a Fag, had pushed him from behind into the swimming pool. Realising almost at once the enormity of his crime he made haste to apologise. "I am very sorry" he said. "I mistook you for a fourth form boy. You are so small." Amery naturally took this as insult upon injury and Winston, aware that his remarks had not yet had the desired effect, added, "My father, who is a great man, is also small." Completely disarmed, Amery laughed, and after telling Winston off about his cheek signified that the incident was closed. Soon after Winston was permitted by Amery to launch out in the magazine under the pen name "Junius Junior" a vigorous attack upon the management of the school gymnasium.

"What I ask," wrote Junius Junior with florid exuberance, "and what the school asks – and will ask – is: Why did so few boys do anything? Why was the performance watched from the gallery by two members of the school eight? . . . All these things serve to suggest that there is something rotten in the state of Denmark. I have merely stated the facts; it is not for me to offer an explanation of them. To you, sirs, as directors of public opinion, it belongs to lay bare the weakness." Amery added in an editorial note "We have omitted a portion of our correspondent's letter which seemed to us to exceed the limits of fair criticism."

Despite these precocious flights, Winston was still very much a little boy, and at home during the holidays loved to play with a complete and beautiful set of toy soldiers. Once on a rare occasion his father, also at home, observed him playing with them and asked if he would like to be a soldier when he grew up. Winston replied, "Yes" without thinking, little realising that by that artless response his future had been decided upon. He was only to discover later that his father considered him too stupid to enter the Law.

The year 1893 therefore found Winston at a special "cram" school where he hoped to acquire sufficient knowledge to pass the entry examination for the military college at Sandhurst. At his second attempt he scraped home.

Just before he was due to enter the college he went on holiday to Bournemouth with his cousins. They were still schoolboys but Winston was not too old to take part in their games. One day being chased by them Winston found himself cornered on a bridge which crossed a deep cliff gully. Certain to be caught by his pursuers, now at either end of the bridge, Winston got the crazy idea that if he jumped and grasped the tip of one of the young fir trees level with him, which were growing from the foot of the ravine, he might slide down safely, trusting to the branches to break his fall. They did not, and he crashed thirty feet and nearly died of a ruptured kidney. He was laid up for the best part of the year.

Convalescence brought Winston one benefit – for the first time in his life he was to get to know his parents better. Although his father Randolph was only a shadow of his former self – exiled to the back-benches since resigning as Chancellor of the Exchequer, and in failing health, prey to a demoralising disease which was wasting away his once magnificent intellect – the Churchill's town house continued nevertheless as a mecca for all the young Tory notables and elder statesmen. In his mother's drawing room Winston drank in day after day the heady wine of politics. In his father's library he read the bound volumes of his father's speeches; and in the members gallery of the House of Commons, during the second reading of the debate on the second Home Rule Bill for Ireland, he watched and listened with wonder. For the first time, he began to understand why his father was truly "a great man," as he had described him with childish pride to his friends at Harrow. Winston admired and wished to emulate the power of his father's words and the ideals for which he had fought. A great gulf though lay between them and Winston, longing to communicate, could not pierce the dark veil of his father's gloomy reserve. However through the power of the printed page his father spoke to him:

"The young men of England are joining the Tory party in great numbers: the youth of England is on our side . . .

"Youth is indeed a great calamity, and it appears to excite the worst passions of human nature among those who no longer possess it. We may, I think, chase away such depressing reflections remembering that youth is a calamity which grows less bitter and less poignant as years go by, and that by the sheer process of living and surviving we must each in our turn approach the summit of the wave."

All through his year of convalescence both Winston and his mother felt a sense of chill foreboding. People were whispering, there was something wrong with Randolph's speeches, the news-papers were kind but they no longer reported them verbatim as they once had done.

His father had been irritated that Winston had come out so low in the list for Sandhurst which meant it would be difficult for him to get any regiment but a cavalry one, where the competition was reduced because of the expense. He warned Winston against ending up as a "social wastrel". Winston however, though he feared his father's contempt, was privately very pleased. He loved horses, enjoyed riding, looked forward to disporting himself in a gorgeous uniform and was captivated by the romantic tradition.

On entering college he found, to his own amazement and to the astonishment of his father, friends, and relatives, that he took to military studies with skilful aptitude. Within the year he had graduated eighth out of his class of one hundred and fifty. His father had little time to appreciate his son's belated success. The following year he died suddenly.

Though he had hardly known him, Winston grieved bitterly. He had hoped that with his own maturity he might have been able to form that bond of affection with his father which he had never known in childhood. The last five years of his father's life had been haunted by the spectacle of the ruins of a political career which had been thrown away in a futile gesture, and Winston was determined that some day, somehow, he would vindicate his memory.

Eventually commissioned as a cavalry officer in the 4th Hussars, Winston soon wearied of the pleasant jollities of peace-time soldiering in England. In November 1895 after seven months duty he was entitled to a period of leave and decided to use it in a search for some real action. Rebellion against Spanish rule had broken out in Cuba and a large Spanish army had been sent out to suppress it. Winston wrote to the British Ambassador in Madrid, an old friend of his father, who succeeded in getting him an introduction to General Campos the Spanish Commander-in-Chief. Permission granted, Winston sailed for Cuba, with a companion of like mind from his regiment, and a commission in his pocket from the Daily Graphic for a series of letters reporting on the war. His father had written for the same paper and though poorly paid on this occasion, Winston could now proudly call himself a journalist.

Although the regular Spanish forces had been unable to make much contact with the elusive enemy, Winston counted himself fortunate enough to be involved, soon after his arrival, in several skirmishes. Fired at in anger by men, with guns, who meant to kill, he was delighted to learn that, far from feeling the sensation of fear which he had dreaded, he found, instead, that he thoroughly enjoyed the experience.

"You might call it tomfoolery," he wrote later, "to travel thousands of miles with money one could ill afford, and to get up at four o'clock in the morning in the hope of getting into a scrape in the company of perfect strangers, is certainly hardly a rational proceeding. Yet we knew there were very few subalterns in the British Army who would not have given a month's pay to sit in our saddles."

His leave was soon up; but before returning to England General Campos presented him with the medal of the Spanish Order of

Military Merit of the 1st Class. Winston was elated; in the long Victorian peace British soldiers had almost stopped winning such decorations.

Back at Aldershot in the early spring of 1896 Winston basked for a short period in the warm admiration of the aristocratic society into which he had been born, and which was then reaching its glittering heyday. He supped at Ministerial banquets, was invited to parties at Devonshire House, Landsdowne House, Stafford House, and met such giants of the Tory establishment as Lord Salisbury who had been Prime Minister at the time of his father's downfall. "In a very large degree" he wrote later "everyone knew everyone else and who they were. The few hundred great families who had governed England for so many generations and had seen her rise to the pinnacle of her glory, were inter-related to an enormous extent by marriage. Everywhere one met friends and kinsfolk."

After six months of this agreeable and luxurious life he and his regiment set sail for India. There, at Bangalore, Winston's active spirit was bored beyond measure by the interminable periods of enforced idleness which made up the long hot Indian afternoons once lunch was over. He wrote to his mother for books, and so before the enjoyable evening rituals of polo, dinnertime, and bed, he read seriously for the first time. Politics already held his interest but now he thirsted for a knowledge of history, science, and philosophy. From the pages of Gibbon, Macaulay, Darwin, Malthus, Schopenhauer, Plato and Aristotle, Winston's mind opened to a wide new world which would, from then on, be dedicated to thought as well as to action.

However, apart from polo, there was little enough of that; and hearing that trouble had broken out between the British and the fierce Pathan tribesmen of the Northwest frontier, Winston itched for active service. He pulled every string he possessed among his influential friends and relatives to get himself transferred away from the life of pleasant idleness, which he might have continued to spend on the high plains, to a posting of great peril.

British soldiers who fell into the hands of the hill-men risked the death of a thousand knives, but fearing nothing, and daring all, Winston fought in hand-to-hand combat, experienced half a dozen hairsbreadth escapes, and earned a considerable sum of money and fame by having all his despatches published by the Daily Telegraph.

The tribesmen soon made peace and hearing that fresh trouble had broken out elsewhere on the Northwest frontier Winston again tried to take part in a punitive expedition mounted by the British Army, risking this time his Commanding Officer's displeasure, but to his disappointment, before a fight had time to begin, peace was made by diplomacy.

Winston was not too disheartened; active campaigning had entitled him to a spot of home leave, and he sailed for England – not to enjoy himself in the conventional way, but to win himself a place on yet another military expedition.

General Kitchener was at that moment assembling a British Army which was to proceed up the River Nile to punish the dervishes of the Sudan who ten years before had hacked to pieces General Gordon, hero of Khartoum.

It did not seem as if Winston would be successful this time. "Medal-hunter and self-advertiser" he wrote later were the opinions held against him "in some high and some low military circles." Apparently sharing these views Kitchener made it abundantly clear that he did not want Winston in his Army. Not at all put off by the rebuff Winston pulled all the strings there were to overcome Kitchener's prejudice. In the end persistence won its reward and he dashed out, with only days to spare, to join the 21st Lancers on their march to Omdurman.

"Nothing like the battle of Omdurman will ever be seen again." Winston recalled euphorically, "It was the last link in the long chain of those spectacular conflicts whose vivid and majestic splendour has done so much to invest war with glamour. Everything was visible to the naked eye. The armies marched and manoeuvred on the crisp surface of the desert plain through which the Nile wandered in broad reaches, now steel, now brass. Cavalry charged at full gallop in close order, and infantry or spearsmen stood upright ranged in lines or masses to resist them . . . This kind of war was full of fascinating skills. It was not like the Great War. Nobody expected to be killed. Here and there in every regiment or battalion, half-a-dozen, a score, at the worst thirty or forty, would pay the forfeit; but to the great mass of those who took part in the little wars of Britain in those vanished light-hearted days, this was only a sporting element and splendid game."

Winston's part in the battle had, in his eyes, the quality of medieval knighthood, and his description of the last cavalry charge in history is vividly electric.

"Once again I was on the hard crisp desert, my horse at a trot, and I had the impression of scattered Dervishes running to and fro in all directions. Straight before me a man threw himself on the ground . . . I had been trained as a cavalry soldier to believe that if ever cavalry broke into a mass in infantry, the latter would be at their mercy. My first idea therefore was that the man was terrified. But simultaneously I saw the gleam of his curved sword as he drew it back for a ham-stringing cut. I had room and time enough to turn my pony out of his reach and leaning over on the off-side fired two shots into him at about three yards. As I straightened myself in the saddle I saw before me another figure with uplifted sword. I raised my pistol and fired. So close were we that the pistol itself actually struck him. Man and sword disappeared below and behind me. On my left, then yards away, was an Arab horseman in a bright coloured tunic and steel helmet with chain mail hangings. I fired at him. He turned aside. I pulled my horse into a walk and looked again."

After the charge, when his troop had had time to regroup, Winston asked his Second Sergeant if he had enjoyed himself. "Well," the young man answered diffidently, still shaken by the ordeal, "I don't exactly say I enjoyed it, sir; but I think I'll get more used to it next time." As his troopers laughed gaily at this ingenuous response Winston records how their attention was drawn by the approach of some of their comrades to whom the recent action was no longer a matter of light-hearted banter: "From the direction of the enemy there came a succession of grisly apparitions; horses spouting blood, struggling on three legs, men staggering on foot, men bleeding from terrible wounds, fish-hook spears stuck right through them, arms and faces cut to pieces, bowels protruding, men gasping, crying, collapsing, expiring."

Casualties like these were fortunately light on the British side though the Dervishes fared less well—in a few brief hours thirty thousand of them had been mown down by disciplined rifle volleys and explosive Howitzer shells. Kitchener had let it be known that the fewer prisoners taken the better he would be pleased and Winston was disgusted by the scale of the slaughter. He condemned especially Kitchener's wanton destruction of the Mahdi's tomb, and the desecration of the Mahdi's body—the head was brought back to England as a trophy and the body thrown into the Nile—and he wrote: "I shall not hesitate to declare, that to destroy what was sacred and holy to them was a wicked act of which a true Christian, no less than a philosopher, must express his abhorrence."

Winston decided to leave the Regular Army. His father's death had brought him little inherited wealth. His parents had been extravagant and when all debts had been paid his mother had barely enough left to keep up her opulent life-style, without providing for Winston as well. It was clear that he could not have remained much longer in the Army on the fourteen shillings a day he received, out of which he had to maintain two horses and provide for an extremely costly uniform.

He had, however, been making preparations against this eventuality by developing his ability to write and the success of his newspaper articles and letters encouraged him to proceed further along this route towards financial security. The tale of his adventures on the North-West Frontier called "The Story of the Malakand Field Force" had already been published and gained great success, and he next tried his hand at writing a romantic novel called 'Savonrola'—a book which in after years he pleaded with his friends not to read! That too was successful, in the financial if not the literary sense, and with an additional three hundred pounds which he had earned for a series of letters sent to the Morning Post about the battle of Omdurman, Winston knew his career as a journalist was assured. He began work on a two-volume account of the Sudan campaign called "The River War" and earned regularly £3 a week for articles published in the magazine The Pioneer.

With all money worries therefore behind him for the time being Winston planned an ambitious programme for the coming year of 1899. He would, he thought sanguinly, "return to India and win the polo tournament: to send in my papers and leave the army: to relieve my mother from paying my allowance: to write my new book and a letter to The Pioneer and to look out for a chance of entering Parliament . . ."

All but one of these ambitions Winston was to accomplish without difficulty, but he did not anticipate the pitfalls which awaited an ambitious young man eager to enter the world of politics.

Early in November he paid a visit to the Central Offices of the Conservative Party to find out how to go about finding a constituency. At first, his father's old friend there was enthusiastic. Winston recalled: "The Party would certainly find me a seat, and he hoped to see me in Parliament at an early date." But, Winston discovered, there was a snag. "He then touched delicately upon money matters. Could I pay my expenses, and how much a year could I afford to give to the constituency? I said I would gladly fight the battle, but I could not pay anything except my own personal expenses. He seemed rather damped by this, and observed that the best and safest constituencies always liked to have the largest contributions from their members. He instanced cases where as much as £1,000 a year or more was paid by the member in subscriptions to charities in return for the honour of holding the seat. Risky seats could not afford to be so particular, and 'forlorn hopes' were very cheap. However, he said, he would do all he could, and that no doubt mine was an exceptional case on account of my father, and also he added, on account of my experience at the wars, which would be popular with the Tory working men."

Feeling somewhat cheered by this news after his earlier disappointment, Winston was on the point of leaving the building when his eye lit upon a large book upon the table which bore upon its cover the inscription SPEAKERS WANTED. He gazed upon it wonderingly for some time before muttering with astonishment, "Fancy that! Speakers are wanted and there is a bulky book of application!"

Winston had always dreamed of making a speech but, he lamented, "I had never on any occasion great or small been invited or indeed been allowed to do so. There were no speeches in the 4th Hussars or at Sandhurst either . . ."

"Tell me about this" he asked his father's friend "Do you mean to say there are lots of meetings which 'want' speakers?" Affirmation of his question brought to Winston a thrill of expectant apprehension as he learned of a crying and unsatisfied demand for speakers at all kinds of gatherings – indoor meetings, outdoor fetes, bazaars and rallies. "I surveyed the prospect" he relished, "with the eye of an urchin looking through a pastry cook's window."

Delight at tackling a new challenge did not however blind Winston to the serious natural disabilities which stood in his way of becoming an effective public speaker. He suffered from an impediment in his speech – an inability to pronounce the letter 's' which made him sound blurred, and worse, he was unable to say anything that he had not written out and committed to memory beforehand. He knew he could never aspire to the sparkle of spontaneity of the natural orator, but he possessed an excellent memory, and with his new-found skill as a writer, with painstaking practice he could in tones of bold rhetoric, create an illusion of freshness in the minds of his hearers.

His debut turned out to be amazingly successful and he was gratified to learn the following day that the product of his labours was reported verbatim in the Bristol press.

The constituency that eventually came his way was, as he had been warned it would be, something of a forlorn hope. A tide of popular support was flowing in favour of the Liberal Party and Winston and his running-mate for the twin-member constituency of Oldham in Lancashire were, even for the Conservative Central Office, singularly ill-chosen candidates. Winston, a fresh-faced aristocratic boy would have a limited appeal to the stolid sober hard-working Lancashire cotton workers, but his partner Mr Maudesley was neither fish nor fowl, and, although a working man and the Secretary of the Millworkers Union, proclaimed his belief in a strange new doctrine called Tory Socialism!

The duo's gallant efforts to hold what had hitherto been a safe Conservative seat failed convincingly. Poor Mr Maudesley was accused by the working folk of deserting his class, while Conservative supporters were outraged by the presence of a wicked Socialist on their platforms. Worse still for Winston, as far as his future prospects with the Tory Party were concerned, he fell foul of his political masters by declaring publicly during the campaign against the Government's intention of raising a selective tax for supplementing the income of the Church of England's clergy.

"Everyone threw the blame on me." Winston bemoaned humorously, "I have noticed that they nearly always do. I suppose that it is because they think I shall be able to bear it best." The high Tories in the Carlton Club said "Serve him right for standing with a Socialist. No man of principle would have done such a thing!"

Accordingly, all his bright hopes evaporated, Winston returned to London, "With those feelings of deflation which a bottle of champagne or even soda water represents when it has been half emptied and left uncorked for a night."

For the rest of the year he concentrated on writing "The River War" and watched with the rest of England the march of events in South Africa, which was seemingly leading to an inevitable collision.

It had been obvious for some time that conflict between the Boer settlers and the incoming Britishers who sought gold, diamonds and adventure, would be bound to lead to a fight. The Boers armed with the best modern weapons from Holland and Germany, resolving to bring their quarrels with the incomers to a head, issued an ultimatum requiring the withdrawal of British forces. War was certain from that moment.

The tickertape machine in the London offices of the Morning Post had hardly chattered out the news for an hour before Winston was offered an appointment as principal war correspondent with that newspaper at £250 per month with all expenses paid, and four months guarantee of employment. A pound then equalled one gold sovereign, which at current values is worth approximately £26. He sailed on the Dunottar Castle on the 11th of October 1899 and everyone aboard, including Winston, was afraid the war would be over before they arrived. No-one knew how ill-matched the British 'Tommy' would be, pitched against the lightning guerilla attacks of the Boer horsemen who were fighting not for King and country but for what they believed was their very survival.

Winston hurried to a front crumbling before the Boers' advance and found himself with a small British contingent which held an extended salient deep within enemy territory. At any moment ten or twelve thousand mounted Boers might sweep forward and cut off their retreat. It was essential to get prior notice of the enemy's advance, and the British General in command of the post conceived an imprudent scheme for recoinnoitring ahead, up the railway line, with an armoured train. Winston immediately realised the train's vulnerability to Boer attack – it would only be necessary to blow up a bridge or culvert to leave it stranded – but he volunteered nevertheless to travel with it, for, besides thinking it his duty to gather as much information as he could for the Morning Post, he also admitted frankly that he was "eager for trouble . . . "

All his misgivings were soon confirmed, for the armoured train had travelled no more than fourteen miles before it was observed that their retreat was cut off by a party of Boers who could be seen tampering with the track. A vain attempt was made to steam back up the line but it was too late. Some obstruction had already been placed across the rails and the centre carriages were suddenly thrown violently off the track. Once immobilized the ambush on the train began in earnest, and the steel armoured plating rang with the richochets of shrapnel, rifle, and machine-gun bullets.

In the excitement Winston forgot that he was a civilian and under the withering fire cajoled and pleaded with the frightened troopers to get them to join with him in an attempt to clear the track of the derailed portion of the train. His plan came within a fraction of success but in the end it was only found possible to free the engine itself. Encouraging the driver Winston got him to open the throttle and they pulled away from the scene of confusion, the engine and tender piled high with blood-stained wounded. Winston remained on the footplate for a short distance until the train crossed the bridge spanning the Blue Krantz river, where he told the engine driver to wait. He was on his way back to join the main party who had had to be left behind, and by then were making their last stand, when he found himself cut off by several approaching Boers. With bullets sucking past his ears Winston scrambled up the steep embankment and through the fence only to find himself covered by the rifle of a Boer horseman. He had no alternative but to give himself up. It was fortunate that in the excitement of the fight he had lost his Mauser pistol loaded with its hated dum-dum bullets, for, as a supposedly non-combatant he could have been shot out of hand. As it was he became a prisoner-of-war to one Louis Botha, who was to gain fame as a brave and resourceful guerilla-General and whom Winston was later to meet in quite different circumstances as the first Prime Minister of the Transvaal.

To be imprisoned was an experience Winston found almost impossible to endure and he was determined to try to escape. His opportunity came a month after his capture. He scaled the wall of his temporary prison, boldly marched past two guards and soon afterwards strolled undetected through the main stret of Pretoria. From there he set off, marching south, and jumped a Boer goods train which was heading towards neutral Portugese territory. At the approach of daybreak Winston, fearing a search, decided to abandon this train and catch another later in the day. He found however, to his disappointment, that few trains ran and walking on foot along the line was impossible with every bridge guarded by armed men. He left the track in sheer desperation but by the following day, soaked and exhausted through crossing streams, stumbling into bogs, and trying to fight his way through impene-trable grass, he realised he must find help soon. A hue and cry had been raised after his escape and £25 was put on his head dead or alive. Winston was unflatteringly described by the Boer notice as "An Englishman of indifferent build walking with a forward stoop, pale appearance, reddish brown hair, small and hardly noticeable moustache, talks through his nose and cannot pronounce the letter 's' properly." By an astonishing piece of good luck the first house he called at belonged to a British mining engineer who had been allowed by the Boers to stay on to keep the coal mine open.

John Howard, the mine manager, told Winston he would have to hide up for a while; and so, liberally supplied by his brave and generous host, with mattress and blankets, a couple of candles, some books, a bottle of whisky, a box of cigars and a cold chicken, Winston found himself comfortably installed two hundred feet down the mine shaft. Eventually, eight days after his escape and with the help now of a Mr Dewsnap of Oldham, of all places, and a friendly Dutch neighbour, Winston made a dash for freedom, first by truck and then by train to Lourenco Marques and the safety of Portugese East Africa. There the British Consul arranged his passage be sea to Durban where he found himself a popular hero acclaimed by bands and flag-waving crowds.

In England however his exploits generated a storm of press criticism in connection with the part he had played as a non-combatant in the incident of the armoured train. One newspaper 'The Phoenix' said that the Boers would have been within their rights if Winston had been executed, ending the editorial in sarcastic vein:– "It is to be sincerely hoped that Mr Churchill will not be shot." This attitude was echoed among the military as well, for Winston in his articles to the Morning Post had made such unwelcome comparison as to state that, "The individual Boer, mounted in suitable country, is worth from three to five regular soldiers." And, had concluded, that to win the war would require a quarter of a million men in the field. Not all responsible opinion was negative though, Sir Redvers Buller the British Commander-in-Chief thought Winston talked much good sense and granted him an interview.

"You have done very well," Buller told him, after Winston had related his adventures behind the Boer lines, "is there anything we can do for you?" Without hesitation Winston asked for a commission. Buller reluctantly demurred; the last time Winston had combined journalism with soldiering the High Command had been greatly displeased, seeing their decisions boldly discussed in print by a junior officer. Buller eyed Winston drolly for a time and at last said, "All right. You can have a commission in Bungo's regiment. (Colonel Byng, later Lord Byng of Vimy) You will have to do as much as you can for both jobs. But you will get no pay for ours." Winston accepted gratefully, and riding alongside the seven hundred mounted men of the South African Light Horse experienced further adventures, taking part in the relief of Ladysmith, and had the satisfaction of liberating his fellow prisoners-of-war when the British finally took Pretoria.

The Boer armies had been defeated, and although the Tory Government's intransigent insistence on unconditional surrender meant that Boer guerillas would fight on for another two years, the British people decided the war was won. To cash in on the popular feeling the Government decided to hold a "khaki" election and Winston returned to England to try his luck once more at Oldham.

This time, he was accorded a triumph, driving in state in a procession of ten landaus through streets crowded with enthusiastic millgirls. After the election, when the votes were counted, it was found that Winston had ousted Stephen Runciman the very able Junior Liberal Member who took second place in the poll by the narrow margin of 230 votes.

In those days a General Election was spread over a period of nearly three weeks; and instead of all the electors voting blindly on one day, only learning next morning that they had overthrown or elected a new Government, national issues were fought out, meeting by meeting, constituency by constituency, before the small, and all-male electorate. As one of the first Tory successes in the campaign Winston became a star turn and was sought as a speaker from every part of the country. On familiar terms now with such important personages in the Tory party as Lord Salisbury, the Prime Minister, and Mr Joseph Chamberlain, the Chancellor of the Exchequer, Winston's cup ran over. "For three weeks," he wrote later, "I had what seemed to me a triumphal progress through the country. The party Managers selected the critical seats, and quite a lot of victories followed in my train. I was twenty six. Was it wonderful that I should have thought I had arrived?"

One thing only remained to be done to ensure the success of his career in politics—he must provide himself with complete financial security. Sales of "The River War" and his two books of war correspondence from Africa, together with the ten months salary he had received from the Morning Post, amounted to more than £4,000 but this alone would not be enough. An opportunity, however, of increasing this reserve was at hand, for he planned to lecture all through the autumn and winter in Britain and in the early part of the following year in the United States of America.

Night after night, moving from one city to the other, never sleeping twice in the same bed, Winston entertained capacity audiences illustrating the account of his adventures and escape in the Boer War with magic lantern slides. He hardly ever earned less than £100 a night and once at the Philharmonic Hall in Liverpool gathered over £300. By November he had safely banked over £4,500, having toured half the towns in Great Britain. In America audiences sympathetic to the Boers were more critical, but the results financially were substantial just the same, and at the end of his tour there, in the middle of February, Winston had in his possession a fortune of nearly £10,000.

Parliament re-assembled later that month and a Liberal attack, spear-headed by the fierce invective of the up-and-coming young Welsh Radical, David Lloyd George, plunged the House of Commons into a bitter debate regarding the Tory Government's conduct of the war. It was of course Winston's subject, and, although warned against speaking too soon, made his maiden speech only four days after taking his seat:

"Though I had done nothing else for many months but address large audiences," he wrote afterwards, "it was with awe as well as eagerness that I braced myself for what I regarded as the supreme ordeal. I learned that a rising young Welshman, a pro-Boer, and one of our more important bugbears named Lloyd George, who from below the gangway was making things very difficult for the leaders of the Liberal Party, would probably be called about nine o'clock. He had a moderately phrased amendment on the paper, but whether he would move it was not certain. I gathered that I could, if I wished, have the opportunity of following him."

This could be Winston's first chance to establish his reputation but already he was torn with anxiety. The problem was that then, and for many years afterwards, he was unable to say anything in public which he had not written out and committed to memory beforehand and to be faced now with following a speaker who was a master of the impromptu rejoinder was daunting. Winston could do little more than gather in his mind a miscellaneous assortment of prepared replies, one of which he hoped would meet the occasion.

Sitting in the corner seat of the gangway, immediately behind the Ministers on the front bench, the same seat from which his father had made his speech of resignation, Winston braced himself for his initiation as an M.P. Then the house began to fill and Lloyd George rose to speak. Winston's heart plummetted when he heard his opponent announce that he did not intend to move his amendment but would speak instead on the main question. Of what use was his "quiverful of arrows of different patterns and sizes" none of which could now be aimed against the quicksilver tongue of the little Welshman, Lloyd George, encouraged by the Irish members and his own left wing in the Liberal Party, grew more and more animated while Winston floundered along trying to keep up with him, constructing sentence after sentence intended to act as an apt and witty link when he rose to speak himself. Each of these improvisations became obsolete in turn and as Lloyd George sat down Winston repressed his despair with an inward gasp. At that moment Tom Bowles, a skilled Parliamentarian sitting on Winston's left, sensed his young friend's predicament and whispered, "You might say 'Instead of making his violent speech without moving his moderate amendment he had better have moved his moderate amendment without making his violent speech.' " Winston recorded with heartfelt gratitude that "Mannah in the wilderness was not more welcome! It fell only just in time. To my surprise I heard my opponent saying he 'would curtail his remarks as he was sure the House wished to hear a new member,' and with this graceful gesture he suddenly resumed his seat.

"I was up before I knew it, and reciting Tommy Bowles' rescuing sentence. It won a general cheer. Courage returned. I got through all right. The Irish—whom I had been taught to detest—were a wonderful audience."

At the House of Commons bar afterwards Winston and Lloyd George were introduced, and it was clear to both men that they would get on well together in the future, though for the moment they sat on opposing benches.

Winston made only two more really successful speeches from the Conservative Benches of that Parliament and both were in its earliest months, for it was not long before he found himself in disagreement with many entrenched Tory attitudes. He was all for carrying on the war against the Boers, which had now flared up again in a desultory manner, to a victorious conclusion, but at the same time he admired their gallant resistance and resented the abuse with which they were covered. He hoped sincerely that an honourable peace might be found which would bind those brave men and their leaders to Britain forever. He abhorred the policy of farm burning and the concentration camps where women and children were dying of starvation and disease.

"I thought" he wrote, "we should finish the war by force and generosity and then make haste to return to paths of peace, retrenchment and reform. Although I enjoyed the privilege of meeting in pleasant circles most of the Conservative leaders, and was always treated with extraordinary kindness and good nature by Mr Balfour, although I often saw Mr Chamberlain and heard him discuss affairs with the greatest freedom, I drifted steadily to the left. I found that Rosebery, Asquith and Grey, and above all John Morley, seemed to understand my point of view far better than my own chiefs . . . I became anxious to make the Conservative Party follow Liberal courses. I was in revolt against Jingoism. I had a sentimental view about the Boers . . . and I was so untutored as to suppose that all I had to do was to think out what was right and express it fearlessly; I thought that loyalty in this outweighed all other loyalty. I did not understand the importance of Party discipline and unity, and the sacrifices of opinion which may lawfully be made in their cause."

When the Secretary of State for War announced a scheme for re-organising the Army on a larger scale, and of course raising taxes to pay for it, Winston could no longer restrain himself from launching a general attack upon his Party's policy. Just as his father Randolph had done at the time he had resigned his office as Chancellor of the Exchequer, Winston urged peace, economy and reduction of armaments. In a speech he had taken six weeks to prepare, and had learned off by heart, he reminded a crowded House of Commons of his father's own sacrifice and quoting from his letter of resignation to Lord Salisbury, said, "I decline to be a party to encouraging the military and militant circle of the War Office and the Admiralty to join the high and desperate stakes which other nations seem to be forced to risk."

"A European war," he said, pulling aside with intuitive prescience the veil of fate which hid the future, "can only end in the ruin of the vanquished and the scarcely less fatal dislocation and exhaustion of the conqueror, democracy is more vindictive than cabinets, the wars of people will be more terrible than the wars of kings."

Concluding, Winston emphasised that Britain should rely for her security upon her Navy and her position of honour among nations: "British influence is a healthy and kindly influence . . . we shall make a fatal bargain if we allow the moral force which this country has so long exerted to become diminished, perhaps destroyed, for the sake of the costly, trumpery, military playthings on which the Secretary of State for War has set his heart."

The Conservatives were startled. The Liberal opposition benches rang with delight.

At this time Winston came under the influence of John Morley, the Liberal philosopher and free-thinker who was the disciple and biographer of Gladstone and who had once been his Chief Secretary for Ireland. Once over dinner Morley commended to Winston a book recently published called "Poverty: A Study of Town Life by Seebohm Rowntree." A classic study of the poor of the city of York. Winston bought a copy of the book the following day and was shocked by what he read. For the first time he realised that Britain was two nations. "Consider," he wrote bitterly, "the peculiar case of these poor, and the consequences. Although the British Empire is so large they cannot find room to live in it; although it is so magnificent, they would have had a better chance of happiness if they had been born cannibal islanders of the southern seas; although its science is so profound, they would have been more healthy if they had been the subjects of King Canute . . . This festering life at home makes worldwide power a mockery, and defaces the image of God upon earth." And in a letter to J. Moore Baillie on the 23rd of December 1902 he wrote "For my own part, I see little glory in an Empire which can rule the waves but is unable to flush its sewers."

A number of Winston's colleagues in the Tory Party were also as concerned with these same social evils and saw their eventual solution in a new economic policy. Although Britain's prosperity had rested, they believed, until then, upon the twin pillars of "laissez faire" and Free Trade, it had been obvious for some time that the country was no longer in a central position as the only workshop in the world, and the flood of cheap foreign manufactured goods, mainly from Germany and the United States, was evidence which testified to that fact for all to see.

Joseph Chamberlain, the Chancellor of the Exchequer, had, before entering politics, made his fortune as a Birmingham brass founder and was a vigorous partisan for the new ideas. He wanted to erect a tariff-barrier against all imported products and to initiate a system of preferential treatment for the countries of the Empire. He argued that most other industrial countries in the world had already moved away from Free Trade and that Britain and its workers would be strengthened by a policy of protectionism. His opponents on the other hand, both Liberal and Tory, argued that the adoption of such measures would incur the retaliation of other countries and that it would, in effect, place a tax on food, which in Britain had mostly to be imported, thus inflicting a blow upon that part of the population least able to bear the burden.

Winston's father had been a devoted Free Trader and so, therefore, was Winston.

Chamberlain's open advocacy of Tariff Reform split the Tory ranks, and although Balfour, who had succeeded his uncle as Prime

Minister, tried to paper over the cracks, disagreement between the two sides was too fundamental for the breach to heal.

Winston, in the meantime, drew more openly towards the Liberals and in a letter to an elector expressed his opinion that "The time has come when Free Traders of all parties should form one line of battle against the common foe." This was followed by a speech at Halifax when he committed the final heresy by saying, "Thank God for the Liberal Party!"

This was going too far. Oldham, nearby Manchester, was Chamberlain country and the constituency party there passed a vote of no-confidence, making it abundantly clear that if Winston wanted to champion the Free Trade cause he would have to find a seat somewhere else. He had, in any case, already made up his mind. In a letter to Lord Hugh Cecil, a fellow Tory, which was, understandably, never sent, he wrote, "I am an English Liberal. I hate the Tory Party, their men, their words, and their message. I feel no sort of sympathy with them—except to my own people at Oldham. I want to take up a clear practical position which masses of people can understand."

But he did not, for the moment, resign his seat and continued to remain, embarrassingly, for some weeks in his usual place behind the Treasury bench while at the same time openly associating with the Members of the Opposition. His old Tory colleagues were infuriated and one night tempers rose to such a pitch that when Winston rose to speak the Prime Minister got up and walked out followed by two hundred and fifty Conservative M.P.'s. Soon afterwards he was invited by the Liberals of North West Manchester to fight the next General Election for them and there, early in May 1904, he made a striking speech at the Free Trade Hall.

"We want," said Winston in ringing tones, moving a vote of thanks to John Morley, "a Government that will think a little more about the toiler at the bottom of the mine and a little less about the fluctuations of the share market in London. We want a Government which, instead of looking mainly abroad, will look mainly, if not, I think, entirely, at home. We want a Government and a policy which will think the condition of a slum in an English city is not less worthy of the attention of a statesman and of Parliament than the jungle of Somaliland.

"That is the kind of Government which we may be able to obtain. That is the kind of Government which Mr Chamberlain says will 'after a brief interval be hissed off the stage.' Well, let us get it first, and then we will show what we will do with the hissing."

A fortnight afterwards Winston moved over, quietly and without fuss, to the Opposition Benches and took his seat beside Lloyd George. Of the move Henry Lucy, with malicious perception, noted in his diary, "Winston Churchill may be safely counted upon to make himself quite as disagreeable on the Liberal side as he did on the Unionist. But he will be handicapped by the aversion which always pertains to a man who, in whatsoever honourable circumstances, has turned his coat."

With his Party disintegrating under him Balfour decided to resign in December 1905 without dissolving Parliament, thinking that the Liberals, with their own divisions, would be unable to form a Government. It was a serious miscalculation, for, at the prospect of real power, the Liberals joined ranks and Campbell Bannerman, the new Prime Minister, was easily able to form an administration.

Winston's former colleagues, regarding him now with contemptuous hatred, were incensed when they learned that he had been appointed Under-Secretary for the Colonies.

The General Election, which the Liberals called in order to get a working majority in Parliament, took place early in the New Year and the "Banner Constituency" upon which all eyes were fixed and where the fighting would be fiercest was North-West Manchester.

Winston's opponent was a young lawyer named Joyston Hicks and, circulating a pamphlet which exploited Winston's Conservative past, he exposed him as a turncoat and a deserter. Electors cried clamorously to Winston at one meeting, "Answer it!" Winston was unruffled. "What about it?" he replied, "I deny nothing. I have said all those things. I have said them because I belonged to a stupid Party which I have left because I did not want to go on saying stupid things!" Amid loud cheers from the delighted audience he tore the pamphlet in shreds and flung it from him with disdain.

He was also attacked by Sylvia Pankhurst and Mrs Drummond, the militant leaders of the Suffragette movement. Winston had always supported votes for women but with supreme logic these ladies, desiring maximum publicity for their cause, picked upon the one newsworthy candidate most favourable to them. Night after night they tried to wreck his meetings. His speeches were continuously interrupted until, amid scenes of confusion and disorder, the banner-waving, dishevelled young women were ejected by ushers and police. Once Winston invited a female interruptor to come up to the platform and put a question before he made his speech. "Will a Liberal Government give women the vote?" she demanded. Winston replied that, considering the treatment he had received and the disruption which had taken place at his meetings, he had witnessed nothing which would induce him now to vote in Parliament for giving women the franchise. He added, however, that the only occasion on which he had actually voted on the question he had supported the proposal. Cheers followed and as his angry interrogator was forcibly removed from the platform Winston told his audience: "I am not so hostile to the proposal as I thought it right to say just now, but I am not going to be henpecked!"

The phrase caught on and became a popular catchword throughout Manchester, echoed in the pantomime and the music-hall. People would turn round as he passed in the street and with a laugh call out, 'Don't be henpecked, Winston!'

The campaign was dominated by his extrovert personality. All his meetings overflowed and afterwards he frequently addressed dense throngs outside in the street. Once, in a hall bulging at the seams, the floor itself seemed in danger of collapse. "What," responded Winston to the cry of panic, "let us do justice even though the floor fall."

Humour was not his only weapon and at a great meeting in the Free Trade Hall he spoke with vitriolic invective of the late Tory Government. "Curruption at home" he blasted, "aggression abroad, sentiment by the bucketful, patriotism by the Imperial pint, the open door at the Public Exchequer, the open door at the public house, dear food for the million, cheap labour for the millionaire."

The poll in the Manchester area was held on January the 13th and after the votes were counted it was revealed that the Liberals had gained a sweeping victory. "Even the most ardent Liberal," wrote Winston, "would never have believed it. When we rose in the morning all the nine seats were held by Conservatives. When we went to bed that night all had been won by Liberals."

Manchester proved to be a barometer for the whole country and the Liberals won by a landslide capturing 377 seats and were able to count on another 136 seats taken by Labour and the Irish Nationalists who could be expected to support the new Government.

In power at Westminster the Liberals were committed, under the leadership of Sir Henry Campbell Bannerman, to implement a long promised policy of Radical reform, dedicated to bind and heal the running sores of nineteenth century capitalism.

Winston returned to the Colonial office. His most pressing problem there was what to do about the Chinese 'slaves'. For a number of years the goldmines of the Transvaal had been worked by indentured labourers brought in from China who had been forced to endure the most appalling conditions and whose existence was not far removed from a state of enslavement. The Liberals, in opposition, had accused the Tories of doing nothing to stop the scandal and during the election the topic had been a major issue. Winston, however, had known since first taking office in December that, despite taking immediate steps to mitigate their hardships, the new Liberal Government had no intention whatever of immediately repatriating the Chinese. How was he now to justify before the Tory benches in the House of Commons the continuance of the very policy over which they had likely enough lost the election? Choosing his words with more care than regard for the unvarnished truth, he said:

"The contract may not be a desirable contract, but it cannot be, in the view of his Majesty's Government, classified as 'slavery' in the extreme acceptance of the word without some risk of terminological inexactitude"!

Having neatly escaped from that trap Winston turned his attention to the main issue — that of conferring self-Government on the conquered Boers. It was an undertaking which could easily have gone badly wrong but Winston welcomed it as a wonderful opportunity. Since his South African adventures he had admired the independent courage of the Dutch settlers and even in the heat of battle had pleaded again and again in Parliament that when the time should come for a settlement the utmost generosity should be shown towards the brave but beaten foe.

This attitude was to be one of the most constant factors in Winston's political philosophy.

"It is extraordinary," he wrote many years later, "how rarely in history have victors been capable of turning in a flash to all those absolutely different processes of action, to that utterly different mood, which alone can secure them forever by generosity what they have gained by force. In the hour of success, policy is blinded by the passion of the struggle. Yet the struggle with the enemy is over. There is only then the struggle with oneself. That is the hardest of all . . . Two opposite sides of human nature have to be simultaneously engaged. Those who can win the victory cannot make the peace; those who make the peace would never have won the victory."

Winston, with his romantic view of history, was determined to do differently, inspired by the noble gesture shown after the American Civil War by General Grant at Appomatiox who sent the sorely needed rations of his own army to the starving Confederates telling General Lee to take his artillery horses home to plough the devastated Southern fields.

The Conservatives received his Bill with incredulous anger, but Winston replied with dauntless optimism in his closing speech:

"We do not ask the Honourable gentlemen opposite to share our responsibility. If by any chance our counsel of reconciliation should come to nothing, if our policy should end in mocking disaster, then the resulting evil would not be confined to South Africa. Our unfortunate experiences would be trumpeted forth all over the world wherever despotism wanted a good argument for bayonets, whether an arbitrary Government wished to deny or curtail the liberties of imprisoned nationalities.

"But if, on the other hand, as we hope and profoundly believe, better days are in store for South Africa, if the long lane it has been travelling has reached the turning at last, if the near future should unfold to our eyes a tranquil, prosperous, consolidated Afrikaaner nation under the protecting aegis of the British Crown, then, I say, the good, as well as the evil, will not be confined to South Africa; then, I say, the cause of the poor and the weak all over the world will have been sustained, and everywhere small people will get room to breathe, and everywhere great empires will be encouraged by our example to step forward—and it only needs to step—into the sunshine of a more gentle and a more generous age."

It is a historical tragedy that Winston's great vision was in this case myopic.

He conceived no place in his South Africa for the indigenous black majority except as kindly used docile domestics.

Not only by the Tories was self-government for South Africa seen as a dangerous and reckless experiment, and the headlines of the Daily Mail the day afterwards summed up the feeling of many:

"Transvaal given back to the Boers—Fruitless sacrifices of the war—22,000 lives and two hundred and fifty million pounds for nothing."

Winston was not disheartened. In order to complete his knowledge of the African continent as Under-secretary for the Colonies he set off on a four months official tour. It was a trip he enjoyed immensely. Conveyed across the vastness of the East African veldt, then unspoilt and crowded with game, in the luxury of a private railway coach, a nod of his head was sufficient to stop the train. He would then alight, rifle in hand, to bag large numbers of wild animals whose heads, in the custom of the time, were destined to hang as trophies upon his study wall. But slaughter alone did not engage all his attention and in his book 'My African Journey', recording his experiences, Winston waxed lyrical on what was to be a lifelong love of butterflies:

"Never were seen such flying fairies. They flaunted their splendid liveries of inconceivable varieties of colour and pattern in our faces at every step. Swallowtails, Flottilaries, Admirals, Tortoiseshells, Peacocks, Orangetips . . . floated in sunshine from flower to flower, glinting in the shade of great trees, or clustered on the path to suck the moisture."

In the spring of 1908 Campbell Bannerman died suddenly and Herbert Henry Asquith, the Chancellor of the Exchequer, a 56-year-old ex-lawyer whose Scottish constituency was in East Fife, was called by Kind Edward VII to take his place as Prime Minister. In the necessary re-organisation of the Cabinet Asquith handed over to Lloyd George his almost completed Budget and long realising Winston's drive and ability, asked him to go to the Board of Trade which carried with it, unlike his Under-Secretaryship, a seat in the Cabinet. Asquith's Cabinet was acknowledged even by his enemies as talented and the credit was to lie largely in the Prime Minister's supreme qualities as Chairman able to maintain a finely balanced equilibrium between his brilliant, though highly individualistic, colleagues. Haldane, the steady and stolid Minister of War however, noted sourly in his autobiography that sessions in Asquith's Cabinet were "More like a meeting of delegates than a controlled discussion under the Chairmanship of the Prime Minister" and Winston he characterised as being "As long winded as he was persistent." The other Members of the Cabinet were no less irritated by Winston's pushing irrepressible energy. Lord Crewe, the Colonial Secretary, had often been rubbed the wrong way by his precocious Junior and once Asquith had to reply wittily and consolingly to Crewe about an importunate letter he had received from Winston as "A typical missive, born of froth out of foam."

The April weekend in which Asquith announced the team that would make up his new Government Winston spent at Salisbury Hall, his mother's house near St. Albans, where a family friend, Lady Blanche Hozier and her daughter, were also staying.

Clementine, the 23 year old daughter of Lady Blanche and Colonel Sir Henry Montague Hozier, besides being intelligent was also a striking beauty. She had been brought up in reduced circumstances. Her parents lived apart, Colonel Hozier not even listing his marriage in Who's Who and, while he had cut a gay and flamboyant figure in London Society, his wife and children were confined in the Sussex countryside and at Dieppe, across the Channel, where living was cheaper. Living abroad had brought Clementine some advantage; she had studied at the Sorbonne and was fluent both in French and German.

The first time Winston and Clementine had met was at a dance given by Lady Crew in 1904. During the evening Winston had asked his mother who the girl was and if he could be introduced to her. Lady Randolph replied that though she didn't know her she would find out. Returning she said: "How very interesting, she is the daughter of a very old friend of mine, Blanche Hozier, whom I haven't seen for years." As Winston was introduced Clementine said, "How do you do," and many years later, recounting the eposide to her son Randolph, she observed:

"Winston just stared. He never uttered one word and was very gauche – he never asked me for a dance, he never asked me to have supper with him. I had of course heard a great deal about him, nothing but ill. I was told he was stuck up, objectionable, etcetera, and on this occasion he just stood and stared." Eventually Clementine had to beckon to another of her admirers to rescue her from the long and embarrassing silence.

Winston had always been awkward when he met women for the first time and found it difficult to chat inconsequentially or engage them in casual conversation. His favourite subject was always himself and then he sparkled, expressing aloud, a constant stream of novel and intriguing ideas as they occurred to him, expressed with wit and humour – but he could hardly do this with strangers! Asquith's 21-year-old daughter Violet, and one of Winston's most constant admirers, describing her first meeting with Winston two years before, wrote:

"For a long time he remained sunk in abstraction. Then he appeared to become suddenly aware of my existence. He turned on me a lowering gaze and asked me abruptly how old I was. I replied that I was nineteen. 'And I,' he said almost despairingly 'am thirty two already. Younger than anyone who counts though.' After a long oration he suddenly ended with the immortal words, 'We are all worms, but I do believe that I am a glow worm.' "

It was four years before Winston and Miss Hozier met again, this time at a dinner party given by Lady St. Helier.

"I had not wanted to go to the dinner at all." Clementine recalled later, "I had come home after giving French lessons at half a crown an hour and was rather tired, when my mother said: 'Your Aunt Mary has just sent a message, she has been let down and is thirteen for dinner and she would very much like you to go to dinner tonight.'

"I really can't," I said, "I don't want to go, I have nothing to wear, and I have no clean gloves."

'That is very ungrateful of you,' my mother scolded. 'Your Aunt has been extremely kind to you. Let's have no more nonsense, go upstairs straight away and get dressed.' "

At 12 Bolton Street a similar scene was taking place. Eddie Marsh, Winston's private secretary, found him in his bath when he should have already left for Lady St. Heliers. 'What on earth are you doing, Winston?' he asked. 'You should be at dinner by now.'

"I'm not going," was the reply, "it will be a great bore."

'But you can't do that—especially not to Lady Jeune,' persisted Marsh appealing to Winston's conscience. 'Remember how kind she was to you when she got Sir Evelyn Wood to get you to the Omdurman campaign.'

Marsh's remonstrance at last had its effect, but, of course, Winston was very late. Coming in halfway through the meal he took his seat beside Clementine and once having taken the plunge, monopolised her company for the remainder of the evening, much to her embarrassment. He asked her whether she had read his 'Life of Lord Randolph' the biography of his father which had been published with great success at the time of the last election. Clementine had been repeatedly told by her mother to brush up on Winston's book but so far she had not got round to it. Admitting honestly she hadn't read it, Winston said: "If I send you the book tomorrow, will you read it?" "Yes" she replied. Winston, however, never did send the book, and she recalled "That made a bad impression on me."

Miss Hozier was not the only lady Winston made a bad impression with that evening. The dinner party was in honour of Lady Lugard, wife of Sir Edward Lugard the great West African Colonial Administrator, and Winston, understandably pre-occupied with beautiful Clementine, had ignored her all night. She wrote later in high pique of "That wild Winston . . . an ignorant boy, so obviously ignorant in regard to Colonial affairs and at the same time full of personal activity that the damage he may do appears to be colossal."

The next occasion Winston and Clementine met he came over with better effect and in a letter to a friend soon afterwards Clementine was to refer to his "dominating charm and brilliancy." And, during that first busy week at the Board of Trade, Winston wrote to her:

"I seize this fleeting hour of leisure to write and tell you how much I liked our long talk on Sunday and what a comfort it was to me to meet a girl with so much intellectual quality and such strong reserve of noble sentiment. I hope we shall meet again and come to know each other and like each other more; and I see no reason why this should not be so."

Winston had been in love before, once proposing and being refused by the famous actress Ethel Barrymore, but that had been a light-heartedly romantic affair. Now with Clementine he felt absolutely serious. Nevertheless, although he had reason to believe she also felt the same way as he, one hurdle would have to be put behind him before he could make his proposal.

At that time, under an old 18th century rule, Cabinet Ministers when newly appointed had to seek re-election by their constituencies, a measure which had originally been intended to prevent corruption, but by 1908 had become an unnecessary and unwelcome ordeal. Though Winston loved a fight and looked forward personally to the contest, it was obvious to everyone else that this by-election would be made a test of confidence in the Liberal Government and bound to attract all the pent-up fury of the discomfited Tory Party. To re-submit himself now to the approval of public opinion at the ballot box was certain to be an exceptionally gruelling experience. As Violet Asquith noted:

"All the forces hostile to the Government, and in particular to himself, were concentrated against him. By Conservatives he was the best-hated Member of the Government and his elevation to Cabinet rank was the last drop of bitterness in their cup."

When the campaign opened Tory faithfuls came from far and near to North West Manchester to speak and work for Winston's defeat, their efforts again reinforced by the Suffragettes, led on by the redoubtable Mrs Pankhurst and her two daughters Christabel and Sylvia who were to launch on this occasion their first full scale campaign of violence and civil disobedience. Winston noted of his public meetings "just when things were going well and the audience was gripped, a high pitched voice would ring out, 'What about the women?' 'When are you going to give women the vote?' No sooner was one interrupter removed than another in a different part of the hall took up the task." Though he tried to appease them, right up to the close of poll on April 23rd, the Suffragettes kept up the pressure.

By-elections, at any time, normally bring before the attention of the electorate a number of minor issues which in a General Election are often swept aside by the mainstream of events and Winston was faced with the demanding task of explaining and defending every aspect of the Government's policy of the past two years.

North West Manchester was a peculiar constituency in a number of ways.

It was a great centre for the large number of Jewish immigrants who had escaped from the pogroms then raging in central Europe. Two years before Winston had promised the Jewish community to amend the Aliens Act which, among other things, imposed a large naturalisation fee, but so far he had been able to do nothing for them and they disappointedly nursed their grievance.

The sizeable Irish community was also up in arms because an Education Bill was then under way threatening, in the cause of reform, to take from the Roman Catholics their denomination schools.

Winston defending his seat at the Manchester by-election of 1908 from the roof of one of his campaign vehicles. No other parliamentary contest generated such interest, no other politician could arouse such enthusiasm and yet no other electorate produced such a dramatic result.

The measure was even more strongly opposed by the Church of England for in this same process they stood to lose their position of privilege. Winston therefore made a special appeal to the Catholics and the Jews declaring incidentally that he also favoured Home Rule for Ireland. The Manchester branches of the Church School Defence League retaliated issuing a manifesto against special favours to Jews and Roman Catholics saying, "If you reject Mr Churchill a safe seat will be provided for him elsewhere. If you elect him you strike a deadly blow at all voluntary schools."

If this alone had not been sufficient, Winston also had to face the whole force and influence of the drink trade who were fighting a desperate rear-guard action against Asquith's Licensing Bill which sought to curb the prevalent degrading drunkenness among the poor by limiting the opening times of public houses and other restrictions. Manchester's part in this agitation, as a great manufacturing and distributing centre for drink had been strong and continuous and the big brewers spared neither money nor effort to misrepresent the proposed legislation.

Much of the heat too, by that time, had been taken out of the Free Trade issue and many of the leading Unionists who had acted as Chairmen at Winston's meetings in 1906 working and voting for him on account of the Tariff Reform split, now returned to their traditional loyalty and he could count on these votes as lost.

Not only were the Conservatives united, under the energetic leadership of their candidate young Joynston Hicks, but a third contender also entered the field this time to plead the cause of Labour and whose candidature, dividing the Radical vote, seemed to Liberals the height of irresponsibility on the part of their ostensible allies.

Right up to the eve of poll, however, Winston thought he could pull it off, but most unbiased observers already sensed the shift in public opinion. Giving popular form to the trend, the following lines, to the tune of "Goodbye Dolly," were printed on a small card and circulated throughout the constituency in thousands.

"Goodbye Winston you must leave us, though you may not like to
    go,
If you stayed you would deceive us, as you did two years ago,
Perhaps they'll have you somewhere, we don't want you here
For Joynston Hicks is winning, Goodbye Winnie dear."

As the campaign drew to its close Winston used every known electioneering device to stem the ebbing tide. A covered van paraded the streets emblazoned with large posters showing the symbol of a "large Free Trade loaf" and alongside in comparison "the small loaf" which Protectionism was supposed to bring. Sticky-back photographs of Winston were posted to every voter captioned "Stick to Winston." Mrs Cornwallis-West – amid much gossip Lady Randolph had remarried a young army officer – vigorously canvassed for her son's re-election. Speaking at an open air meeting on April 23rd she remarked, "I hear a good deal about dear coal, and dear beer. But what I say is 'Vote for *dear* Winston.'"

On polling day the weather was beautifully fine and from 9 a.m. onwards hundreds of vehicles sporting the rival colours of the candidates dashed about the division bringing voters to the polling booths. In the evening the scene in the counting room was of intense excitement, but Winston must have felt some presentiment. He only arrived after 9 o'clock and then, the result was known. He had been defeated.

Putting a bright face on it, accompanied by his mother he walked up to his successful rival and congratulated him. Joynston Hicks replied with feeling – "I must say you are a real brick to say what you have done."

Many reasons were put forward to account for his defeat – Winston himself blamed a hostile Press – but the constituency, a marginal one, was always liable to swing towards the alternative Party and the intervention of the Socialist stealing away many of the much needed Radical votes was the decisive factor in giving Joynston Hicks his small majority of 429 votes.

One correspondent, writing in a letter to the Manchester Guardian, lamented: "Manchester will be sorry for what she has done today." Tory supporters, however, were jubilant. Churchill "memory" cards were peddled in the crowded streets and the Sheffield Telegraph gloated:

"Churchill out – language fails us when it is most needed. We have all been yearning for this to happen with a yearning beyond utterance. Figures – Oh! yes, there are figures – but who cares for figures today? Winston Churchill is *out,* OUT, *OUT!"*

A joke quickly circulated about a stock exchange telegram supposedly sent to Winston the day after his defeat. "To Winston, Manchester: What's the use of a W.C. without a seat?"

Winston however received his setback with equanimity.

"It took only five or six minutes" he wrote, "to walk from the City Hall where the poll was declared, to the Manchester Reform Club. I was accompanied there by tumultuous crowds. As I entered the Club a telegram was handed to me. It was from Dundee and contained the unanimous invitation of the Liberals of that City that I should become their candidate in succession to the sitting member . . . who was about to be promoted to the House of Lords.

It is no exaggeration to say that only seven minutes at the outside passed between my defeat at Manchester and my invitation to Dundee . . . ''

The citizens of Dundee, the Scottish constituency placed at Winston's disposal, had followed the events of the by-election in Manchester with great interest and viewed now with mixed feelings – despite the decision of their Liberal Club – the prospect of gaining the President of the Board of Trade as a Member of Parliament. And, when it became clear that Winston was in no hurry to accept the invitation, and was in fact considering three other possible constituencies, local pride was outraged.

"Wire if possible tonight," the Dundee Liberal Association had asked. But when Winston's reply came on the Saturday he said merely that he was giving their invitation his best considerations, and arriving from Manchester at London's St. Pancras railway station at two o'clock on Saturday afternoon told an enquiring journalist: "Nothing is yet settled with regard to my standing for Dundee or any other constituency."

It was not until Tuesday, April 28th, seventy-two hours after he had received the invitation, that he made it known that he had accepted Dundee's offer. The Dundee Courier, a newspaper of Conservative sympathies, noted sourly: "On thinking matters over Mr Churchill has decided to come to Dundee . . . which may or may not be willing to take in 'second hand goods from Manchester.' ''

Telling his mother that he had finally accepted Dundee's invitation on the advice of the Prime Minister and Party whips, he wrote:

"They all seem to think it is a certainty – and even though a three cornered fight will end in a majority of 3,000. *It is a life seat and cheap and easy beyond all experience*"!

Winston was discreet enough not to offer those reasons for his choice to Dundee's electors and, although he did not know it at the time, there was to be a fourth candidate which would make the fight for the constituency anything but easy.

Dundee, a dark mass of dirty grey sandstone tenements, punctuated by high chimney stacks and church spires, lies beautifully situated between green hills, the cultivated patchwork-quilt of the Angus countryside and the silvery water of the river Tay. A bustling industrial and commercial centre, Dundee's activities were then summarised by three commodities, "jute, jam and journalism" to which should have been added shipbuilding and engineering. Like other Scottish cities which had been transformed by the Industrial Revolution, Dundee had a chronic imbalance in its pattern of manufacture and relied too heavily on the textile trade:

The weaving flat in Baxter Brothers Dens Works in 1908. The jute industry employing predominantly child and female labour was unhealthy, paid subsistance wages, and subject to frequent trade recessions caused by foreign competition offered no job security.

Failing to champion their interests Winston was to win no loyalty from jute workers for maintaining his principles on free trade.

unemployment among men was consequently high not only for the reason that this staple industry used mainly female and child labour, but also because, almost wholly dependent on foreign trade, it suffered badly from frequent trade recessions.

In 1908 Dundee was suffering one such recession and to make matters worse the Caledon shipyard, involved in a national dispute between employers and labour, had locked out its total work-force. Over half the population were in dire need. All the charitable organisations in the town tried to bring some relief to the desperate poverty which festered in the damp and miserable slums. Door to door collections were organised, soup kitchens were erected, farmers from the surrounding areas provided vegetables free and the local butchers donated beef and bones.

Here, Winston was to see for himself, the kind of poverty he had read about, and had pledged himself to eradicate.

A BAD SIGN.

As minister at the Board of Trade Winston's major task was to try to get some of these two million back to work. But then, as now, the roots of the problem lay in a worn-out industrial base requiring massive injections of capital for new machinery and equipment.

Crowded tenements five and six storeys high with outside stair-cases and open connecting balconies called 'plats' nestled close to the factories, their inhabitants dominated, at work and out of it, by the sound and smell of jute manufacture. Each dwelling had a kitchen and perhaps two bedrooms, and with the usual large family that meant the male children slept in one room, females in the other and the parents in the kitchen. The kitchen, hub of family life, was provided with a black iron sink with cold running water, and a single gas light which served for heating, cooking and baking. There were no baths and no lavatories. In the back courtyard stood an open midden for general rubbish, used by the males as a urinal while the women used a pail indoors emptying the contents later. The "scaffies" or scavengers employed by the Town Council cleaned the midden out weekly, and in the dark early mornings of winter seeing their way in the noisome darkness with the aid of little head-held brass paraffin lamps attached to their foreheads like coal miners, wheeled out the muck onto the street. Some of the newer, better-class tenements possessed the luxury of a water closet on the stair landing which was shared also by the four other families in the same 'plat'. Not surprisingly disease, especially tuberculosis, was rife.

Jute manufacturing, from raw fibre to burlap, gunny bag, or carpet backing, the work upon which almost everyone was engaged, was, and is, hard, dirty, and unhealthy; and the sight then of the bobbin shifters, small boys and girls running about on bare feet covered from head to toe with white "mill stoor," and harrassed bedraggled women, old before their time, tending the inexorable noisy machinery, would have angered the heart of any reformer.

Dundee had an evil reputation for drunkenness. The innumerable public houses with their stale stench of beer, sawdust floors, spittoons, and salt fish kept on the counter by the publican to give his customers a thirst, promised a brief illusory comfort and accordingly did a roaring trade. Pay-day was Saturday night and the workers fought and brawled the length of the Overgate, the jostling heart of the medieval part of the city, and the police were kept busy with their specially constructed wheelbarrows carting away the casualties after the battles had subsided. Winston observed that he had "never seen parallel to any part of the United Kingdom" such "bestial drunkeness."

Since the days of the French Revolution, when its citizens sent money to the Jacobins, Dundee had been politically Radical. Then, the Government in London thought revolution so likely that an army garrison had to be stationed in the town and two of her citizens were transported to Australia merely for composing an address on the subject of reform. Later it became a centre of Chartist agitation and by the 1880's and 1890's Dundee was the home of Radical Liberalism, whose voice, the People's Journal, published strong reformist opinion. In 1892 however political opinion moved further leftwards when, with the formation of the Scottish Labour Party a Labour candidate stood in Dundee for the first time and polled 345 votes. Attracted by the puritan perfectionism of the new Labour party the Dundee Temperance Men, a body of idealistic but impractical reformers, soon afterwards deserted the Liberals bringing to their new allegiance their own distinctly illiberal views on the "demon drink" and in 1895 when the same Labour candidate stood on a prohibition pledge against the Liberal one of restrictions on opening times, he polled 1,313 votes. By the General Election of 1906 fifty one Labour candidates had been returned as Members of Parliament, including men like Keir Hardie and Ramsay Macdonald. Growing political support from Trade Unionists did not immediately foster the same measure of self-confidence in Labour party leaders and the infant national organisation chose to remain allied with the great Liberal tradition. Representative of this transitional period in Dundee, Alexander Wilkie, General Secretary of the Shipwrights union and no doctrinaire Socialist had, since entering Parliament, made a point of co-operating with his senior Liberal partner Edmund Robertson, now Lord Lochee. Nevertheless, considering the economic plight in which many Dundonians found themselves, it appeared likely that political opinion in the city would continue to swing further to the left. The Dundee Courier, the Tory daily, fishing in troubled waters put the matter succinctly:

"Mr Churchill takes the field not only against, a Unionist, but also against a representative of Labour whose candidature has been approved and endorsed by every trade organisation that can possibly be concerned. Here, then, we have the President of the Board of Trade deliberately endeavouring to keep out of Parliament a chosen representative of the working classes, who form the bulk of the citizens of Dundee. There cannot possibly be excuse for his actions. He had, as we have seen, the option of going to Merionith; he could have had Pembrokeshire; and he might have tried Stirling Burghs, where, as yet there is no Labour candidate in the field. Mr Churchill has ignored these constituencies, and has, in his capacity of Cabinet Minister, entered the lists against the accredited champion of Labour."

Could Winston, the Edwardian swell, with his silk top hat, silver-topped cane and overcoat with astrakhan collar, convince the Dundee workers that he was truly, a Radical among Radicals?

The Liberal Party organisation in London clearly did not think so, for there were rumours, soon substantiated, that the Labour

The Caledonian Railway Station, Dundee West, in 1908 – the scene of many of Winston's arrivals and departures, as a horse-drawn hackney carriage waits for custom beneath the canopy.

Party Executive still dependent on Liberal goodwill had been pressurised into asking their Candidate in Dundee, George Harold Stewart, a thirty six year old ex-postman from Oldham to withdraw from the contest.

Stewart however soon made it plain that whatever the Labour Party Executive decided, he himself had no intention of standing down. Referring publicly to the rumour about his withdrawal from the contest, Stewart, "alert and boyish looking," before a huge audience in the Gilfillan Hall declared with ponderous humour:

"If they (the Labour Party Executive) really do favour Mr Churchill and are to withdraw it will not be the first time in the history of these kingdoms that the House of Churchill has gained an advantage in an indirect and subtle way at the expense of the House of Stewart . . . Winston the Wanderer—(laughter and cheers)—who, having been defeated in Manchester, now makes Dundee the first stage of what to him will be a pilgrimage of sorrow." (renewed laughter and cheers)

Winston was expected in Dundee on Friday May 1st and long before his train arrived from the south, large numbers of people gathered at the West Station to greet him. Liberal dignitaries were present in full array and quite a stir was created when, upon the scene arrived an army of Suffragettes. Repudiating the suggestion that they had come to give Winston a warm reception, their leader assured the Station Superintendent they were there only to welcome Miss Christabel Pankhurst who was also due in on the same train to take part in the campaign. "We will be extremely decorous if you allow us onto the platform," said Miss Gothard, and their request granted, the Suffragettes joined the apprehensive reception party beyond the ticket barrier. To everyone's relief they were as good as their word.

As the train came alongside the platform Winston was seen at once, standing at the doorway of his First Class carriage. Cheers were raised as he stepped down accompanied by his brother Jack and friends and after introductions all round, the party moved towards the station exit where they were met by volley upon volley of cheers. In the booking hall the crush was so severe that Winston practically had to fight his way forward. Some groans were heard intermingled with the cheers when he reached the open but in response to shouts for a speech, Winston responded warmly saying:

"Gentlemen of Dundee a great conflict is going on in our country between the forces of progress and reaction, between the forces of freedom and restriction, between private interests and public rights. That battle has now reached a critical stage. The fortunes of the struggle hang in the balance, and at this juncture Dundee has

ARRIVED.

Courier cartoon from the 1908 election depicting Winston's arrival in Dundee hotfoot from his defeat in Manchester carpetbag in hand, the city's landmarks smoking chimneys and St. Mary's tower in the background.

stepped forward into the forefront of the fighting line. (Cheers) What has she done it for? She has done it to strike a good blow. Yes, gentlemen, not only a blow, a good blow. (Cheers) If you are to strike a blow before all the country, before the whole of this island in which we live, let it be a smashing blow." (Loud cheers)

Winston then entered his horse-drawn carriage and was driven off to the Queen's Hotel.

WILL WINSTON KEEP THE WIND FROM VEERING ?

A "Courier" campaign of the 1908 election which although scoring a telling point against Winston, nevertheless brings out the fact that it was his brilliant oratory that made victory possible considering the swing of public opinion against the Liberal Government.

The editor of the Courier was not so easily impressed;

"Mr W. S. Churchill, who arrived in Dundee this morning," he wrote scornfully, "has come to be known as a Promising Young Man in politics. The best sketch of this rising statesman was that offered to a Manchester audience last week by Mr Victor Grayson: – 'When you go to Mr Churchill and you ask him. Are you in favour of this?' He looks you straight in the eyes and says, 'Are you?' You answer, 'Yes'; he says, 'So am I. It's the very thing I have been wishing for ever since I was rocked in my cradle.' "

This sally set the pattern for each day's publication of the newspaper right up to election day; large articles prominently displayed in the centre pages virulently explored Winston's political past, seeking out the public statements he had made as a Conservative and contrasting them with his present opinions. He was lampooned mercilessly in cartoons and scurrilous little ditties such as –

"Winston's Way"
Promise any mortal thing anybody wants to get
   that's the art of canvassing.
Promise any mortal thing that might look as if t'would bring
   one more fish into the net hidden –
Promise any mortal thing anybody wants to get!

He was reminded he had once said, "The Radicals as a class are very peculiar people . . . A squabbling, disorganised rabble, who have neither a purpose, plan, policy, nor power . . . It (the Liberal Party) reminds me of some hoary-headed profligate overtaken in his old age by the results of the sins and follies of his youth." And, "The Radical Party is not dead . . . It is hiding from the public view like a toad in a block of coal, but when it stands forth in its hideousness the Tories will have to hew the filthy object limb from limb."

IF HE HAD ONLY KNOWN !

Two Dundee Liberal electors in the 1908 election discussing an anti-Churchill poster which cast up his anti-Liberal past as a Tory M.P. at Oldham. Winston's parliamentary career hung in the balance, another defeat after Manchester would probably have committed him to the political wilderness.

Press abuse however scathing was something Winston had learned to live with — he almost enjoyed it!

He had much ground to make up — the other candidates had been campaigning for some weeks — and in the few days left to him he had to make himself acquainted with all the quirks and peculiarities of his intended constituency.

"If you wish to know about elections" he wrote in retrospect, "I am the person to tell you . . . The visits to the prominent people, the tour of the constituency, and the study of its industries, interests, character and particular idiosyncrasies. Then decision as to the main line of the campaign. Writing the election address: Alarms and excursions in the local press! Opening of the contest! Nomination day! You walk with your principal friends to the Town Hall or other appointed place. Here you meet your opponent or opponents for the first time. Smiles of forced geniality are exchanged. 'Good morning, I am delighted to meet you. I hope we shall have a very pleasant contest! ' "

THE VALUE OF A GENIUS.

1908 election. Winston's reputation as a genius whose ability was marred by an enthusiasm for hare-brained schemes and projects was one from which he could not escape.

And so it turned out, each candidate fought hard and fiercely, yet each behaved in a spirit of chivalry and good humour.

Besides Labour, which Winston considered to be his greatest threat, the Unionist, Sir George Washington Baxter could not be lightly dismissed, for, although no Tory had ever been elected in Dundee since the great Reform Act of 1832, as a local man he was highly respected. A jute manufacturer, Sir George, despite that normally unpopular designaton, had his workers' interests at heart and was celebrated as a local philanthropist keenly interested in

AND THEY CALL THIS SAFE !!!

Courier cartoon from the 1908 election showing Winston perplexed by the problem that what had so recently been a safe seat in Dundee was on this occasion being contested by three other candidates plus the complicating issue of Woman's Suffrage which was not expected to help him. Though not against voting rights for women he had shown himself an opponent of their violent methods.

improving educational prospects for the underprivileged. He was no reactionary, his father had been in fact a Liberal Member of Parliament and Sir George himself had only left the Liberal Party in 1886 after Gladstone had introduced his Home Rule proposals for Ireland. He was however a champion of Tariff Reform and fought under the slogan 'Something must be done'. The jute trade

THE OLD, SWEET SONG.

Winston who defended Free Trade could not deny that Britain's main competitor was Germany protecting her industry by tariff barriers on our goods while theirs flooded into our market without hindrance. In this one-sided arrangement Dundee, heavily dependent on jute, suffered more than most and Winston's rival Sir George Baxter, the respected local candidate, comes to the rescue with the Tory life-belt entitled 'Protection'.

especially had suffered badly from foreign competition, mainly German, and Baxter's strongest card was, that if Protectionist policies had been followed by the Government, the present distress in the city could have been avoided.

The fourth candidate, Mr Edwin Scrymgeour, was well-known as a local councillor but any chance of his being elected was regarded by most responsible opinion as a forlorn hope. An idealistic Socialist not recognised by the Labour Party, his main platform was the abolition of intoxicating drink, and "Neddy", as he was known affectionately by his fellow Dundonians, was regarded as a harmless eccentric.

Winston could not afford to be complacent, for with a franchise of nearly 19,000 and as one of the three of the candidates competing for the Radical vote his share was bound to be diminished.

On the evening of his arrival he spoke in the Drill Hall. Packed to capacity with between five and six thousand people the demand for admission was so great that thousands more had to be turned away from the doors more than an hour before proceedings began.

Surrounded on the platform by Dundee's leading Liberals Winston's audience rose to their feet, waved handkerchiefs and cheered again and again.

"There is certainly, ladies and gentlemen," was his opening phrase upon the lull, "a keen and bracing air about the politics of Dundee–(Hear hear)–and I look forward with great exhilaration to having some opportunity of discussing political questions in the city and to upholding the whole argument which I desire to submit to you on this important occasion–(Hear hear) . . .

"I do not come here to apologise for His Majesty's Government. (hear hear) I say it is a fine record at home and abroad that we put before a Scottish constituency after two years administration. Foreign affairs, conducted with the dignity and the specific intent and with a success which even our opponents do not challenge. (Hear hear) India governed with wisdom and with sobriety and at the same time a just and earnest effort to reform administrative abuses and to give the people some share in their Government. (Cheers) South Africa–who is going to challenge our policy on South Africa? (Hear hear and cheers) A policy which has really brought a valiant people within the circle of the British Empire, which has not confined itself to the acquisition of territory or the conquest of goldmines, but which has won the hearts of men, and has made the most formidable of military antagonists today a colonial Prime Minister, (Louis Botha who had captured Winston at the Kranz River) serving loyally under the Crown (Cheers) No; I say we have nothing to be ashamed of . . .

"And yet," he continued "it would be foolish to suppose that we are not confronted with the elements of reaction and discontent . . . we cannot be blind to the fact that the influence of money (the brewers) expended through a dozen unauthorised associations and outside leagues, with the influence of a Press directed by millionaire proprietors who are awarded Life Peerages for their pains– (laughter)–and with the banding together of the great vested interests who consider themselves to be affected by Radical legislation enables a pressure and force to be brought to bear upon a particular constituency in which a bye-election occurs . . . "

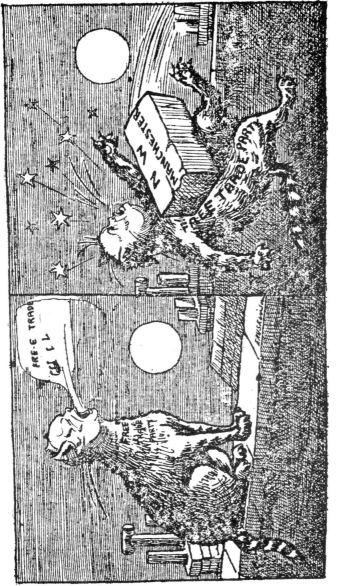

In 1908 a flood of cheap foreign imports mainly from Germany was adding to Britain's rising unemployment and Winston's defeat at North West Manchester had been largely attributed to his steadfast support for the continuance of the policy of free trade, after a large section of the Tory party proposed to help Britain's growing industry by imposing a stiff tariff barrier.

Winston then warned that the whole Liberal programme of Reform would be imperilled by the obstructive power of the House of Lords if the Upper Chamber judged that public opinion had swung back in favour of the Tories.

Defending the economic policy of Free Trade, he admitted there had been a distinct setback, but denied it was more than temporary:

"My confidence in the future of British industry is high" he assured his listeners. "I have no patience with those croakers who go about crying down the credit of their own country, making out that we are broken down and played out as an economic and commercial force in the world. (Cheers) . . . If you allow Tariffs to be imposed or restrict the free enterprise or rights of every trader to buy where he will . . . in the markets of the whole world . . . you will hamper your business, and if you allow people for private profit to impose taxation upon bread and meat you will cheat and starve your children." (Cheers)

The Liberal Government, he assured his audience, had reduced taxes and had produced a healthy balance of payments:

"Why, look at Germany" he pointed by comparison, "Look at their own pet Germany – (Laughter) – that they admire so much and want to imitate so often. Look at Germany. Germany has got taxes on everything that man or woman can desire, (Great laughter and cheers) . . . and yet, in spite of all these devices which we are asked to adopt, Germany in the last year showed a deficiency on the financial side of more than six millions."

Tariff Reform he explained would alter the balance between direct and indirect taxation and in such a way as to decrease the amount paid by the wealthy while increasing the amount paid by the wage-earner:

"Nothing" he said "more clearly indicates the capitalistic and undemocratic character of the Tariff Reform movement . . . I say to you with all solemnity that this talk about broadening the basis of taxation which you hear on very side means one thing and one thing only – it means making the poor pay more . . . no, no, we don't want to broaden the basis of taxation. No, it is the basis of society we want to broaden. (Cheers) We don't want to raise the levels of our tariff. It is the standard of life and labour we should elevate." (Cheers)

He referred to Tory attempts to prevent the passage through Parliament of the legislation which would limit the coalminer's working day to eight hours:

"Yes," he said scathingly, "they come and try to get votes from working men by telling them, if you pass the Miner's Eight Hour Bill, coal will cost you more. Well, gentlemen, I do not think it will, but even if it did, I would urge you to vote for that measure. (Cheers) Why, when you think of the danger of the work; of the lives that are lost every day; of the hardships of working underground in a cramped position in a high temperature; of the great distance to travel before the surface of the coal is reached; of the darkness — when you think of all these elements which constitute the daily life of the coal miner; when you read the medical evidence which is put before you on every hand; I say that eight hours work underground is quite enough. I am all for Free Trade, but I am not for Free Trade in labour or liquor." (Cheers)

For chronic unemployment Winston admitted, he had no easy answers, but looking ahead to the future proposed by simple analogy a revolutionary scheme for bridling the ruthless energies of the capitalist economy:

"You are all familiar with machinery" he said. "I spent a very pleasant afternoon going over a great mill, and I was looking at the powerful engine driving all the machinery in the mill, and I saw a governor spinning round, which corrected, by closing or opening the throttle of the valve, the rapidity with which the machinery revolved. Now, is it beyond our science in the 20th century, beyond our political knowledge and power, to place upon the industry of this country, perhaps through the agency of the Board of Trade, something which would have the effect of enabling us a little to increase the demand for unskilled labour in times of exceptional stringency and preserve a more uniform level?"

Concluding his speech with a rousing appeal he reminded his listeners:

"There is no short cut to prosperity. (Cheers) There is no conjuring trick, no wizard's incantation whereby the hard facts of daily life can be suddenly or strikingly altered or ameliorated but there are principles of policy, of economics, of morals . . . open to us more widely by the science of modern times, by which we may lead the millions onward and upward to better and brighter lives to happier and nobler destinies. There is a great cause of international peace and goodwill among nations of the earth. There is education . . . the scientific and technical training of the youth of the country in skill of hand and in qualities of heart and character indispensible to success. There is the cause of religious equality . . . there is the cause of temperance . . . well worth fighting for, well worth running risks for, (Cheers) well worth losing bye-elections for. (Cheers) There is freedom of trade which we have still to guard; there is freedom of land which we have yet to win (Cheers) yes, but if these things are to be gained you have to fight. It is to come forward at your head in this battle that you have asked me to come to Dundee. (Loud cheers) I accept the duty. (Prolonged cheers) Tonight we go on active service, (Hear hear) tonight we unfurl our standard. It is the old flag of civil freedom of social justice under which your fathers conquered, and under which you in turn shall be unconquerable. (Cheers) Let us so ask that it comes to no misfortune or dishonour at our hands."

Amid the reverberations of crash upon crash of sustained cheering Winston resumed his seat after speaking for an hour and a quarter.

With what he must have considered to be a magnificent beginning to his campaign Winston threw himself energetically into the contest.

"Every morning," he wrote later, with his Dundee experience very much in mind, "between nine and ten the Committee, all the heads of departments represented—posters, canvassers, the reports from the different committee rooms, progress of the canvass, press notices, advertisements, motor cars, meetings, prevention of disorder (at your own meetings), cautioning everyone about the election laws, prominent persons who required to be attended to, and so on. Then out and about round the constituency . . . in a two horse landau, at about seven miles an hour. Meetings early in the morning when the workmen have their lunch, meetings in their dinner hour, meetings in the afternoon . . . three meetings every evening, rushing from one to the other."

Winston spoke in the following days of the new dynamic Liberalism and the social policy which he intended to pursue personally at the Board of Trade. He announced plans for an old-age pension scheme for the half a million people over seventy which would cost the Exchequer six millions a year and introduced Lloyd George's equally revolutionary proposals for unemployment insurance.

Still, his opponents resisted stubbornly. Some observers even felt that Baxter might well gain the seat by the combination of his quiet moderation and the open divisions in the forces of the Left. Winston himself, referring to Labour, had denounced "the wanton division of the forces of progress" and "the false friends upon our flanks stabbing at us even while we fight for them." His opposition in the Commons to Ramsay MacDonald's 'Right to Work' Bill, a well-meaning, but ill-conceived piece of legislation, was used against him by both Stewart and Scrymgeour, and Keir Hardie, the cloth-capped leader of the Parliamentary Labour Party, in a letter of support to Stewart, spoke of Winston's "shameless prevarications" on the subject. The old age pension scheme was greeted with derision by many of the more articulate working class, few believing they would ever live to receive it and regarded Winston's stirring rhetoric with hostile scepticism. A Mr Robert Stewart, then Scrymgeour's election agent and later a founder member of the British Communist Party, remembered of one meeting in the Drill Hall when Winston shouted to the crowd "Britain has great Imperial strength. We have belted the world with free Institutions." Churchill was, Stewart reflected sardonically, "Speaking in Bell Street, next door to the Sheriff Court, across the road from the Salvation Army Home for Fallen Women; next door to that was the Parish Council Lunatic Department, nearby the Night Refuge for homeless people to get a cup of tea in bed before they started their wanderings next day. The gulf between Churchill's oratory and the living reality was there in the street where the meeting was held."

However by the end of the first week Winston felt sufficiently confident of the adherence of the middle class traditional Liberal voter that he was able to make an extraordinary attempt to capture additional support from the two opposing ends of the political spectrum.

On the Monday preceding the poll, before an audience of thousands in the Kinnaird Hall he addressed a meeting which, according to the Manchester Guardian, evoked memories of the great days of Gladstone. After being received with loud and prolonged cheering and putting forward an eloquent case for Irish Home Rule, Winston made a direct appeal to working class voters asking them to form a united front against Tory reaction, and yet, at the same time, turning upon the very principles of his Socialist opponent and defining once and for all his own political attitude to the new creed:

"Let me first say a word about Socialism", he explained quietly, "There are a great many Socialists whose opinions and whose views I have the greatest respect for − (Hear hear) − men, some of whom I know well, and whose friendship I have the honour to enjoy . . . I am dealing rather with those of violent and extreme views who call themselves Socialists . . . To the revolutionary Socialists I do not appeal as the Liberal candidate for Dundee. I recognise that they are perfectly right in voting against me and voting against the Liberals, because Liberalism is not Socialism and never will be. (Cheers) . . . There are many steps we have to take which our Socialist opponents or friends, whichever they like to call them- selves, will have to take with us; but there are immense differences of principle and of political philosophy between the views we put forward and the views they put forward.

"Socialism" he continued, going on to contrast the two systems of political thought in a series of terse epigrams, "seeks to pull down wealth; Liberalism seeks to raise up poverty. (Loud cheers)

"Socialism would destroy private interests; Liberalism would preserve private interests in the only way in which they can be safely and justly preserved, namely by reconciling them with public right. (Cheers)

"Socialism would kill enterprise; Liberalism would rescue enterprise from the trammels of privilege and preference. (Cheers)

"Socialism assails the pre-eminence of the individual; Liberalism seeks . . . to build up a minimum standard for the mass. (Cheers)

"Socialism exalts the rule; Liberalism exalts the man.

"Socialism attacks capital; Liberalism attacks monopolies. (Cheers) These are the great distinctions which I draw . . . between our philosophies and our ideals.

"Ah! gentlemen, I don't want to embark upon bitter or harsh controversy, but I think the exalted ideal of the Socialist—a universal brotherhood, owning all things in common—is not always supported by the evidence of their practice. (Laughter)

"They put before us a creed of universal self-sacrifice, they preach it in the language of spite and envy . . . They tell us that we should dwell together in unity and comradeship. They are themselves split into twenty obscure factions, who hate and abuse each other more than they hate and abuse us. (Hear hear and laughter) They wish to reconstruct the world. They begin by leaving out human nature. (Laughter) Consider how barren a philosophy is the creed of absolute collectivism. Equality of reward irrespective of service rendered! It is expressed in other ways. You know the phrase—'From each according to his ability, to each according to his needs.' (Laughter) How nice that sounds. Let me put it another way—'You shall work according to your fancies; you shall be paid according to your appetite.' (Cheers) Although I have tried my very best to understand these propositions, I have never been able to imagine the mechanical heart in the socialist world which is to replace the ordinary human heart that palpitates in our breast. What motive is to induce men, not for a day, or an hour, or a year, but for all their lives, to make a supreme sacrifice of their individuality? . . . And what then are we to make this sacrifice for? It is," said Winston scornfully answering his own question, "for the sake of society. And what is society? I will tell you what society is. Translated into concrete terms. Socialist society is a set of disagreeable individuals who obtained a majority for their caucus at some recent election, and whose officials in consequence look on humanity through innumerable grills and pigeon-holes and across innumerable counters, and say to them, 'Tickets, please.' (Laughter) Truly this grey old world has never seen so grim a joke." (Applause)

Winston admitted that State enterprise had an important part to play in Britain's economy but, he concluded, "When we are told to exalt and admire a philosophy which destroys individualism and seeks to replace it by collectivism, I say that is a monstrous and imbecile conception which can find no real foothold in the brains and hearts of sensible people." (Loud cheers)

He paused for a moment and thanking any convinced Socialist who might have been present, for the courtesy and patience with which they had listened to him, he asked for the help of all Trade Unionists:

"Labour in Britain," he said "is not Socialism. It is quite true that the Socialistic element has imposed a complexion on Labour, rather against its will, and has been largely supported in its actions by funds almost entirely supplied by Trade Unions. But Trade Unions are not Socialistic. They are the antithesis of Socialism . . . and I have the right, as a member of His Majesty's Government to speak with good confidence to Trade Unionists, because we have done more for Trade Unionists than any other Government that has ever been. (Cheers) We have," he said pointing to the security enjoyed by Trade Unions since the passing of the Trades Disputes Act, "given them a Charter . . . Do they really believe – I put this question to them fairly – do they really believe that there is no difference whatever between a Tory and a Liberal Government? (A Voice – 'None') Winston smiled, "One gentleman in this great gathering, believes that there is no difference between a Tory and a Liberal Government. (Laughter) Now, his cure is simple. He has only to listen to Sir George Baxter. (Laughter) . . . Do Trade Unionists really desire the downfall of the existing Liberal Government? Would they really like to send a message of encouragement to the House of Lords . . . such as this – 'House of Lords, you were right in your estimate of public opinion when you denied the extension of the provision of meals to schoolchildren in Scotland, when you threw out the Scottish Land Valuation Bill, when you threw out the Scottish Smallholders Bill – when you did all this you were right.' Do you wish to send that message to the House of Lords? (Cries of 'No') That will be the consequence of every vote subtracted from the Liberal majority. (Hear hear) . . . What would happen if this present Government were to perish? On its tomb would be written – 'Beware of Social Reform.' (Laughter) The working classes – will not support a Government engaged in Social Reforms. Every Social Reform will cost you votes. Beware of Social Reform. Learn to think imperially." (Tremendous cheering)

Almost every wealthy Dundonian of any note had turned up to hear Winston and they now sat, drawn by curiosity from the plush comfort of their mansions in the fashionable West End of the city and the seaside suburb of Broughty Ferry, listening intently for his next thought-provoking revelation. He paused to allow the enthusiasm of the generality of his audience to subside:

"To those," he said speaking quietly again, revealing with eloquent sincerity his own belief in the essential conservatism of the British people, "who say 'We like Free Trade and we are Liberals at heart, but this is too Radical . . . why can't they let well alone, what do they mean by introducing all these measures . . . which disturb credit and trade and interfere with the course of business and cause so many class struggles in the country?' I turn to those who say that . . . and I say to them . . . Why is it that life and property are more secure in Britain than in any other country in the world? Why is it that our credit is so high and that our commerce stretches so far? . . . I will tell those wealthy and powerful people what the secret of the security of life and property in Britain is. The security arises from the continuation of that very class struggle of which they lament, of which they complain, and which goes on ceaselessly in our country . . . with perpetual friction, a struggle between class and class in this country, which never sinks into lethargy, and never breaks into violence, but which from year to year makes a steady and constant advance. It is on that class struggle that the security of life and property in our country is fundamentally reposed. We are always changing; like nature we change a great deal, although we change always very slowly. We always change, and consequently we are always reaching a higher level after each change, but yet with the harmony of our life unbroken and unimpaired. And I say also to those persons here, to whom I now make my appeal—wealthy men, men of light and leading have never all been on one side in our country. There have always been men of power and position who have sacrificed and exerted themselves in the popular cause, and that is why there is so little class hatred in our land in spite of all the squalor and the misery which we see around us. There, gentlemen, lies the true evolution of democracy. That is how we have preserved the golden thread of historical continuity when many others have lost if forever. That is the only way in which your island life as you know it and love it, can be preserved in all its grace and in all its freedom, can be elevated, expanded, and illumined for those who will occupy our places when our share in the world's work is done."

Amid tumultuous cheering and applause Winston resumed his seat.

"I think," he wrote later, "this was upon the whole the most successful election speech I have ever made. The entire audience, over two thousand persons, escorted me, cheering and singing through the streets of Dundee to my hotel."

ANOTHER MANCHESTER ?

During both campaigns Winston was to be plagued by bell-ringing targers demanding votes for women.

A number of his other meetings went less smoothly. The local Suffragettes, joined by their compatriots from Manchester, were determined to see Winston repeat his recent humiliation. "And," he recollected, "a peculiarly virulent Scotch virago armed with a large dinner bell interrupted every meeting to which she could obtain access . . ." At one open-air meeting at the Blackness Foundry during the dinner hour Miss Malony, the persistent bell ringer, forced Winston to beat a tactical retreat and then, driven in his car some distance up the road, was chased by the poster-covered horse carriage of the Womens Freedom League with the indefatigable Miss Malony balanced on the drivers seat vehemently ringing her bell. Pursued and pursuer were soon surrounded by the noisy expectant crowd which had followed them up the road. "I will make no attempt to compete" Winston remarked to his listeners with studied coolness, "with a lady in a high state of excitement." And sitting down, leisurely took out and lit a cigarette. Another attempt was made to throw off the Suffragettes by driving still further west but they soon caught up again. Mr George Ritchie, the dignified Chairman of the Dundee Liberal Association, bursting out in exasperation, "Disgraceful is not the word for this." Winston stood up in the back of the car, his flushed face betraying his anger. "I call your attention," he shouted above the racket of Miss Malony's bell and the chatter of the gathering crowd, as he contemplated his imminent rout, "to the methods adopted by the women who want a vote. They want to obtain a vote but observe what regard they have for the rights of free speech. If she thinks she will advance her cause before the working men of Dundee by adopting such tactics as this let her do it. It only saves me the trouble of making a speech to you and I only say good afternoon."

On Friday 8th of May, the eve of the poll, the situation, as far as Winston was concerned, remained obscure with several important factors contributing to the uncertainty. That morning in banner headlines the Courier ran news of the 'impending' closure of one of the city's biggest jute mills which threatened to lay off hundreds of workers, and, making the most of it, the editorial savagely laid all the blame on Winston and Free Trade. On top of all the other afflictions suffered by the Dundee economy this could have proved devastating—if it had been true! It was however only a clever and unscrupulous Tory ruse designed to lose Winston votes. The Caledon shipyard lock-out also ground on and although Winston had returned to London on the evening of Tuesday the 5th to join Alexander Wilkie, Dundee's existing Labour M.P. and the Board of Trade conciliation team to try to bring an end to the dispute, his one day's absence at the capital had been without apparent result. Nevertheless, the Courier's "London Letter" writer grudgingly admitted of his efforts that "If Mr Churchill can show he is as good a conciliator as Mr Lloyd George, and, moreover, can lay claim to have settled one of the biggest labour disputes of the last twelve months, this will help him in his candidature. Mr Churchill has already come near to doing this."

Winston's appeal to the fifteen hundred-strong Irish vote— descendants of the despised immigrants who had come over in the last century to work the linen trade—had so far met with a mixed reception. It was true that O'Donnel Derrick, Secretary of the Irish League in Scotland, convinced of Winston's sincerity when he promised Home Rule had advised his fellow Catholics in

THE MORNING OF BATTLE.

Though the Liberal Dundee "Advertiser" was owned, like the Dundee "Courier", by Winston's severest critic, David Couper Thomson, the paper was to retain for some time a certain degree of editorial independence which is amply reflected by this cartoon published on the eve of the 1908 election which hero-worshipped Winston as an idealistic knight-errant pledged to defeat Tory reaction.

FIGHTING THE GOOD FIGHT.

An "Advertiser" cartoon of the 1908 election. Winston in the role of Robert Bruce at Bannockburn strikes furiously Liberal sword in hand, against Sir George Baxter the Tory candidate.

blasphemous terms to "go to the polling booths and make the sign of the cross opposite the name of Winston Churchill." And, the offices of the Dundee Catholic Herald formed an active centre for pro-Winston propaganda by distributing his favours and propaganda leaflets. But, the local priesthood, no doubt motivated by their conservative hierarchy, fearing a revival of Protestant persecution, instructed their flock to vote for Baxter.

That evening in the Kinnaird Hall Winston made his final address to the electorate. For three minutes his audience cheered and sang "For He's A Jolly Good Fellow" and when he rose to speak he was met with the cry, 'Three Cheers for the Smashing Blow'!

Pointing to the recent swing of by-election defeats for the Government, mentioning among them amid great laughter his own at North West Manchester, Winston stressed the crucial nature of the present fight. And to the Party's faithful he declared flatteringly:

"The stage is cleared, and into the middle of the National arena march the electors of Dundee. (Cheers) . . . I have been here now for eight days, moving up and down your streets, meeting face to face the electors, and I have never yet seen audiences where people thought more about the fundamental acts of politics, and where they were more ready to give a fair hearing to every view that I have found in your great city. (Cheers)

"When you asked me to come to Dundee you knew perfectly well you were plunging into the storm . . . You did not hesitate to give me a unanimous invitation—(Cheers)—to a great industrial centre—a great manufacturing and labouring city, and I accepted that invitation. Other seats—safe seats, seats where there would have been no contest at all—were placed at my disposal by patriotic Liberals who were willing to make sacrifices of their personal position in order to carry the cause forward (Cheers) I chose Dundee. (Cheers, again and again renewed) Now, it is for Dundee to choose. (Cheers)

"Our opponents," he continued, elaborating on his Manchester speech and making a last merciless assault on the Tory enemy, "have left us in no doubt about their policy. We know what to expect when they return to power—a Party of great vested interests, banded together in a formidable confederation; corruption at home, aggression to cover it abroad; the trickery of Tariff jungles; the tyranny of wealth-fed Party machines; sentiment by the bucketful—(Great laughter)—patriotism and imperialism by the Imperial pint—(More laughter)—an open hand at the public Exchequer, an open door at the public house—(Laughter and great cheering)—dear food for the millions, cheap labour for the

The Overgate in 1908 looking east to the High Street from Tally Street.

The foot of the Wellgate, in 1908, at its junction with the Murraygate.

73

millionaire. (Laughter) That is the policy which the Tory Party offers you, and that is the policy which I ask you tonight to strike at with the battle axe of Scotland. (Cheers)

"We may differ amongst ourselves," he entreated finally of the working class members of his audience, " . . . about how far, how fast, and in what direction we are to move forward. But in one thing we are agreed; we are not going back – not one inch. (Loud cheers) We are not going back; we are going on. Our movement is towards a better, fairer organisation of society; and . . . the time will surely come . . . when the dull, grey clouds under which millions of our countrymen are monotonously toiling will break and melt, and vanish forever in the sunshine of a new and noble age." (Loud cheers)

For Winston, during the closing moments in the counting of the votes, the tension became almost unbearable. Bob Stewart, the Election Agent for the Prohibition candidate recalled:

"I noticed Churchill standing alone in a corner twisting little rubber bands around his fingers, and as each one broke he threw it away. He was obviously in a very agitated condition. I went over and started a conversation with him about stopping the sale of strong drink, asking what he would do in Parliament to bring this into law. It was obvious that he was only interested in one thing – the result. 'How do you think it is going?' he asked me. 'You're in by a mile, worse luck,' I said. You didn't have to look at the vote counting very long to see that."

Mr George Ritchie, the Chairman of the Dundee Liberal Association, gravely dignified with his white goatee beard, also had words of encouragement, and giving Winston and his self-doubts a wintry smile, observed, "The majority will be about 3,000."

Just before midnight around 30,000 people crowded into Courthouse Square to hear the announcement of the result. At ten minutes past twelve the Sheriff Courthouse door opened and Sheriff Ferguson, with Winston by his left hand, stepped onto the balcony. Instinctively the crowd knew he had won and a roar grew, from the front of the open square, which was taken up by the streams of people who were out of sight of the event packing Bell Street to the left and Lochee Road to the right, and swelled out into a crescendo of noise. Winston was the hero of the hour. He had won by a comfortable 2,709 majority over the other candidates. Sir George Baxter was runner up with 4,370, George Stewart got 4,014 and Scrymgeour, last of all, lost his deposit with only 655.

The score of policemen guarding Winston's car linked arms against the surge of people but when he took his seat, the crowd, delirious with enthusiasm and excitement, crushed round and Winston stood up waving acknowledgement to the frantic mass.

Daily Mirror

THE MORNING JOURNAL WITH THE SECOND LARGEST NET SALE.

No. 1,414.   Registered at the G.P.O. as a Newspaper   MONDAY, MAY 11, 1908.   One Halfpenny.

ASK FOR the Special Extra
BEAUTY NUMBE[R]
of the "DAILY MIRROR."
PRICE ONE PENNY.
NOW ON SALE.

[M]R. WINSTON CHURCHILL FINDS "A SAFE SEAT" AT LAST: REJECTED MANCHESTER, HE IS ELECTED M.P. FOR DUNDEE.

Victorious at last in Dundee Winston waves jubilantly from the back of his open landau to the crowds lining Reform Street. But with a majority of only 2709 votes his "safe seat" had been hard won and in no future election could he ever consider a favourable result as certain.

75

Slowly, the car passed along Bell Street, with the twenty policemen hanging onto its sides for dear life while the sergeant, seated ludicrously astride the bonnet, energetically waved his arms as a signal for a clear passage. Outside the Liberal Club in Reform Street the scene was one of intense excitement and as Winston passed by the lined street thousands were added to the mighty crowd which followed in his wake. Passing the east end of the Overgate and turning right into the High Street, by the Old Town House, the car proceeded at a snail's pace into the Nethergate past the Old Steeple. Winston must have felt as if he would never make the last two hundred yards to the Queen's Hotel. There too, thousands were waiting and passage seemed impossible as his police escort were, in the surge, suddenly brushed off the car like flies. Regaining control however, both car and police reached the hotel entrance where they elbowed and pushed to make a clear way. As Winston stepped out of the car he was surrounded on every hand.

Pulled this way and that he had literally to be hauled into the door of the hotel, breathless from his ordeal.

Safe inside and after resting for a few minutes he appeared on the balcony above the entranceway and was met with an outburst of cheering which continued for fully five minutes though he held up his hand several times for silence. With his eyes sparkling and his voice choked with emotion he spoke haltingly at first, "Gentlemen for the first time I have the honour to address you as the Member for Dundee. (Cheers) This has been a memorable election. Four candidates have been in the field. Let me say of these other gentlemen that they have fought this fight like Britons. But gentlemen when all these just courtesies have been paid the result remains and that result is what I told you it would be, a thunderbolt from the north. (Cheers) It is a triumph for the people's cause. It is a triumph for the grand old Liberal Party. (Cheers) It is a victory for Free Trade. (Cheers) It is a victory for temperance. (Cheers) It is a victory for Ireland. When all the cross-currents and all the conflicting issues have passed away this election will be regarded as the decisive expression of the true instincts of a great people.

"Gentlemen let us follow the main road. Let us march straight forward, seven thousand strong upon that road of progress to peace, justice, and to truth. Dundee forever! (Great cheers) Scotland to the fore! I bid you all goodnight. You have done a good day's work for democracy." (Great and prolonged cheering)

The crowd would not let him go. Winston took out his handkerchief and waved it with all his might in every direction for several minutes then turned and went into the hotel.

Dundee Election.
May. 9th 1908

Winston S. Churchill

Arthur C. Murray

Charles F.G. Masterman

De Forest

A.m. Anderson

Edward Marsh

John S. Churchill

George Ritchie

Frederick E. Guest

alex M: Maclean

A page dating Winston's first Dundee election from the autograph book of Miss Flora Scrymgeour – her father was a reporter in the D. C. Thomson organisation.

CHAPTER II

PEOPLE'S TRIBUNE

FOR SEVEN EXHAUSTIVE weeks Winston had been at the hustings in Dundee and as he wrote later, "It was with the greatest relief that I returned to London, and was introduced into the House of Commons by the Prime Minister, Mr Asquith, took my seat as a Member of the Cabinet and settled down to enjoy the Board of Trade."

Although during the two election campaigns they had kept in touch by letter, now at last Winston had time to resume once more his neglected courtship of Clementine. The Duke of Marlborough invited her to visit Blenheim and Winston, adding to his cousin's plea, wrote, "I want so much to show you that beautiful place, in its gardens we shall find lots of places to talk in and lots of things to talk about." Welcome as the invitation must have been, it could not have come at a more awkward time, for, Clementine later told her son Randolph, she was down to her last clean cotton frock – "everyone except me had a maid and I remember having to stand for fear of getting it crushed." Nevertheless, she accepted and arrived at Blenheim on Monday August 10th with Lady Randolph to act as her chaperone.

The following morning Winston slept late as usual while Clementine, by complete contrast, was up and about early and Marlborough had to entertain her himself with a drive around the park. In the late afternoon – wide awake this time – Winston took her for a walk. The rain came on and they took shelter in the ornamental temple which stands in the ground overlooking the lake. He proposed, and was accepted.

That night Clementine wrote Winston a loving note before going to bed, illustrating it with a drawing of a heart inscribed inside with his name, and the following morning he brought to her a bunch of roses.

They were married in St. Margaret's Westminster in September 1908 and from then on, as Winston observed, they lived together "happily ever afterwards."

Winston's guide and mentor at the Board of Trade was the forty five year old Welsh Radical David Lloyd George, a man of great and original genius who was to exert immense influence upon his career in Government. Born actually in Manchester, Lloyd George's schoolmaster father had died young and at the age of three he and his mother had to go and live in North Wales where they were looked after by her brother Richard Lloyd a village cobbler, whose second name he adopted. Though desperately poor, enough money was scraped together to allow him to study for the law and at the age of twenty-one Lloyd George was admitted to practise as a solicitor where he soon made his mark by fiercely defending the rights of the Welsh non-conformists, who, though forming a majority religious faith in Wales, were forced to support the established church. He was soon afterwards elected as Liberal M.P. for Carnaervon−a seat he was to hold for forty years−and in Parliamentary debate speedily won attention for his fearless attacks on Tory Government policies which he delivered with a quick and often malicious wit. Unlike Winston, whose antipathies were only skin deep, Lloyd George actually hated the upper classes, holding them responsible for the deprivation of his childhood. No mere meek and mild reformer, Lloyd George was a crusader with a mission, whose self-chosen task was to humble the rich and raise up the poor.

Winston, writing much later of his relationship with him, said: "No-one can have worked as closely as I have with Mr Lloyd George without being both impressed and influenced by him. At his best he could almost talk a bird out of a tree . . . I have seen him turn a Cabinet round in less than ten minutes, and yet when the process was complete, no-one could remember any particular arguments to which to attribute their change of views . . . One of his most impressive faculties was the power of seeing, in moments when everyone was asking about the next step, the step after that . . . "

Unfortunately, Lloyd George's skill as a conciliator was eventually to burden him with a reputation for double dealing, and his vanity which equally matched Winston's would place severe stresses on their long relationship.

During his two years in the Board of Trade Lloyd George had already worked out the details for his scheme of social betterment for some at least of Britain's deprived millions, laying the foundations for what was to become the Welfare State. But, when Winston took over it remained for theory to be translated into practice and it was mainly due to Winston's driving energy and determination, in the fact of obstruction and red tape from his unimaginative civil servants that was to put the necessary legislation on the Statute Book. As the historian Professor R. K. Webb was to note, "There was nothing automatic about Social Reform, even when the ground was well prepared; to enact it required stamina, authority and egotism." W. H. Beveridge, later Lord Beveridge and the founder of the National Health Service, observed of Winston's period at the Board of Trade that it was a most "striking illustration of how much the personality of the Minister in a few critical months may change the course of social legislation."

Winston set up Trade Boards to curb the excesses of sweated labour in certain of the worst industries—although significantly, and unaccountably, he left out jute. This was followed by the Miners' Accident Bill, the Coal Mines Bill and most important of all, he played a major parliamentary role in the passage of the National Insurance Act and the setting up of employment exchanges.

To persuade and argue against the doubts and objections of his permanent administrative staff that his proposals were unworkable or unrealistic, Winston's grasp of what was an entirely new concept of Government intervention in industry was severely tested. But his homework had been done thoroughly. In 1907, prior to going off on his African trip, he had visited the Kaiser's Germany where the most all-embracing system of social welfare was already in operation, and the wonder of the world, though mainly financed by large deductions from the weekly pay packet of the German worker, sweated at his labour for twelve hours daily. He had also made frequent visits in a spirit of humble enquiry to the home of Sidney and Beatrice Webb, the great Socialist intellectuals who founded the influential Fabian Society.

The reforms which Winston and Lloyd George introduced seemed to the upper classes to verge on revolution, but, despite that, they came too late to satisfy either the British workers' rising tide of expectation or even their sense of economic justice. Food prices were soaring. Unemployment was continuing its dramatic rise—between 1907 and 1908 the rate had nearly doubled—with the hardest hit, engineering, shipbuilding and coalmining, and as profits declined owners tried to cut wages. The workers naturally resisted.

Winston's support of the eight hour day for the miners seemed to city financiers and capitalist industrialists, like economic suicide. His answer to them in Parliament was that Britain's industrial workers, "are not content that their lives should remain mere alternations between bed and the factory. They demand time to look about them, time to see their homes by daylight, to see their children, time to think and read and cultivate their gardens, time, in short, to live. That is very strange perhaps," he added with heavy sarcasm, "but that is the request they have made and are making with increasing force and reason as the years pass by."

When Lloyd George had been at the Board of Trade he had attempted to cope with the industrial unrest by setting up conciliation machinery, but the problem had so increased that Winston found himself now with as many cases to solve as in the two previous years put together. It was work he relished though, and was good at. After returning from the election in Dundee his first job, as he had promised his electors, was to find a settlement of the shipyard lockout. He managed to get the workers to accept a compromise cut of one shilling and sixpence (7½p) per week in wages, promised them permanent negotiation machinery and persuaded Reginald McKenna, the first Lord of the Admiralty, to bring forward the Naval construction plans for 1909, which would give the Dundee yard fresh orders and reduce unemployment.

As Winston had feared, hostility to all of the Liberal Party's programme continued to build up in the House of Lords. Lord Landsdowne forecasted with fatuous insensitivity that non-contributory pensions for the aged would "Weaken the moral fibre of the nation and diminish the self-respect of the people." The issue was finally brought to a head when Lloyd George introduced his **People's Budget in 1909.** "I made up my mind," said the little Welshman, "that . . . no cupboards should be barer, no lot harder to bear." Winston too, angry that the Lords had already rejected the previous year's Licensing Bill, was eager for a showdown. Once at dinner he said with menace, "We shall send them up a budget in June that shall terrify them, they have started the class war, they had better be careful."

To find the revenue for the old age pension scheme, and for the seven new battleships insisted upon by the Navy, Lloyd George placed a 5% Estate Duty on property of one million pounds or over, together with a series of other land taxes, and increased the Income Tax from one shilling (5p) to one shilling and twopence (6p) in the pound. Though tiny by today's standards, the wealthy propertied classes regarded the new taxes as nothing short of confiscation, and, through the power of the House of Lords to so amend a Commons Bill that it would to all intents and purposes be rendered ineffective, they intended to resist.

Prime Minister Asquith tried to come to some kind of gentleman's agreement with King Edward, that if the Liberal Party were returned with a fresh mandate, then he, the King, would if necessary, create enough new Peers to make certain that the budget would pass through the Lords without amendment. Though the

King was equivocal and would give no definite undertaking, rather than see all their reforms mangled, the Liberals prepared to fight an election anyway, and with the slogan 'Peers versus People' Lloyd George and Winston, the Party's two biggest crowd-pullers spoke up and down the country to marshall the support of public opinion.

On July 18th 1909 addressing the Scottish Liberal Association in Edinburgh, in words which would not be quarrelled with by any modern Socialist left winger or neo-marxist, Winston spoke of the esential nature of land ownership.

"Examine," he said, "the enrichment which comes to the landlord who happens to own a plot of land on the outskirts or at the centre of one of our great cities, who watches the busy population making the city larger, richer, more convenient, more famous every day and all the while sits still and does nothing. The roads are made, the streets are made, the railway services are improving, electric light turns night into day, electric trains glide to and fro, water is brought from reservoirs and hundred miles off in the mountains, and all the while the landlord sits still.

"Every one of these improvements is effected by the labour and at the cost of other people—yet his (the landlord's) land value is enhanced. When the land is finally sold, it is sold by the yard or inch at ten times, twenty times or even fifty times its agricultural value on which alone it hitherto has been rated for public service."

Lloyd George in his famous Limehouse speech—a masterpiece of invective—savagely attacked the aristocracy:

"A fully equipped Duke" he said, with devastating humour, "costs as much to keep us as two Dreadnoughts, (battleships) and Dukes are just as great a terror and they last longer." He held up to ridicule the wasteful, indolent, parasitic life of the patrician—"Who has one man to fix his collar and adjust his tie in the morning, a couple of men to carry his boiled egg to him at breakfast, a fourth man to open the door for him in and out of his carriage, a sixth and a seventh to drive him."

Winston published a one hundred and fifty page pamphlet entitled "The People's Rights," and at St. Andrews Halls in Glasgow on January 12th, 1910, thundered accusingly of the House of Lords that it was "Filled with old doddering Peers, cute financial magnates, clever wire pullers, big brewers with bulbous noses. All the enemies of progress are there—weaklings, sleek, smug, comfortable self-important individuals."

At Inverness the following day, five days before polling day, he said of the Lords at first in gentler, more humorous mood—

"You have been told by one of these proud Peers that civilisation was the work of aristocracy. He would have been nearer the truth if he had said, 'The upkeep of aristocracy has been the hard work of all civilisation.' " (Laughter)

Then, outdoing even Lloyd George in the violence of his expression, he said of the Tories that: "Just as they clutched greedily at the last sour unpalatable dregs of the bottle before it was torn away from them at the last election, so now when they see a possible chance of obtaining power and place, they kick over the whole table in an ugly wish to jam their noses in the trough."

As the campaign came to its climax the emphasis changed suddenly in character, from the issue of the Lords to the long disputed question of Free Trade, for by their insistence that Tariff Reform would reduce unemployment, the Tories were undoubtedly winning working class support. At Dundee on January 15th Winston was forced to argue in language of a markedly higher level than he had been using of late, that:

"The lie of protection has been inverted to give the property classes means of warding off the insistent claims of the social and remedial legislation for the masses of the population . . . Every advocate of reaction and monopoly would know, that by blatant newspapers, by public house organisation and influence, by the pressure of the privileged class on their dependents and upon those who are affected by them, by flagrant misrepresentations, by thrusting humbugging statistics, false misleading theories before the electorate, it was possible to go on in the old evil ways, trample on reform, and cast all progress underfoot."

The Dundee Courier had watched Winston's lightening progress up and down Britain with profound distaste, calling him a quack doctor after his Glasgow speech and on the following Monday, petulantly demanding to know why he had been invited to Germany—as had recently been reported—to study the Kaiser's Army maneouvres when he ought instead remain in Britain and look after the Board of Trade. Speculating that Winston might be about to take over the War Office from Haldane, the article went on to say that if that were true, it "would be regarded as most objectionable . . . it is very certain that ninety nine hundreds of the Army officers and men are Unionists, to this extent, that they believe in upholding the present Constitution of the British Empire, against which Mr Winston Churchill and his socialistic allies declared war."

Speaking of his election methods the Courier editor commented: "Mr Churchill is a political contortionist like the three-legged symbol so favoured by the Isle of Man, he seems to point in all directions but really concentrates attention upon himself all the time."

Then, referring to Winston's double candidature on the same platform alongside Alexander Wilkie, which cemented the close partnership the two men had established in Parliament, the Courier

WINSTON BACK AGAIN.

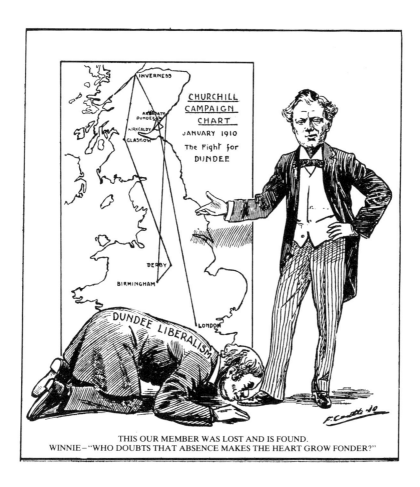

THIS OUR MEMBER WAS LOST AND IS FOUND.
WINNIE – "WHO DOUBTS THAT ABSENCE MAKES THE HEART GROW FONDER?"

Winston was considered the Liberal Party's greatest asset and besides his ministerial responsibilities was required to speak the length and breadth of the country. The first of the two elections held in 1910 over the issue of the House of Lords versus Parliament was a gruelling ordeal yet Winston's one brief visit to the city was misrepresented as a case of ill-considered neglect for his constituents.

concluded; "It is in his election literature that we find the President of the Board of Trade at his best. To his electors he has sent a card which is Mr Churchill all over—Mr Churchill at the top of the bill and Mr Wilkie pushed to the foot.

"Let the Labour sympathisers and the Trade Unionists take note of these tactics when recording their votes . . . The President of the Board of Trade fights only for Churchill."

Polling day in Dundee fell on Saturday the 22nd of January. The snow of the previous week had cleared and for the time of year the weather was ideal. Besides the colourful rosettes everyone was wearing, large numbers of dogs were out on the streets wearing coverlets embroidered with the various party slogans. A bulldog named "Jimmy," well known in the locality, roamed about Albert Square with a big blue ribbon in his collar—obviously a Tory!

After making an early tour of the polling stations Winston motored down to Carnoustie to put in a round of golf before lunch, only returning to the city in the afternoon to make a last tour of the booths after six o'clock. Clementine on the other hand, accompanied by her sister and Mr George Ritchie, dutifully kept up the work of visitation during his absence. Going in to record his own vote later, Winston met Scrymgeour—his only rival now standing from among those who had fought the previous election—as he was coming out. It was noted wryly that "they did not hug one another in a fond embrace."

When the results were announced it was seen that the Lib-Lab partnership had proved a winner, Winston coming top of the poll with 10,747 votes and Wilkie close behind with 10,365. The Conservative, a Mr Seymour Lloyd—Baxter had declined the candidature—got 4,552, a Mr Glass a complete newcomer to the field as a Liberal Unionist got 4,339, and Scrymgeour, doing marginally better this time, still lost his deposit with 1,512.

In the country as a whole the Liberals did less well. The Conservatives made a massive net gain of 116 seats giving them 273 Members in the House of Commons, and left with just 275, the Liberals now had only a parliamentary majority of two. The great gains in the victories of 1906 had vanished. Asquith, however, was determined to soldier on, but his Government's continuance in power depended entirely on the 41 Labour Members and 71 Irish Nationalists.

Many Liberals blamed the loss of seats on the virulence of Lloyd George's and Winston's speeches. Asquith's sharp tongued, but perceptive wife Margot, wrote to Winston and severely took him to task for his conduct: "Believe me," she said, "cheap scores, hen-roost phrases and all oratorical want of dignity is out of date . . .

Only say to yourself . . . I have got a beautiful young wife, an affectionate heart and a love of amusement. I will make the Court, the Colonies, the West and the East end of London change their whole view of me. I won't see a Press man, and I won't have my name coupled with anyone, I shall thrive on being liked instead of loving abusive notice and rotten notoriety."

Asquith himself, though, seemed to approve Winston's recent performances. Offering him warmest thanks and best congratulations on his work during the election he wrote: "Your speeches from first to last have reached high-water marks and will live in history." He also thanked Winston in terms more materially gratifying. All the spade work had now been accomplished at the Board of Trade and he offered Winston, first the Irish Office and after that was tactfully refused, the Home Office. Only one other Home Secretary, Sir Robert Peel at thirty three, had been younger, and the post was not only considered a great honour but in addition paid a far larger salary. Winston needed the money. What he had saved from his lecture tours and his "Life of Lord Randolph" had long been spent; like all Members of Parliament at that time he received no salary and his fairly extravagant life-style had quickly soaked up the £2,500 a year he had received at the Board of Trade.

At the Home Office, never forgetting his own experience cooped up in a cage as a prisoner-of-war of the Boers, he set to work to reform the Penal System. He introduced regulations which would reduce the number of people imprisoned merely for being unable to pay a fine. Despite ridicule in Parliament and from the Press he put through plans for prison lectures and concerts to lighten a little the terrible boredom of convict life. Deeply moved by the lot of boy prisoners when he visited Pentonville Prison, many of whom were in prison for sleeping out because they had no home, he encouraged the police to form a more generous interpretation of the Laws of Vagrancy and fostered the idea of residential homes. Deciding whether to recommend to the King to reprieve a murderer awaiting execution weighed heavily on his conscience—Dr. Crippen was hanged during his period of office—he once told Wilfred Blunt his adviser that, "It had become a nightmare to him to exercise his powers of life and death . . . "

Only by the Suffragettes was his penal policy regarded as too severe. It was at this time that a number of the Movement's leaders, arrested and finally sentenced for their various crimes and misdemeanors, started a series of hunger strikes inside prison. Winston incurred the entire blame for the painful disgusting process of force-feeding, temporary release after the victim's health broke down, and re-arrest, with the whole miserable procedure to go through all over again, until the sentence was served in full.

He remained privatey in favour of women's suffrage but as a member of a government pledged to a tight parliamentary programme of more important legislative priorities Winston was not prepared to assist in formulating a Bill which would, as things stood, give votes only to upper class women, thereby in all probability, assisting the Tories.

For the remainder of that year the House of Lords and the Tory "Die-hards" continued to put up a desperate struggle to maintain their hereditary prerogatives, and they were aided by the unexpected death of Edward VII, upon whose unspoken promise Asquith had relied. George V, his successor, a wholly inexperienced young man could not handle the conflicting advice given by his private advisers, and Asquith with so much at stake, revealed, not for the first time, the granite-faced politician which he was normally at great pains to keep hidden behind a mask of pleasant urbanity. He bullied the King for hours on end to make him agree to create the necessary unlimited number of Peers if the House of Lords refused to accept the Parliament Act. An immediate influx of newly enobled Liberal peers would seriously reduce the Lords powers to hold up legislation concerning finance. When King George asked what Asquith would do if he refused, the latter answered promptly: "I should immediately resign and at the next election make the cry 'The King and the Peers against the People.'" Under this threat the young King surrendered, making only one condition, that Asquith would go to the country again for a fresh mandate. And so, before the end of the year yet another General Election had to take place.

Winston protested of the unprecedented situation of deadlock in his manifesto to the Dundee electors:

"The whole machinery of representative Government has been brought to a standstill, . . . the Tory Party regard themselves as the ruling caste, exercising by divine right a divine superior authority over the whole nation." Speaking in the city on November 14th, 1910, and referring in terms of studied moderation—Margot Asquith's advice must have had its effect—to the many attempts the Government had already made to come to some amicable arrangement with the House of Lords, he said: "All that friendly discussion, prolonged in earnestness and candour for so many months, could do, has been done and been done in vain . . . at the end of every legislative avenue loomed the portals of Lansdowne House." At a meeting at Highbury Athenium on November 22nd he said, in the strongest terms he now allowed himself:

"I have not come here tonight to attack individual Peers. There is no hatred of Peers, as Peers among the British people. It is their function and power that are deservedly the objects of popular displeasure."

As he warmed to his work however, some of Winston's suppressed fire flickered forth again and at Sheffield on November 30th—his thirty sixth birthday—he poured scorn on Arthur Balfour the Tory leader quoting him mischieviously after the latter had announced "I am a Leader who means to lead." "Balfour," said Winston referring to the recent theatrical comedy success "is now like Charley's Aunt, still running."

Winston was back in Dundee again by 9.20 the following morning, and because he had been assaulted with an umbrella the previous week by a young man violently pleading the cause of the Suffragettes, was accompanied by three Scotland Yard men and met at Tay Bridge Station by a large bodyguard of city detectives. In the evening he spoke before a crowded audience in the King's Theatre. In his speech dealing with Home Rule for Ireland and the issue of the House of Lords he devoted a considerable part to a reply to Lord Rosebery, who he described as "A bitter and excited partisan in deep and desperate argumentative distress." Afterwards while Winston was answering questions from the floor a city official tried to take a flashlight photograph but the sudden ignition of the magnesium powder, set fire to the clothes of a young man sitting nearby and brought temporary consternation to the party on stage. Winston and his burly protectors must have thought for a moment that they were to be the victims of a Suffragette outrage. All of these ladies however, had been kept safely outside the theatre, and there, the waiting crowd became so threatening to them that a body of police had to escort the demonstrators to safety.

Twelve hours after his arrival Winston left by train for Manchester.

"An Insult to Dundee," headed the Dundee Courier editorial the following morning, "Mr Winston Churchill holds the electors of Dundee in cheap estimation. Not only does he give them little of his time, but his speeches indicate that he does not rate their speeches highly.

"In the King's Theatre last night he insulted a Liberal audience telling them that Lord Rosebery's speech the previous day was 'vulgar, silly ranting.' This is not argument, the wonder is that language of the kind should be tolerated in Dundee, where some of Lord Rosebery's most noteworthy rhetorical triumphs have been achieved."

After a drill display outside the Bell Street Fire Station around 1910. Sir George Ritchie is on Winston's right and both he and Captain Weir, Dundee's Firemaster, appear to be amused that their companion from the Town Clerk's office has been surprised by a sneeze.

You vote FREE TRADE TO-DAY

One of Winston's handbills from the January election of 1910.

In the centre pages of the same newspaper the last verse of what was entitled "A Little Poem to Winston," written by a Mr Andrew T. Wilkie, exhorted:

> Throw him out, ye men of jute;
> Tell him Scotsmen he won't suit
> When Englishmen won't have him
> Why should you?

Speaking the previous evening, Miss Murray of Cardross told a meeting of her fellow Suffragettes at Dundee Y.M.C.A.: "We are dissatisfied with Mr Churchill. He may be a great man in his way, but he has been a traitor to the women." A Miss Husband, one of the deputation who had gone to see Winston at the Home Office reported that they had accomplished nothing. "I did not expect much" she said, "Mr Churchill might be clever but he is never cleverer than when getting out of his promises. (Laughter) My impression of Winston Churchill is simply this—he is concerned only for Winston Churchill, he does not care one little bit for the men and women of Dundee."

There were some, nevertheless, among those not normally his admirers, who had to admit a measure of praise for the boundless energy shown by him and Lloyd George during the campaign. The London Correspondent for the Dundee Courier wrote:

"The General Election of last January is generally admitted to be the most strenuous of its kind this country has known. The present fight is shorter but so far as some of its principal combatants in it are concerned will not be a whit less strenuous. For instance, Mr Lloyd George and Mr Winston Churchill are delivering on the average something like two speeches a day, and are speeding over the country as fast as special trains and motor cars will carry them."

POTTING THE PEERS.

The Dundee "Advertiser" (still sympathetic to Winston) looked forward sanguinely to his projected nationwide campaign in January 1910. The intransigent opposition of the House of Lords to the reforming Legislation of the Liberal Government, marked out peers as prime targets in Winston's caustic speeches.

BILLS VERSUS POSTERS.

January election 1910. In this "Advertiser" cartoon Winston proudly displays his "babies" against a hysterical background of Tory propaganda.

So keen was Winston to maintain the initiative that on the 3rd of December, the day after leaving Dundee, and the eve of the poll in Grimsby, he took a train for Crewe Junction after speaking at Fraudsham in Cheshire, and from there he travelled by a specially chartered private train to arrive in Grimsby by midnight. Balfour the Tory leader had spoken there earlier in the evening and a verbatim transcript of his speech was rushed by motor car to Sheffield, halfway between Crewe and Grimsby, to intercept Winston and give him time to make a reply.

On Tuesday he was back in London, called as a witness at the Bow Street Magistrates Court, in the case against the young man who had assaulted him. After giving his evidence in a strained and husky voice, which revealed the sheer physical punishment involved in non-stop campaigning he asked for leniency to be shown to his attacker. The Court however was less merciful and the young man was sentenced to six months.

Dundee High Street in 1908 looking east.

Back in Dundee the following evening, Winston accepted a challenge which had been thrown down by Seymour Lloyd the Unionists' second candidate this time—Sir George Baxter was also standing again—for a public debate. In a perhaps too gentlemanly exchange of views, which could hardly have matched the expectation of his Drill Hall audience, Winston by general agreement won the honours and after an exchange of good humoured courtesy between the two rivals, Seymour Lloyd left the meeting amid loud cheers.

Continuing the meeting, Winston gave his listeners what they had been waiting for, demolishing the latest Tory red herring which called for a referendum—the novel electoral device practised in Switzerland—which the Tories said would decide more democratically than Parliament the various issues facing the electorate. "The referendum," said Winston, "means that though a Government is defeated through it, it will occupy the degrading position of remaining in office. I see no reason why Tariff Reform and the Referendum should not be tied up in a bag together like the Kilkenny cats until there is nothing but the tail left." (Laughter)

"Tariff Reform," he continued, returning with mocking humour to the long and tedious controversy, "is like the famous 'Jewjah' song which would cure anything from a sore throat to a smoky chimney, and so efficacious was it that it was once administered to a dead cat, and twenty four hours afterwards the cat had kittens." (Great laughter)

The Courier, ignoring these later remarks and considerably mollified by the spectacle of the dud duel between Winston and Seymour Lloyd was almost complimentary:

"Both Mr Churchill and his supporters are entitled to a word of praise for the courtesy extended last night to a political opponent. The debate at the Drill Hall was unique in Dundee electioneering, and it may not be without its results."

Dundee's voters went to the poll on December the 8th, 1910, and Winston and Alexander Wilkie were again returned, this time with slightly decreased majorities, though this was to be expected. Electoral enthusiasm was bound to flag through the surfeit of stimulation. Even Winston was beginning to feel over-exposed. The figures were: Churchill 9,420; Wilkie 8,957; Baxter 5,685; Lloyd 4,914; Scrymgeour 1,825.

For Asquith the results nationally were also disappointing. With only 272 seats, the Liberals were now matched exactly by the Conservatives, and the balance of power continued to be held by the 84 Irish Nationalists and the 42 Labour M.P.'s. Just the same, the Parliament Act received its third reading in the Commons though there was one last unhappy attempt by the Lords to stave off defeat. But realising the disasterous consequences of unconstitutional action, Arthur Balfour, albeit unwillingly, eventually repudiated his Tory backwoodsmen in the House of Lords and by the following year the power of the Hereditary Chamber to stop progress, was destroyed forever.

Winston was picked out for retaliation, as incensed and angry Conservatives levelled every kind of slander against his personal character. He had run away from the Boers; he had broken his parole; as the grandson of a Duke he ought to have known better; he had betrayed his class for self-advancement. The Duke of Beaufort, obviously a hunting man, said he would like to see him and Lloyd George, "In the middle of twenty couple of fox hounds." "What have you got to say for him now – your treacherous little gutter genius?", Violet Asquith the Prime Minister's daughter was taunted on one occasion.

"Winston," she wrote "headed the list of untouchables. No epithet was too uprorarious to hurl at him, and the doors of many houses were closed against him." Speaking of the burden this threw upon his wife, she continued: "Clemmie met these affronts with cool defiance and never wavered from her militant loyalty. His cause was her cause, his enemies were her enemies . . . I asked her once in later years how much she had minded those early days and she replied, 'I didn't mind a bit. It was so exciting – it made me feel heroic and proud!' "

These personal setbacks, however, were hardly to be counted, measured against the sea of troubles Winston was having to contend with as Home Secretary. Besides the reputation he earned as "the most humane and human Home Secretary in our history," he was also labelled for posterity with the other, almost wholly mythological one, as the arch-enemy of the working classes!

As Home Secretary, Winston, as well as his general duty of maintaining law and order, had the extremely difficult responsbility for controlling the then almost inevitable civil disturbances which occurred during periods of industrial action and unrest. The severe economic conditions of 1908 had improved a little and the unemployment rate had been reduced to around four per cent, but the continual erosion of working class living standards by inflation and wage-cutting, had produced a growing militancy among rank and file Trade Union members which forced the hands of their hitherto mild and moderate leadership. During Winston's first year of office a whole series of strikes broke out. The first was in Wales in May 1910 where the employers wanted to use outside labour to break a strike among their own dockers who were demanding more money. The dispute involving two or three hundred men had brought the docks to a standstill and there were soon reports of looting. The employers approached the Home Office for help in suppressing the workers but Winston uncompromisingly instructed his permanent official Mr Edward Troup to tell them that they would get no help from him:

"Do not," he insisted, "on any account give them or the public the impression that we approve their actions." Winston also refused a plea from the Newport Magistrates for troops to put down the riots which were expected to erupt in sympathy for the dockers in Cardiff and other towns in South Wales. He sent instead a small contingent of Metropolitan Police, which was never used, and the dispute was settled peacefully by the intervention of the Board of Trade conciliation team.

The second strike he had to contend with that year began in the coal mines of the Rhondda Valley in early November and it arose this time from a dispute concerning wage differentials in the working of hard and soft seams. Many different pits were affected and nearly 30,000 men were involved. Again there was looting, and once more the local authority appealed for troops. Winston decided to send again another contingent of Metropolitan Police, at the same time making an appeal to the miners to go back to work, promising them an immediate Board of Trade enquiry into their grievances.

These precautions incurred the displeasure of The Times:

"Mr Churchill hardly seems to understand" announced the reactionary voice of Lord Northcliffe, "that an acute crisis has arisen, which needs decisive handling. The rosewater of conciliation is all very well in its place, but its place is not in face of a wild mob drunk with the desire of destruction."

The following day, November 10th, the Liberal Manchester Guardian rebuking The Times in their editorial said:

"Mr Churchill was violently attacked in yesterday's Times for a decision which in all probability saved many lives. It needed some courage after the Chief Constable had asked for troops to stop the troops which were on their way and send policemen instead. But, as usual, the brave course was also the wise one."

Only later as the crisis worsened and after consultation with Lord Haldane the Minister of War did Winston consent to send a limited number of troops as a precautionary measure but the only occasion they were used was at a village called Tonypandy when police were being heavily stoned and had suffered a number of casualties. Their intervention did not lead to bloodshed.

At the time, serious enough as these incidents were, they made little impact upon the public mind and it was not until January the

3rd 1911 that a quite unrelated incident took place that was to brand Winston forever in the public consciousness as the man who was always, in any situation, only too ready to bring about a solution by violent confrontation.

The affair began in the middle of the previous month when a Mr Isenstein, who kept a fancy goods shop in London's Whitechapel, heard mysterious noises at the rear of his premises. A body of police investigated and in a running fight through the dark and twisting streets after the intruders, three policemen were shot dead and several others wounded. With only truncheons to protect themselves the police gave up the chase and the killers escaped. The authorities, however, had for some time been keeping an eye on a man named Peter Straum, commonly called Peter the Painter, who was suspected of revolutionary activities and was the leading figure in a small colony of Lithuanian immigrants in Whitechapel. Ten days after the shooting a series of ruthless police searches revealed in a house in Stepney an anarchist's armoury consisting of an automatic pistol, ammunition and bomb-making equipment.

Early in the morning of January 3rd, at 100 Sidney Street, fifty police, a number of them armed, tipped off that Peter the Painter was inside, closed in on the narrow terraced house. The police summons breaking the dead silence was suddenly met by a burst of fire from the windows on the second floor. Fortunately only one policeman was slightly wounded and by mid-day the gunmen were held at bay by a police contingent now seven hundred and fifty strong assisted by a number of Scots Guardsmen.

"This was the position when I saw Mr Churchill arrive in a car from Whitehall," wrote Hugh Martin a reporter at the scene. "He was wearing a silk hat and a fur-lined overcoat with astrakhan collar—altogether an imposing figure in the exceedingly drab surroundings . . . I watched him moving restlessly hither and thither among the rather nervous and distraught police, a professional soldier among civilians, talking, questioning, advising."

Soon after one o'clock wisps of smoke were seen coming from the broken windows and within half an hour the house was in flames. The Fire Brigade arrived but was held back by the police. The firing from the house ceased and after ten minutes of silence a police inspector, Winston, and a guardsman armed with a double-barrelled shotgun, marched up to the front door and kicked it down. The firemen then were allowed to douse the flames. From the ruins two charred bodies were recovered, but no trace was ever found of Peter the Painter.

The incident, sensationalised by the popular Press, passed into legend, but Winston, "The Hero of Sidney Street" lost a great deal of credit in the eyes of many people who resented the spectacle of a King's Minister wanting to play at soldiers.

On May 28th an event occurred in Winston's domestic life which drew him for a time at least from his single-minded devotion to affairs of State. Clementine bore him his only son Randolph. He was their second child, their first, Diana, had been born on July 11th 1909. Clementine's health was delicate at this time, and her frequent separations from her husband, she in the country, and Winston in London with his demanding public life, have left to posterity the touching correspondence which passed between them. Before Randolph arrived both of them clearly expected a boy and they gave the unborn child the nickname Chumbolly. "I hope" wrote Clementine, referring both to her husband's personal appearance and to his persistent late-coming, "he (Chumbolly) will not have inherited the Pug's unpunctual habits!" Besides keeping his wife fully informed on political events and the incidents which occurred in his social life, Winston's letters are sprinkled with such phrases as "two thousand kisses my sweet birdling," "your ever-loving and devoted Pug." In one letter after Randolph was born he wrote, "precious pussycat I do trust and hope that you are being good, and not sitting up or fussing yourself. Just get well and strong and enjoy the richness which this new event I know will have brought into your life. The Chumbolly must do his duty and help you with your milk, you have to tell him so from me. At his age greediness and even swinishness at table are virtues." Both Winston and Clementine illustrated their letters with affectionate cartoons of kittens and pug dogs.

Domestic happiness however did not keep the problems of government away and in June, 1911, the country was paralysed by a strike which began in Southampton docks and spread quickly to other ports. Winston warned Asquith that these events were tending towards a general stoppage throughout the whole of industry and his fears were confirmed, when, from the beginning of August, groups of railwaymen, who had their own grievances, but who also supported the dockers, staged a series of wildcat strikes in various parts of the country.

Britain had never experienced the effects of a national strike and Winston exaggerated the effects one might have had on the security of the nation. In his mind's eye—his imagination no doubt coloured by his recent experience at Sidney Street—he pictured a catastrophe where hundreds of thousands of people might starve and a situation where the Government itself might break down to be immediately followed by a Red Revolution. Cool judgements were not made easier by the stifling summer weather with unusual temperatures as high as a hundred degrees being recorded at Greenwich, or by the inflammatory international situation.

Kaiser Wilhelm of Germany alarmed every country in Europe when he dispatched the gunboat Panther to the port of Agadir on the Atlantic coast of Morrocco with the deliberate intention of provoking France, Britain's ally. It was feared the incident might even spark off a European war and that at any moment the Germans might attack the British fleet.

Winston was not the only one to over-react to the situation at home. The Lord Mayor of Liverpool and the Mayor of Birkenhead sent him a joint telegram asking for a warship to be sent to the Mersey, and Lord Derby, who reported that the city of Liverpool was in a state of siege wrote, "The hospitals have but two days supply and within forty eight hours all poor people will be face to face with starvation and God alone knows what happens when that moment arrives." Winston received a telegram from the King which echoed the autocratic sentiments of his Royal relatives the Czar and the Kaiser, strongly deprecating the half-hearted employment of troops. "They should not be called" he said, "except as a last resource but if called on they should be given a free hand and the mob should be made to fear them."

The international situation eased after the Kaiser backed down, but on August 18th after Asquith had offered the railwaymen a Royal Commission into their grievances the invitation was refused on the grounds that it would be too slow to report. Asquith, in anger, is reported to have said: "Then your blood be on your own heads." That evening, every railwayman received from Union headquarters the same telegram: "Your liberty is at stake, all railwaymen must strike at once."

Winston immediately sent in troops to garrison the railway stations and to protect the lines, epecially the signal boxes.

Despite his use of such an unfortunate phrase, Asquith sympathised with the railwaymen, for their fight to have their Trade Unions recognised by their hard, greedy and reactionary employers was a fight for common justice and he tried once more to get a settlement. The leaders of the Rail Unions no more wanted a revolution than did the Government and after only two days the strike ended, thanks to the genius of Lloyd George for negotiation. By a tragic irony, two days after agreement was reached a dismal incident occurred at Llanelly in South Wales when four people were killed by troops after a train had been held up and the engine driver knocked senseless by looting rioters.

Working class mythology was to transfer these deaths to the earlier incident at the coalmining village of Tonypandy, and for it, Winston was given the blame. Clearly, the notoriety he had gained earlier in the year was at least partly responsible for converting truth, half-truth and sheer libel in the mind of the ordinary man into sinister legend.

These crises, unique in British history, did not however deflect Asquith's Government from its stated programme. The time had now come to honour its obligations to the Irish Nationalists, and Home Rule once more became one of the chief issues in political debate.

Home Rule for Ireland had been the declared policy of the Liberal Party for over twenty six years but their Bills had always been defeated in the Commons by the intransigence of the Ulster Unionists, backed up by the Tory Party and the House of Lords. Winston's father Randolph had himself coined the ominous slogan "Ulster will fight and Ulster will be right" and this time, yet again, the Protestants of Ulster threatened to fight a Civil War if the British Government handed over sovereignty to Dublin and Roman Catholic domination. Although in most other respects Winston had faithfully followed many of his father's political beliefs, he saw with a modern eye the crying need to grant Ireland its independence and bring about a reconciliation between its divided populations. Ever since his first speech had been cheered by them in the House of Commons, Winston had had a soft spot for the Irish Nationalist members of Parliament and speaking at Islington at the time of the previous election had said of them:

"For thirty years these same men have laboured with that hope deferred that maketh the heart sick and they have laboured without taint of personal motive—without thought of personal gain—for one cause, the cause which every Englishman who loves freedom and honour of his country, and whatever his opinion for or against Home Rule—must treat with consideration and respect . . . "

In February 1911 Winston circulated a paper to the other members of the Cabinet giving his views on devolution and later in the year on October 4th he spoke at Dundee on the same subject with sympathy and understanding:

"Next year we propose to introduce the Home Rule Bill and we propose to carry it forward with all our strength. It is eighteen years since this subject has been debated in Parliament and many things have happened in the interval.

"All the self-governing colonies are favourable to Home Rule— we are now in the full tide of successful experiment in regard to self-government. South Africa and Canada are the fruits of the imperialism of peace and freedom . . .

"It is our duty to exhaust every effort which sympathy and earnestness can inspire to understand the reasonable difficulties of Ulster and to allay unfounded alarm – and provide sure and effective safeguards for civil and religious equality and freedom."

The city of Belfast was in the front line of the controversy and in January 1912 Winston announced his intention of holding a meeting in the Ulster Hall. A roar of fury greeted the news from the Unionists. "What a man to select!" thundered Sir Edward Carson, ex-Law Officer of the Crown and a violent, sentimental, but Protestant Dubliner. "The most provocative speaker in the whole Party, and going under the most provocative circumstances to a place where the words of his own father are still ringing in the ear . . . "

The Press seethed with reports of the violence which awaited if Winston dared to violate this Orange sanctuary. Armed Ulstermen took over the hall hired for the occasion and refused to leave. Instead, a huge marquee was procured, sent to Ulster in advance and erected in the football ground at Celtic Park on the outskirts of Belfast within the Roman Catholic enclave. Accompanied by Clementine, Winston had a hostile reception at presbyterian Stranraer in Scotland and in the sea-crossing, made sleepless by Suffragettes who shrieked 'Votes for Women!' into their cabin windows, they arrived in Belfast only to be told that the glass had had to be removed from the windows of their car because the dockworkers had armed themselves with rivets which were to be used as missiles. They were to stay at the Grand Central Hotel and a hostile crowd of nearly 10,000 was there to greet them. On February the 9th, the day of the meeting, the atmosphere was explosive.

"As each car made its way through," wrote the reporter from The Times describing the drive from the Hotel to the Celtic Road, "men thrust their heads in and uttered fearful menaces and imprecations, it seemed to me, that Mr Churchill was taking a greater risk than ever he expected . . . Yet he never flinched and took hostility visualised as well as vocalised calmly . . . "

Although four battalions of infantry guarded the route, before the police could beat them off the angry crowd were able to lift Winston's car eighteen inches off the ground. However, when the party reached the Faulds Road district occupied mainly by Roman Catholics the booing gave way to cheers, and at last in the pouring rain they reached the stadium.

At two o'clock on a high rickety platform Winston addressed a vast meeting of supporters and non-supporters and made a moving plea for justice to Catholic Ireland. Adapting his father's famous slogan he played a brilliant variation in counterpoint:

"It is in a different sense," he said, "that I adopt and repeat Lord Randolph's words 'Ulster will fight and Ulster will be right.' Let Ulster fight for the dignity and honour of Ireland; let her fight for the reconciliation of races and for the forgiveness of ancient wrongs; let her fight for the unity and consolidation of the British Empire; let her fight for the spreading of charity, tolerance and enlightenment among men. Then indeed Ulster will fight and Ulster will be right."

Winston and his wife left Ireland safely but Civil War was now openly threatened, both in Ulster, and even by the Conservative leadership at home.

The strain of opposition had wearied good-natured Balfour and his place as head of the Tory Party had been taken by Mr Bonar Law, a Nova Scotia born son of an Ulster Presbyterian minister, who had piled up a fortune as a Glasgow steel-baron. Law was expected by the Conservatives to be a fighting leader, though his aggression was never more than forced and once at the annual procession of the Commons to hear the King speak at the House of Lords had confided diffidently to the Prime Minister, "I am afraid I shall have to show myself as very vicious, Mr Asquith, this session. I hope you will understand."

In July, however, at a great Unionist demonstration at Blenheim, Bonar Law took up the extreme position on the right of his supporters when he declared: "I can imagine no length of resistance to which Ulster will go and in which I will not be ready to support them." Every night in the House of Commons Bonar Law hurled insult and abuse at Asquith and made it clear he held strongly a particular distaste towards the latter's foremost spokesman in the controversy.

Hostility merely strengthened Winston's resolve and on August 12th, 1912 he indicted the Unionist leaders in an open letter addressed to George Ritchie the Liberal Chairman of his Constituency, a man he often turned to when he wanted immediate Press coverage. Bonar Law and his "lieutenant" Sir Edward Carson he accused of inciting "the Orangemen to wage Civil War . . . " and further, said that their example as public men gave inspiration to, "every street bully with a brickbat and every crazy fanatic who is fumbling with a pistol."

Winston followed up this powerful salvo with a speech at Dundee in September underlining Asquith's statement that the Government advocated Home Rule, not only as a solution to the problem of Ireland, but also as a first step, in establishing a federal parliament in Britain, with self-government for Scotland and Wales.

The signing of a Covenant pledged to defeat Home Rule was staged in Ulster accompanied by torchlight processions, bands, Union Jacks and religious services. Carson, who was the first to sign, had announced a few months earlier in his speech at the Criterion Restaurant that he intended, when he went over to Ireland, to "break every law that is possible." Mr F. E. Smith, later Lord Birkenhead, and Carson's associate, a highlight of the English Bar nicknamed "The Galloper" after his brisk gait and impetuous nature, who was incidentally, a great personal friend of Winston, declared that "he would not shrink from the consequences of his convictions not though the whole fabric of the Commonwealth be convulsed." Predictably, rioting broke out in Belfast and two thousand Catholics and five hundred Protestants were forced to leave their jobs in Harland & Wolfe's Shipyard, the biggest employer of labour, because of threats made against their lives; large consignments of arms began to arrive in Ulster while the Bill was meeting its stormy passage through the Commons; and the Ulster Volunteers discarded their dummy rifles and drilled openly with real ones, reviewed by Carson and Smith. Before the Bill's first rejection by the House of Lords, Bonar Law asserted that Ulster would prefer foreign to nationalist rule. Winston scorned, "This then is the latest Tory threat; Ulster will secede to Germany!"

By the summer of 1914 only a refusal of the Royal Assent stood between the Bill and it becoming Law but even secret negotiations held at Balmoral with the King as Chairman could not resolve the difference between the Liberal government and the Tory Unionists. In Ulster a hundred thousand men stood to arms with German rifles. In the South, volunteers to oppose them were enrolling by the thousand. Then, at the Curragh, the British Army Headquarters outside Dublin, nearly all the officers sent in their resignations. It was mutiny, only thinly disguised. Civil War seemed certain.

Winston, now holding the post of First Lord of the Admiralty, but without any specific and direct instruction from the Prime Minister, sent the 3rd Battle Squadron of eight Battleships to concentrate at Lamlash on the Isle of Arran; stationed a cruiser near Carrick Fergus, and sent two or three destroyers to cover the South of Ireland. Though he, personally, was again criticised by the Tory Press for this action, a storm of bitter recrimination broke out against the Government in the world of Labour and the Trade Unions for not doing enough and allowing the mutinous Army officers to get off scot-free, while they the workers had had to submit patiently to the slow, unsatisfactory but democratic means of settling their grievances. The railwayman's leader, G. H. Thomas, said that if Tory doctrine held good, his duty would be to tell the railwaymen to organise their forces and spend the Union's half a million of capital in buying arms and ammunition. John Ward of the Navvy's Union asked ordinary soldiers to remember that if officers were able to exercise an option in obeying orders then they too had a duty never to fire a shot at their own class.

In the Commons, Winston was accused by the Opposition of deliberately provoking violence and disorder but he turned on them roundly saying: "What we are now witnessing in the House is uncommonly like a vote of censure of the criminal classes on the police." He then castigated the Conservatives as:

"The Party of the comfortable, the wealthy . . . who have most to gain by the continuance of the social order, being committed to a policy of armed violence, in utter defiance of lawfully constituted authority . . . to tampering with the discipline of the Army and the Navy . . . to overpowering police, coastguards and customs officials . . . to smuggling arms by moonlight . . . to the piratical seizure of ships to the unlawful imprisonment of the King's servants . . . the Conservative Party is committed to that. That is their position." He then reminded the Tory members, sitting uncomfortably on their benches wincing under the lash of his tongue, of the millions who "are forced to live their lives . . . stripped of all but the barest necessities who are repeatedly urged to be patient under their misfortunes . . . to wait year after year . . . until, in the due workings of the Constitution some satisfaction is given to their claimant needs . . . all the time this great audience is watching and learning from you, and those who have hitherto called themselves 'the Party of law and order,' how much they care for law how much they value order that stands in the way of anything they like! If that great audience is watching here at home, what of the great audiences that watch in India? Think of the devastating doctrines of the leader of the Opposition. The Right Honourable gentleman may laugh in a brief leadership of the Conservative Party but he has shattered treasure which greater men than he have guarded for generations." Winston concluded by accusing the Conservatives of teaching the Irish Nationalists the truth of John Bright's saying that "Ireland never gained anything except by force."

CHAPTER III

SOLDIER OF MISFORTUNE

THOUGH THE IRISH question had succeeded in generating power-ful emotions on both sides of the Irish sea, the issue was soon to be eclipsed by the far more ominous events which had been taking place in Europe.

Until the German gunboat Panther had been despatched in the month of July 1911 to Agadir on Morrocco's Atlantic coastline, Winston had never seriously considered that war might come with Germany some day. Since his early days in the House of Commons when he had opposed Brodick's extravagant Army estimates he and Lloyd George had been strong opponents of all military aggrandise-ment. Although as a young man Winston had been keen enough to become involved in Britain's little Colonial wars, as far as Europe was concerned, he was virtually an isolationist. His colleague Lloyd George was proud to be called by Tory imperialists "a little Englander."

In August 1908, on the morning of his engagement to Clementine, at the same time as Lloyd George was in Germany cementing Anglo/Prussian goodwill, Winston spoke at Swansea condemning the anti-German statements of Lord Cromer in the House of Lords:

"I think it is greatly to be deprecated" he said "that persons should try to spread the belief in this country that war between Great Britain and Germany is inevitable. It is all nonsense. In the first place, the alarmists have no grounds whatever for panic or fear. This country is an island, and no Government which is in power in this country in the near future, or likely to be in power will depart from any degree to the naval policy which shall secure us effectively from the outside invasion . . . I say there is no collision of primary interests—big, important interests—between Great Britain and Germany in any quarter of the globe. Why," he pointed humour-ously "they are among our very best customers, and, if anything were to happen to them, I don't know what we should do in this country for a market . . . I believe" Winston continued, speaking in the language of socialism, "that working classes all over the world are recognising that they have common interests and not divergent interests. *I believe that what is called the international solidarity of labour has an immense boon to confer upon all the people of the world.*" Concluding his speech Winston told his audience of a story he had read about France in 1870. "The Germans" he said, illustrating his strong belief in the essential decency of human nature, "were occupying part of the French territory, and the visitor saw the German soldiers, who were of the hostile garrison, and not on duty, working in the fields by the side of French peasants and helping them to get in their crop. One of the German soldiers was asked, "Why do you do that to your enemy?" Said the German "War is all very well for the swells, but poor people have to help one another." I have come here this afternoon to ask you to join with me in saying far and wide throughout the masses of the British Dominions there is no feeling of illwill towards Germany, I say we honour that strong, patient, industrious German people, who have been for so many centuries a prey to European intrigue and a drudge among the nations of the Continent."

Secure in these convictions, Winston, for the time being, had concentrated all his energies on pushing through his programmes of social reform at both the Board of Trade and Home Office and during these years became prominent as a particular opponent of any increase in the building of warships. The Sea Lords at the Admiralty had pleaded that they needed at least six new Dreadnoughts—enormous armourplated monsters which with one salvo from their powerful guns could equal all the fire-power of Nelson's Fleet at Trafalgar. Winston and Lloyd George refused to agree to more than four and McKenna, the First Lord, supported by the Foreign Secretary Sir Edward Grey, threatened to resign. In the end Asquith arranged a compromise and it was agreed to build eight such battleships but over a more extended period, thus satisfying the Admiralty and allowing Winston and Lloyd George to adequately finance their social programme.

Perhaps it had been the sight, sound, and smell of battle at Sidney Street which rekindled Winston's basic instincts as a soldier but certainly, after the incident at Agadir, he saw for the first time the danger in which Britain stood from Germany. Simultaneously Lloyd George too was suspicious and it was his uncompromising speech at the Guild Hall which caused the Germans to turn away from the brink, though he considered the incident in itself as no more than a diplomatic manoeuvre. With Winston it was different. From then on he was convinced that something more deep-rooted and dangerous than a desire for "a place in the sun" lay behind the Kaiser's protestations.

Winston in 1913 by the side of the Kaiser observing German army manoeuvres. In this last year of peace before the Great War which killed and mutilated millions, shattering forever the calm certainties of European civilisation, Winston was tortured by an anxiety of foreboding. He knew that the Kaiser's blustering affability no more than cloaked Germany's sinister purpose of world domination.

On August 23rd 1911, after Parliament had risen, Asquith called a special and secret meeting of the Committee of Imperial Defence. Although the Home Office was not concerned, Winston was asked to attend along with Sir Edward Grey, Lloyd George and the principal Officers of the Army and Navy. Winston was there because ten days before he had sent the Prime Minister a lengthy memorandum which explored unshrinkingly the consequences of war with Germany. The events he forecast turned out to be uncannily accurate—so much so, that an earlier age might have considered that Winston was possessed of second sight. Sir Henry Wilson, Chief of the General Staff at the time, called it "this silly memo" and Winston wrote modestly enough in reply to the criticism that it was, of course, only an attempt to pierce the veil of the future; to balance the incalculable; to weigh the imponderable. "Nevertheless," he continued, with the self-assurance of a seer, "it will be seen that I named the twentieth day of mobilisation as the date by which the French Armies will have been driven from the line of the Meuse and will be falling back on Paris and the south and the fortieth day as that by which Germany should be extended at full strain both internally and on all her war fronts . . ."

The battle of the Marne, the first allied counterstrike of World War I after continuous retreat before the German steamroller, opened on the forty second day after the Declaration of War!

Asquith was suitably impressed. He once remarked to his daughter Violet, "Winston is always admirable on paper. I often wish he used the same economy in speech as in writing." The Prime Minister had, as a matter of fact, become more and more reliant on Winston over the past years. Asquith was a wise and patient leader but he disliked the hurly-burly of faction and his period of Premiership had been rocked by a succession of crises. The strain was beginning to tell. All through 1910 much of the weight of piloting the anti-Lords Parliament Bill through the Commons fell upon Winston. He was often in charge of Government business, particularly after dinner, and Asquith had delegated to him the task of writing the nightly letter to the King covering the day's proceedings in the Parliament. From a letter Winston wrote to his wife in April 1911 it is clear Asquith was drinking heavily. " . . . On Thursday night the P.M. was very bad: And I squirmed with embarrassment. He could hardly speak: And many people noticed his condition. He continues most friendly and benevolent, and entrusts me with everything after dinner. Up till that (time) he is at his best—but thereafter! I is an awful pity, and only the persistent freemasony of the House of Commons prevents a scandal, I like the old boy and admire both his intellect and his character but what risks to run. We only got him away the other night just before Balfour began the negotiations which I conducted but which otherwise would have fallen to him – with disastrous consequences. The next day he was serene, efficient, undisturbed . . ."

Winston, though he desperately wanted to, had no way of knowing what was going on in the Prime Minister's mind regarding the events in Europe, because as usual, in public or in the privacy of the Cabinet Room Asquith remained always the good listener, precise and cheerful, and as the Chairman of his Cabinet kept any anxiety he might have shared regarding the future to himself. Winston on the other hand, during the holiday weeks of the summer of 1911, lived obsessed by the prescient knowledge of coming war. He thought of that day ten years before when he had told his Conservative colleagues "A European war cannot be anything but a cruel, heart-rending struggle . . . The bitter fruits of victory . . . The whole manhood of the nation . . . Democracy is more vindictive than Cabinets . . . The wars of peoples will be more terrible than those of Kings." Years afterwards he remembered how, one hot August day, after climbing a hilltop and looking out across the peaceful beauty of Somerset, he became haunted by the words of Houseman's poem, "The Shropshire Lad."

> On the idle hill of summer, sleepy with the sound of
>   streams
> Far I hear the steady drummer drumming like a noise in
>   dreams.
>
> Far and near and low and louder on the roads of earth
>   go by,
> Dear to friends and food for powder,
> Soldiers marching,
> All to die.

Day and night a drum beat in his brain to the tune of "Is England Ready?" And the tattoo replied, "I don't know, I don't know."

Winston could have cried with frustration at his own impotence to halt the inexorable march of events, and it was while he was in this strange state of nervous excitement that Asquith invited him to join him for a few days holiday in Scotland.

Though not in such highly coloured and emotional form, Asquith too was plagued by the same fears as Winston. He was content that Britain's small army was in a state of readiness, for Haldane at the War Office (Lloyd George called it the Ministry of Slaughter!) had completed a wonderful job in re-organising and creating an efficient staff. But the Navy, under McKenna, was not in such a happy position. Divided command, entrenched conservatism and long years of peace-time apathy had brought a kind of slow paralysis to what had once been a magnificent fighting machine. As Winston wrote afterwards, "When I went to the Admiralty I found that there was no moment in the career and training of a naval officer when he was obliged to read a single book about naval war, or pass even the most rudimentary examination in naval history." Pay for seamen had remained almost unchanged for almost sixty years, able seamen receiving 1/8d (8½p) per day and petty officers 2/8d (13½p). Although for fire power no foreigner could match a British warship, they were comparatively slow-moving, inefficient coalburners, spread throughout the world in the haphazard way which was thought to be a defence of Britain's trade routes.

It was clear to Asquith, McKenna would have to go. In the face of Admiralty intransigence he had been unable to create a Naval War Staff on the Haldane pattern and ironically as it turned out, had been unable to force his case for more Dreadnoughts because of the determined attacks from Winston and Lloyd George. To replace him Asquith considered Haldane as the obvious choice but he knew in advance the storm from the Admiralty if the same new broom was sent there which had already cleaned up the War Office.

Accordingly, after losing a desultory game of golf to the Prime Minister on the private links of Archerfield House on the East Lothian coast, Winston was offered the job of First Lord of the Admiralty. Violet Asquith remembers how he received it. "Winston left us for a night, I think to go to Dundee, and on the day after his return he and my father played golf together in the afternoon. I was just finishing tea when they came in. Looking up I saw in Winston's face a radiance like the sun. 'Will you come out for a walk with me—at once?' he asked. "You don't want tea?" 'No, I don't want tea.' We were hardly out of the house when he said to me with grave shining eyes. 'I don't want tea—I don't want anything—anything in the world. Your father has just offered me the Admiralty.' " She remembered walking with Winston through darkening woods down to the sea, where Fiddres Lighthouse was flashing out its signal, and how "the fading light of evening disclosed in the far distance the silhouettes of two battleships steaming slowly out of the Firth of Forth." The significance of the sight was not lost on either of them. Forgetting for a moment his own inconsistency—that he had once been offered the Admiralty and refused it—Winston burst out in heated disparagement of his job at the Home Office, "Look at the people I have had to deal with so far—judges and convicts! This is a big thing—the biggest that has ever come my way—the chance I should have chosen before all others, I shall pour into it everything I have got."

His first act on taking office was to send for, as his private and unofficial adviser, his old friend Lord Fisher, a crusty old sea dog living in retirement in Switzerland. Fisher, then seventy, had once been an innovator of genius, joining the Navy when ships had sails and leaving it—almost entirely by his own efforts—the most technically and materially advanced in the world, with submarines, battleships with twelve-inch guns, and a reorganised educational system for the lower ranks. He had wanted to do more, much much more, but his revolutionary methods had split the Navy into two rival camps with the consequent blow to morale from which it had since suffered. Worried by the mighty German fleet being built on the other side of the North Sea, Fisher believed that British Naval superiority could only be maintained by superior speed and completely new tactics. To get speed, however, every man-of-war would have to be re-equipped to burn oil and this would be difficult in a country which had none, but had instead vast reserves of cheap coal, and for years Fisher's enemies in the Admiralty had scoffed, nicknaming him the "oil maniac." Future tactics, Fisher believed, must not be by blockading and bottling up the enemy in his home harbours as practised by Nelson and St. Vincent in the war against Napoleon, but instead tempting him out onto the high seas where he could be destroyed by superior speed and heavier guns. The events of history were to prove Fisher's theory as fundamentally wrong, though his other improvements were to win for Britain the war at sea.

Within a month of his appointment Winston changed the whole Board of Admiralty. One Sea Lord after another was scrapped ruthlessly, and at Fisher's urging he appointed Sir John Jellicoe over the heads of several senior Admirals to be Second-in-Command of the Home Fleet with the intention that he would automatically succeed to the Supreme Command before the end of 1913. Rear Admiral David Beatty, who was under a cloud and had been languishing on half-pay for two years, became Winston's First Secretary—Winston had met him once years before at the Battle of Omdurman when Beatty, in a gesture of good comradeship, had tossed him a bottle of champagne from his gunboat on the Nile and he approved his ability to express his Naval expertise in language he a layman could understand.

Always in the background was Fisher, addressing his letters to "My Beloved Winston," and signing them "Yours to a Cinder" or "Yours till hell freezes" or "Yours till charcoal sprouts." Fisher had once written in the log at Dartmouth Naval College, "Favouritism is the secret of efficiency." And for the first time, automatic promotion by seniority ceased to operate in the Navy and young go-ahead officers soon found themselves in positions of trust and authority. Sir Arthur Wilson, the First Sea Lord, resigned his post prematurely to Sir Frances Bridgeman, but his appointment too soon fell before the axe and was given to the talented Prince Louis of Battenburg, a German-born member of the Royal Family.

In the House of Commons, Charles Beresford, Tory M.P. for Portsmouth, spokesman of the old school and an ex-Admiral himself, foamed at the mouth with impotent rage. Winston defended his actions: "The Honourable and gallant member," he replied, addressing Beresford with reckless impudence, "can best be described as one of those orators who before they get up do not know what they are going to say, when they are speaking do not know what they are saying, and when they have sat down do not know what they have said." Asquith, sitting beside Winston on the front bench, might have hoped that he would have proceeded in a more conciliatory spirit but nevertheless listened with tight-lipped aquiescence, knowing the job Winston had been set to do was necessary and that he must do it in his own way.

During the summer and autumn of 1911 Winston spent most of his time afloat in the Admiralty yacht Enchantress. It was both his office and his home, enabling him to see with his own eyes the full scope of the Navy's activities. As often in the stokehold as he was on the bridge, in visiting ships of the line he was never happier than exchanging a yarn with the officers and men of the upper and lower decks.

Early in 1912 he went to Malta with the Prime Minister to discuss with Lord Kitchener a unified defence strategy, and by the end of the year a Naval War Staff had been created; in Winston's words "a brain far more comprehensive than that of any single man."

On February 7th (the same year he was leaving London for Belfast to speak in support of the Home Rule Bill and while waiting for his train to leave) he picked up a late edition of the evening paper and read that at the opening of the Reichstag the Kaiser had announced increases in both the Army and Navy. Winston already knew from his contact in Berlin, Sir Ernest Cassel his personal finncial adviser, that the Germans were intent on increasing the size and efficiency of their Fleet and after actually reading the Kaiser's words in an English newspaper he felt deep down "a strong impression . . . of the approaching danger." On returning from Belfast two days later, realising that the widely advertised trouble in Ireland would give false confidence to Germany, Winston determined to sound a warning.

"The purposes of British Naval power" he said at Glasgow, after inspecting some new shipbuilding works on the Clyde, "are essentially defensive. We have no thoughts of aggression, and we attribute no such thoughts to other great powers. There is, however, this difference between the British naval power and the naval power of the great and friendly Empire—*and I trust it may long remain the great friendly Empire*—Germany. The British Navy is to us a necessity and, from some points of view, the German Navy is to them more of a luxury. Our naval power involves British existence. It is existence to us; it is expansion to them. We cannot menace the peace of a single Continental hamlet, no matter how great and supreme our Navy may become."

At home and abroad there was a storm of protest. The German Press, in the pockets of her armament manufacturers, described Winston's assertions as outrageous and insolent; the use of the word luxury was branded as a deliberate insult and the 'luxus Flotte' became an expression passed angrily from lip to lip. Liberals in Britain disliked the speech's threatening tone and Winston was attacked by The Daily News which had always, until then, been one of his strongest supporters. Even his colleagues were critical and the Tories were delighted that their "bette noir" had dropped another brick. Nevertheless when Lord Haldane returned from Berlin, where he had been discussing closer Anglo-German relations, he reported to the Cabinet that so far from being a hindrance to him in his negotiations, Winston's Glasgow speech had been the greatest possible help. Haldane's mission had been fruitless however for he brought back with him only the text of the new German Navy Law which provided for large increases in her naval strength and a re-organisation of the existing Battle Fleet which in Winston's words "practically amounted to putting four ships out of five of the German Navy permanently on a war footing."

Introducing his first Navy estimates in March Winston could not at that time reveal to the House of Commons the Government's fore-knowledge of the new German Navy Law, and had therefore no alternative but to submit an estimate based on no further increase in the German Fleet. He announced however that for the next five years Britain had to maintain a sixty per cent superiority in Dreadnoughts over Germany and would lay down two keels for every one laid down by her; and that the bulk of the Navy re-organised into four Fleets would concentrate in the North Sea. At the same time, Lord Fisher was recalled from nominal retirement to be Chairman of a Royal Commission on Oilfields.

Winston made one more effort to reach an understanding with Germany. "Suppose," he invited his opposite number Admiral von Tirpitz, "we were both to take a naval holiday in 1913, and introduce a blank page into the book of misunderstanding!" The appeal met with no response. He received a mesage through Sir

Ernest Cassel from the Kaiser saying that such arrangements would only be possible between allies, meaning that Britain must detach herself from her friendship with France. After twenty four hours of anxious waiting it was clear Admiral Tirpitz wanted no holiday.

Winston got back to the job of putting the Fleet into a state of instant readiness in case of a sudden attack by Germany. It brought him no joy. In May 1912 as one of the speakers at the annual Royal Academy banquet he prophesied: "I believe that if any two great civilised and highly scientific nations go to war with one another, they will become heartily sick of it before they come to the end of it."

Behind the squibs and crackers of Parliamentary politics, the Government and responsible members of the Opposition were coming together under the threat of the common menace. Arthur Balfour, the former Prime Minister, and now a member of the Committee of Imperial Defence, wrote familiarly to Winston on 22nd March 1912:

"My dear Winston," he said, "I return you the documents you were so very kind as to send me. I have read them with the deepest misgiving.

"A war entered upon with no other object than to restore the Germanic Empire of Charlemagne in a modern form appears to me at once to be so wicked and so stupid as to be almost incredible! And yet it is almost impossible to make sense of modern German policy without crediting it with this intention."

Winston too was perplexed. How could it be contemplated that the largest, most advanced and powerful of all the civilised family of European nations, could for some mad dream of self-aggrandisement, attack without warning its peaceful neighbours. And yet, the facts stared him in the face. As he reported to the Committee of Imperial Defence on July 1912:

" . . . The whole character of the German Fleet shows that it is designed for aggressive and offensive action of the largest possible character in the North Sea or the North Atlantic . . . The structure of the German battleships shows clearly that they are intended for attack and for Fleet action. They are not a cruiser Fleet designed to protect Colonies and commerce all over the world. They have been preparing for years, and are continuing to prepare, on an even larger scale a Fleet which, from its structure and character, can be proved by naval experts to have the central and supreme object of drawing out a line of battle for a great trial of strength in the North Sea or in the ocean . . .

"I do not pretend to make any suggestion that the Germans would deliver any surprise of sudden attack upon us. It is not for us to assume that another great nation will fall markedly below the standards of civilisation which we ourselves should be bound by; but we at the Admiralty have got to see, not that they will not do it, but that they cannot do it.

"I say," he concluded, pointing out the danger of a surprise attack, "that there is a great deal of truth in the statement made last night in the House of Commons by Mr Bonar Law, when he said that this great concentrated Fleet, ever growing in efficiency and strength within twelve or fourteen hours steaming of our shores, was almost a loaded cannon continually pointed at us. Of course they may say that our Fleet is similarly pointed at them, but nothing that we can do on the sea can menace the freedom or security of Germany, nothing that we can do on the sea can make any difference to that which makes life worth living for them. For us the matter is very different."

Requiring now little inspiration from Fisher, Winston pressed forward the secret manufacture of a fifteen inch gun which, if fitted to his five new Dreadnoughts at present under construction, would turn them into super-Dreadnoughts. Named humourously by the Service as the "Hush and Push Guns," development of the new weapons strained existing naval technology to the limit but when they were manufactured and tested were found to be capable of throwing a shell weighing nearly a ton for a distance of twelve miles! Fisher, gleeful as a little boy with a new toy, said to Winston, "What was it enabled Jack Johnstone to knock out his opponent? It was the big punch." Later in the House of Commons Winston explained the nature of a battle fought with such weapons. "If you want to," he said "make a true picture in your mind of a battle between great ironclad ships you must not think of it as if it were between two men in armour striking at each other with heavy swords, it is more like a battle between two eggshells striking at each other with hammers."

Though he wanted to do much more, Winston was successful in raising the pay of older able-seamen by threepence a day and of petty officers by sixpence, at the same time reforming the harsh naval discipline hardly changed since Napoleonic times. He made it possible for bright young men of talent to rise from the lower deck to be officers and he reduced the fees at the Naval Colleges of Osborne and Dartmouth to encourage a wider entrance. He ended the practice of officers in command of ships in port disappearing off home at weekends, leaving their ships virtually immobile should a sudden emergency occur. He encouraged the playing of war games by his Senior Staff so as to free their minds from peace-time complacency—a method of instruction which has been adopted today by all the Armed Services including the civilian forces of police, ambulance and fire brigades. At the time, however, these exercises were received less than enthusiastically by some of his Service Chiefs. "I am sorry you do not like the style of the paper called 'The Timetable of a Nightmare,' Winston replied, unruffled, to a critical memorandum by Sir Henry Jackson, "it was written with the intention of raising certain very serious issues, and which I think will be apparent the more the facts and arguments are studied with attention. The title was chosen with the object of justly and accurately describing the character of the paper and of disarming and discounting the very criticism which you make. Leaving, however, the question of style, on which opinions may easily differ, and which in any case is not of serious importance, and coming to the question of fact, I do not gather from your minute that there is much dispute . . . "

To give the Navy speed as well as striking power in accordance with Fisher's belief that "speed is armour" Winston took the irrevocable decision to change over to oil fuel. A tremendous number of problems had to be surmounted. Although oil was to give a speed of twenty-five knots to his new battleships, occupied less space aboard, reduced the manpower used for stoking by more than half, and above all, enabled ships to be refuelled at sea by tankers, the prime disadvantage was that Britain had the best and most plentiful fuelling coal in the world and the oil would have to be imported. Undeterred Winston set up a Royal Commission presided over by Lord Fisher and the British Government took a controlling share in the Anglo-Persian Oil Company by investing two million pounds to develop the Persian Oil Company by investing two million pounds to develop the Persian oil fields. Considering Winston's later attitudes on the state-ownership of private industry the result was, ironically, the first case in Britain of the nationalisation of a private company. It turned out to be an extremely profitable venture and by 1923 Winston estimated the return on the original investment had amounted to forty million pounds. Winston also fostered the new technology of wireless telegraphy and the infant Fleet Air-arm, even taking flying lessons himself which, however, amply demonstrated that he possessed more daring than aptitude!

All this was costing, and was going to cost, a great deal of money—money, which Lloyd George in particular, felt could be far better spent on the social services. He was blind to the real danger from Germany and although Winston had loyally spoken up on his behalf when Lloyd George had become implicated in a shady deal involving Government participation in the Marconi Company which, in all probability, could have cost him his political career, he was, on this occasion, his most determined critic. In Cabinet a series of brief accusative notes passed between them and on January 3rd 1914 Lloyd George made the argument public by giving an interview to The Daily Chronicle. He recalled that Winston's father had resigned because he thought money spent on armaments was "bloated and profligate" and yet the sum Lord Randolph had opposed being spent on the Army and Navy was only thirty two millions, while his son was now preparing an estimate of fifty one millions on the Navy alone.

This outburst seriously impaired the Government's credibility. Asquith pleaded with Winston to make a few economies so that he could affect a compromise, writing picturesquely: "Very largely in deference to my appeal, the critical pack (who know well that they have behind them a large body of Party opinion) have slacked their pursuit.

"I think that you on your side, should . . . show a corresponding disposition and throw a baby or two out of the sledge."

But Winston could make no concessions, he had already done his utmost to keep the estimates as low as possible and the following day, 2nd of February 1914, he replied, saying in the concluding paragraph of his detailed report, "I do not love this naval expenditure and I am grieved to be found in the position of taskmaster. But I am myself the slave of facts and forces which are uncontrollable unless naval efficiency is frankly abandoned. The result of all this pressure and controversy leaves me anxious, chiefly less the necessary services have been cut too low . . .

"The sledge is bare of babies, and though the pack may crush the driver's bones the winter will not be ended."

His colleagues now spoke openly of his imminent resignation but with the Tories, for once supporting Winston's point of view, Lloyd George dared not put it to the test and with sudden and characteristic grace he conceded defeat. "Come to breakfast tomorrow at No. 11" he invited Winston, "and we shall settle the matter." Winston duly arrived fully expecting that he himself would have to resign. Greeting him Lloyd George said, "Oddly enough, my wife spoke to me last night about this Dreadnought business. She said, 'You know, my dear, I never interfere in politics; but they say you are having an argument with that nice Mr Churchill about building Dreadnoughts. Of course I don't understand these things, but I should have thought that it would have been better to have too many than too few.' So I have decided to let you build them."

That of course was not the end of the battle, for when Winston presented the greatest Naval estimates the world had ever known to the Commons in March 1914 the Liberal Party's left-wing and the Labour Party, on whom the Government's majority depended, fumed with rage and Winston's record as a leading critic of the comparatively moderate MacKenna estimates was thrown in his face. Their anger, however, proved impotent because of Opposition support for the measure and they had to be content with Winston's meagre concession of the promise of a reduction in the estimates for the following year and that instead of the usual naval maneouvres this coming summer, a more economical trial mobilisation would be held instead, the highlight of which was to be a Grand Review by the King at Spithead.

It was to be fortuitous that the date chosen for this event was July 18th 1914.

At Sarajevo in Serbia, now Yugoslavia, on June 28th, Archduke Franz Ferdinand of Austria-Hungary was assassinated along with his wife. The British public hardly noticed the event but the Foreign Offices of Europe were in a ferment. A threatening, arrogant, ultimatum was sent to the Serbs by Austria, egged on by Germany. The stack of dominoes was about to be knocked over. Russia was the protector of the Serbs and would intervene to save them. She in turn was allied with France who in turn was allied with Britain.

Sir Edward Grey, in an attempt to lower the temperature, asked the newspapers not to describe the naval review in detail but to be content with giving a general impression of the power of the fleet and the spirit of the officers and men.

It was an amazing and breathtaking spectacle. Steaming at fifteen knots, it took six hours for the two hundred ships to pass the saluting point.

Winston wrote of the grand review that "It constituted comparably the greatest assemblage of naval power ever witnessed in the history of the world."

The ships of the Third Fleet were about to disperse to their home ports when it was learned by Winston on July 26th that Austria had curtly rejected Serbia's conciliatory reply to her ultimatum and with his approval, Prince Louis of Battenburgh immediately issued orders for the demobilisation to be halted and that the Fleet should remain in a state of readiness.

Sir Edward Grey strove to convene a European Peace Conference but the Kaiser and his advisers dismissed the offer, suggesting instead for Britain the role of a dishonourable neutral which would allow Germany, with her overwhelming military superiority, to smash France, strip her of her Colonies, and at the same time invade

Russia to find "Liebenstraum" to the East. The French realised their peril but at British insistence, so that no obstacle would be placed in the path of peace, they abstained from every form of provocative action. Her covering troops were held a long way back from the frontier with Germany and although the Germans made ready, mobilisation in France was delayed to the last moment. Not until the attack began on Russia did France propose to defend herself. As Winston recorded examining the Fundamental cause of the Great War:

"There never was any chance of France being allowed to escape the ordeal. Even cowardice and dishonour would not have saved her. The Germans had resolved that if war came from any cause, they would take and break France forthwith as its first operation. The German military Chiefs burned to give the signal, and were sure of the result. She would have begged for mercy in vain. She did not beg."

Full of exultant foreboding Winston wrote to Clementine from the Admiralty at midnight on the 28th of July:

"My darling one and beautiful, everything tends towards catastrophe and collapse. I am interested, geared up and happy. Is it not horrible to be built like that? The preparations have a hideous fascination for me. I pray to God to forgive me for such fearful moods of levity. Yet I would do my best for peace, and nothing would induce me wrongfully to strike the blow. I cannot feel that we in this island are in any serious degree responsible for the wave of madness which has swept the mind of Christendom. No one can measure the consequences. I wondered whether those stupid Kings and Emperors could not assemble together and revivify Kingship by saving the nations from hell but we all drift on in a kind of dull catileptic trance. As if it was somebody else's operation!"

Asquith's Cabinet was very much divided, the majority being in favour of maintaining a strict neutrality and to let those who wanted war in Europe, get on with it. By Sunday, August 2nd 1914, Germany was officially at war with France and Russia, and had violated the neutrality of Luxembourg. That evening she delivered an ultimatum to the Belgians, demanding free passage across their territory for her troops in preparation for the invasion of France. At the Cabinet Meeting on Monday morning Asquith held the several resignations of his colleagues in his pocket, but, when the news came, while the Cabinet was still in session, that Belgium had refused the German ultimatum, all but three of these ministers realised Britain was now honour bound to go to war. Sir Edward Grey made a moving speech to the House of Commons outlining the situation that faced the country, and though the main purpose of his life's work, to keep the peace in Europe, had failed, he sat down sadly amidst the cheers of the overwhelming majority of the members of the House of Commons. The same sentiment went for the country at large. Ulstermen and Irish Republicans forgot their differences and pledged their loyalty, and even the Welsh miners, who only a week or two before had denounced the prospect of war, before going on their holidays, satisfied now of its justice, returned to work prepared to cut all the coal Britain needed.

"What do we do next?" Violet Asquith had asked her father when she had said goodnight to him that evening. He replied, "We shall send an ultimatum to Germany to stop the invasion of Belgium tomorrow."

Winston had already acted some days before. Confiding only in Asquith, for he feared his colleagues would mistake what he was about to do as provocative action which might damage the slender chance that still remained for peace, he told him that he intended moving the Fleet to its war station on the 30th of July. "He looked at me with a hard stare" recorded Winston "and gave a sort of grunt. I did not require anything else."

And so in secrecy and with sealed orders the great Fleet sailed, commanded by Admiral Jellicoe, northwards through the Straits of Dover. When at 11 p.m., or midnight German time, on Tuesday August the 4th, the British ultimatum to Germany demanding the maintenance of Belgium neutrality expired without an answer, Britain was prepared.

"We were now in a position," wrote Winston "whatever happened to control events . . . If war should come no-one would know where to look for the British Fleet. Somewhere in that enormous waste of water to the north of our islands cruising now this way, now that, shrouded in storms and mists, dwelt this mighty organisation . . . The King's ships were at sea."

Lord Fisher, who like Winston was also a prophet, was only two months out when he had forecast in 1911 that the Battle of Armageddon would take place on October 21st 1914. The world survived the cataclysm but the Great War erased forever the calm and assured certainty that European civilisation would in the full-ness of time automatically improve man's lot upon earth. Spreading like a cancer over a large part of Africa, Asia, Europe and finally drawing into the conflict the New World across the Atlantic, the coming struggle was in a few brief and agonising years to make the stable, solid, sometimes brilliant and progressive world that existed before August the 4th 1914, seem like "the picture of a vanished age." Winston was to observe later how the very character of society, the foundations of politics, the outlook of youth, the scale of values, all changed to an extent which would not have been

Black Watch reservists being piped off from Dundee West Station on the outbreak of war in 1914. Winston had dreaded this moment as far back as 1911 when the haunting lines of A. E. Houseman's poem 'The Shropshire Lad' had rung in his mind their dread warning:

"Dear to friends and food for powder
Soldiers marching
All to die."

believed possible. He had been brought up as a child in the age of Victoria when Britain's position in trade and upon the seas was unrivalled, and when the realisation of the greatness of her Empire and the sense of duty in her citizens to preserve it was growing ever stronger:

"In those days" he wrote, "the dominant forces in Great Britain were very sure of themselves and of their doctrine. They thought they could teach the world the art of government and the science of economics. They were sure they were supreme at sea and consequently safe at home. They rested therefore sedately under the convictions of power and security. The Great War shattered these illusions forever."

To understand what happened look at a map.

On the east of France, running along the boundary between France and Germany, lay a line of strong fortresses which the Germans thought would be too difficult to break through; and for this reason they decided to by-pass them by marching through neutral Luxembourg and Belgium, and thrust their invading force of nearly a million men through France's undefended border with these countries. Having done that, they intended to sweep round in an encircling movement to the south of Paris and march north again to the German border, hopefully destroying or capturing the bulk of the French army within their ring of steel.

Kitchener was brought by Asquith into the newly constituted War Cabinet, and Winston undertook to get the British Expeditionary Force of six Divisions, nearly one hundred thousand men, under the command of Sir John French, across the Channel to aid France. This maneouvre, which in any other circumstances might have been hazardous, was carried out behind the shield of the Fleet, which, by keeping its war station at Scapa Flow, held Germany's Grand fleet impotently in port. Kitchener, despite the smoothness with which the embarkation was accomplished, was pessimistic. He prophesied to a dismayed Cabinet that the war would last for many years, and that it would be necessary to raise and put into the field, armies of millions. Winston wanted to introduce conscription immediately, but it was decided to rely for the moment on volunteers, and Kitchener's famous poster "Your Country Needs You" went out asking for the first hundred thousand.

Helped by the unexpectedly heroic resistance of the Belgian fort of Liege which held up the German advance, and with the advantage of surprise (for no reports had appeared in any of the newspapers) the British Expeditionary Force took up a defensive position alongside the French before the middle of August. However, as Winston had predicted three years before, the Germans for the first few weeks seemed to carry all before them.

They smashed in waves, a grey tide upon the British line, and the 'Old Contemptibles' were forced to conduct their heroic retreat from Mons and Charleroi. For a time it looked as if Paris itself would fall. Joffre, the French Commander, retreated until he was behind the River Marne, but there he decided to give battle. He believed correctly, that although the German army greatly out-numbered the French and British, it was now too far from its base of supplies to sustain a determined resistance. By September the 10th, after four days of bloody fighting, the enemy were defeated, and Germany's plan for a swift victory with a peace dictated to Britain and France before winter lay shattered.

But the losses sustained by both sides were terrible, and as the armies and the armaments of the combatants continued to increase behind an unbroken system of barbed wire and trenches stretching from the Swiss frontier to the English Channel, casualties were to get much worse.

The war at sea, too, brought a number of unexpected reverses, this time to the British.

Ever since the day before the Declaration of War Winston had been suffering tortures of anxiety over the fate of the Goeben, the one German warship at large in the Meditteranean. Outstripping in speed and power every vessel in the Franch Navy, only the British battle cruisers the Indomitable and Indefatigable were her match. Ordered to hold and shadow her in the hours before the expiry of the British ultimatum, Winston would have given them the order to engage her in battle had he not been restrained by Asquith's old-fashioned sense of honour. The chase went on, and, at five o'clock on August the 4th, Prince Louis reported that there was still time to sink Goeben before dark; but, bound by the Cabinet decision, Winston was unable to give the word. Italian neutrality hampered the pursuers, and under cover of darkness the Goeben escaped to temporary shelter in Messina in Sicily. Some days before war had broken out, Winston and Sir Edward Grey had taken the decision to commandeer two warships currently being completed in British yards for delivery to Turkey, and this act hastened agreement between the Turks and the Central powers. The Goeben's commander received news of a Treaty and was given orders to proceed at once to Constantinople. For Winston this incident was to be fateful in its effects.

At the Admiralty he and his colleagues were now working at full stretch. His days began at nine, and with the long day broken by a siesta of one hour after lunch he worked on until 2 a.m. the following morning. The powerhouse of his mind dealt cleanly and logically with a flood of confusing and often conflicting reports which piled onto his desk by the hour. During the dark days of August his courage never faltered, and as the armies of Britain and France fell back under the hammer blow of the Hun, he circulated once more amongst his colleagues in the Cabinet the memorandum he had written in 1911. The German attack, he then had stressed, would break through the line of the Meuse on the twentieth day and the French in retreat would fall back on Paris and the south. "All plans based on the opposite assumption ask too much of fortune." Now, he told them encouragingly, "If the unfavourable prediction about the twentieth day had been borne out, so also would be the favourable prediction about the fortieth day."

By the end of the month he cheered the depressed and anxious Cabinet with the news of the Navy's audacious action in the Heligoland Bight, when three enemey cruisers and a destroyer were sunk and three other German ships were crippled without loss or serious injury to a single British ship.

On August 27th Winston despatched a squadron of his Royal Naval Air Service aircraft to Dunkirk and Calais, where they carried out a series of daring raids over the Zeppelin sheds at Cologne, Cuxhaven, Dusseldorf, and Frederickhaven. Within the year these frail contraptions of canvas, wood and wire, had destroyed at least six Zeppelins, caused confusion to the enemy and gave inspiration to the demoralised French. Before the trench lines were fixed, Winston encouraged his Air Commander to carry out a number of Commando raids using commandeered cars with improvised armour, and the proud plumed German cavalry had to resort to the humiliating stratagem of digging up the roads in order to obstruct their passage. Winston was sure that problem too could be overcome; and thinking of a caterpillar tractor design, or perhaps a car carrying a bridge in front of it, he set up a Land-ships Committee to come up with an answer—it did, with astonishing results.

In September, 1914, Joffre suggested that an additional British force should land at Dunkirk, create a diversion and, hopefully, force the Germans to ease their pressure on the French left flank. Britain's Army was of course fully committed but Winston agreed— with alacrity—to dispatch there a brigade of three thousand Marines with also a similar force to Ostend, whose landings were deliberately given the maximum publicity. Winston's 'Marine Promenaders' came in for a great deal of Press criticism—there was no censorship—but, coming at the psychological moment as the Germans retreated from the Battle of the Marne, the ruse turned the tide of war in favour of the Allies. With Winston's Marines, exaggerated in the imagination of the German High Command to something like forty thousand, they believed their rear was seriously menaced. However, before Germany could turn its attention to this threat Antwerp, the sentinel of the Channel ports, would first of all have to be reduced. If Antwerp fell, so, soon after, would Dunkirk, Calais and Boulogne and thus the brief advantage won by the allies would have been lost, leaving their armies again face to face with disaster.

On September the 28th, under the direction of General Falkenhayn, the Germans began to bombard the apparently impregnable fortifications surrounding Antwerp with heavy Howitzers which fired shells weighing over a ton, and their cavalry swept down the broad sandy beaches of the Belgian coastline.

In a state of panic the Belgian Government decided to leave Antwerp for Ostend, and, led by King Albert, prepared to withdraw their Army to Ghent to protect the coastline. But, as far as the Allies were concerned, Antwerp had to hold out for five more days. In the area around Ypres the British Army was fighting with matchless courage to consolidate its sector of the line, and, if Antwerp fell, the whole left flank of the Allies would be laid open by the mighty German war machine and rolled up in total defeat.

At Kitchener's house a midnight conference was held. Winston required little urging to take on the job of persuading the Belgians to hang on. A brigade of Marines and two of the newly formed brigades of naval volunteers were dispatched immediately to reinforce the defenders, and a Regular Army force of twenty thousand was scraped together under General Rawlinson to land at Ostend and Zeebrugge and which was to march overland and raise the siege.

Winston's arrival in the shell-torn city was noted with wry but too comfortably detached humour by an American correspondent:

"At one o'clock that afternoon" he wrote "a big, drab-coloured touring car filled with British Naval Officers drove down the Place de Mer, its horn sounding a hoarse warning, took the turn into the March-aux-Souliers on two wheels, and drew up in front of the Hotel. Before the car had fairly come to a stop the door of the tonneau was thrown violently open and out jumped a smooth-faced, sandy-haired, stoop-shouldered, youthful looking man in undress Trinity House uniform . . .

"As he charged into the crowded lobby he flung his arms out, in a nervous characteristic gesture, as though pushing his way through a crowd. It was a most spectacular entrance, and reminded me for all the world like a scene from a melodrama where the hero dashes up bare-headed on a foam-flecked horse, and saves the heroine, or the old homestead, or the family fortune as the case may be."

Melodramatic or not, Winston's presence brought a whiff of resolution to the crumbling morale of the Belgians. The British Marines took their places in the Antwerp trenches allowing the hard-pressed defenders their first relief in several days; and within two days of his arrival the Belgians gave up their idea of retreating, determined now to resist the German battering, until relief came.

On October 5th Winston telegraphed Asquith, offering to resign the Admiralty, and undertook to assume the command of the defence and relief of Antwerp. Though Kitchener would willingly have made him a Major-General, Asquith was, understandably, astounded, and when Winston's extraordinary gesture, made in the heat of the moment, was known, it was scornfully ridiculed by his political enemies and the Press.

The following day, the 6th of October, Winston went down to the Headquarters of General Paris to meet the two newly arrived naval Brigades.

Observing the scene was the London War correspondent of an Italian newspaper:

"In the battle line near Lierre" he wrote "in the midst of a group of officers stood a man enveloped in a cloak and wearing a yachting cap. He was tranquilly smoking a large cigar and looked at the progress of the battle under a rain of shrapnel which I can only call fearful. It was Mr Churchill, who had come to view the situation for himself. It must be confessed that it is not easy to find in all Europe a Minister who would be capable of smoking peacefully in that shell-fire. He smiled and looked quite satisfied."

But courage now was not enough; Antwerp was doomed. A Counsel of War was held on the evening of General Rawlinson's arrival, presided over by the Belgian King. Winston and Rawlinson assured their allies that they were prepared to carry on the fight, but fearing their lines of communication might have already been cut off, the Belgians decided instead to carry out their original evacuation plan. Winston telegraphed Kitchener that Rawlinson had already ordered a general retreat to the inner line of forts which would be held long enough for the Belgian Army to withdraw.

That night Winston left Antwerp with General Rawlinson and after an anxious drive to the coast arrived in London next day.

The naval division held on in Antwerp to the last, then stole away by night across the pontoon bridge spanning the river Scheld along roads choked with refugees. Most of them got home safely, but two battalions strayed over the Dutch border and were interned for the duration of the war.

An apparent fiasco, Winston's intervention applied a brake to the German advance down the coast and foiled this, their second attempt, to gain a decisive victory on the western front. It prolonged the defence of Antwerp for a week after it should have surrendered on the 3rd of October, and that seven days respite enabled Dunkirk and Calais to remain in allied hands. It also provided time for the main British force transferred from the Aisne to the new left of the allied line to arrive, and allowed the heroic British Tommies aided by the French and Belgians, standing against huge odds at Ypres, to stabilise a line along the river Yser to the sea. As Sir Basil Liddell-Hart the military historian has acknowledged, that maneouvre "succeeded by so narrow a margin that the Antwerp expedition must be adjudged the saving factor." At the time, though, when many of the facts had to remain secret, Winston was flayed publicly by a vindictive Press. So anxious had he been, they said, to lead the expedition that he had run away from Kitchener before Kitchener had had time to say 'No'. When that story was exploded, another was substituted, that Kitchener had been persuaded by Winston's silver tongue, and that he had absurdly mis-interpreted his instructions. The action upon which most scorn was heaped was his offer to resign the Admiralty, and even Asquith is alleged to have declared, "I can't put an ex-Cavalry subaltern in command of Major-Generals." The accusation which stuck in the consciousness of the public however, was that he had led a futile action and caused "a pitiful loss of brave men's lives."

For the first time Winston's self-confidence was shaken. "I ought," he later admitted ruefully, " . . . never to have gone to Antwerp. I ought to have remained in London in an endeavour to force the Cabinet and Lord Kitchener to take more effective action than they did . . ."

Even in strictly naval matters, as far as the public were concerned, events were not going as had been hoped. With Kaiser Wilhelm himself holding the greatest say among his Naval Chiefs of Staff, Germany was content for the moment to wear down gradually Britain's margin of sea power by the stealth of raid, mine and submarine. Admiral von Tirpitz was furious to be held back with his main fleet straining at its hawsers while the British escaped into the North Sea after Beatty had led his daring raid into the Heligoland Bight. But the Kaiser was no fool, at least in naval matters, and did not intend to risk his all on a "battle in blue water."

Just before the Antwerp foray on September the 21st, Winston, irked with impatience, had declared that "So far as the Navy is concerned we cannot fight while the enemy remains in port . . . If they do not come out and fight they will be dug out like rats from a hole." Unfortunately, early the following morning, while steaming off the Dutch coast, the decoy ships Aboukir, Hogue and Cressy were torpedoed in quick succession by a hidden submarine with the loss of fourteen hundred men.

Of course, Winston, as "an ignorant amateur," who knew nothing of the risks which had to be run at sea, was blamed for the disaster; King George remarked pointedly to Asquith "The rats came out of their own accord and to our cost." It was not known until later, that if Winston's order for the withdrawal of the 'Live bait squadron' had been promptly obeyed, the incident would never have occurred.

In the Indian Ocean too, the armed raiders Emden and Konigsberg were harrying Britain's Merchant fleet, and in the South Atlantic lurked the small cruiser squadron led by the Gneisenau and Scharnhorst. An impatient public asked, 'What is the Navy doing?' How could Winston explain, that by continuing to hold the mighty German Grand Fleet in check the great bulk of Britain's world commerce for the moment could go on virtually undisturbed while Germany's life blood was choked off.

Public frustration turned on Prince Louis of Battenburg, a dignified and loyal Englishman, for no better reason than his German birth and name, and he was hounded from office. To restore confidence in the Admiralty Asquith's obvious and popular choice was Fisher. Winston assured the Prime Minister that he could work with no-one else. Only King George wisely observed, "I think it is a great mistake, and he is seventy four."

Winston loved the old man and even altered his own timetable to fit in with him, but their personalities were too much alike for their relationship to stand the strain for long. Violet Asquith wrote of Fisher: "His conversation (if so it can be called) was torrential. I tried to imagine a tete-a-tete between him and Winston, and wondered which of them did the listening!"

Less than twenty four hours after he took up the job Fisher was brought news of the disastrous defeat at Coronel in the South Atlantic. With a small fleet of superannuated vessels Rear Admiral Craddock had been keeping station between the Magellan Straits and the Falkland Island when he was spotted by Admiral Graf von Spee in the Gneisenau. Hopelessly outgunned by the German squadron all but one of Craddock's ships were sunk with all hands, and once more Winston received the blame.

Taking the risk of weakening temporarily the Grand Fleet, Fisher immediately dispatched the battle cruisers Invincible and the Inflexible to the scene of the action, and within five weeks they had located von Spee south east of the Falkland Islands. This time the Germans were outpaced and outgunned. Von Spee in the Gneisenau fought to the end but he and his two sons and every sailor aboard his five ships were sent to the bottom.

Of course, Fisher got all the credit.

Then came the German naval bombardment of Hartlepool, Scarborough and Whitby, when more than five hundred civilians were killed and wounded. Winston got the blame again.

On January 22nd 1915 the Navy got its revenge when Admiral Beatty fought the battle of Doggerbank, sinking the armoured cruiser Blucher along with two cruisers and although this decisive action too was attributed to Fisher's genius, Winston had the solid satisfaction of the knowledge that the German Navy had been swept from the seas. It was not to venture forth again for nearly fifteen months. The British fleet could now concentrate on its traditional war strategy of maintaining a tight continental blockade. However, with the first phase of the war at sea won, both Winston and Fisher wished to see some of the Navy's spare capacity freed from these routine duties and put to work on some sort of dynamic offensive against Germany. In this the two men were agreed, but as to how the Navy was to be employed was a different matter.

Fisher had a scheme, which as yet he kept to himself, of invading the Baltic Sea with a great fleet; landing an Army on the north shores of Germany, striking at the very vitals of the enemy and ending the war with one blow. Just as imaginatively, Winston's idea, proposed as early as August, 1914, was for a naval operation which would force its way up the narrow strip of water dividing Greece and Turkey, sail into the Black Sea and capture the city of Constantinople. This action he believed would at one stroke separate the Central powers from their ally Turkey; destroy the German battle cruiser Goeben and light cruiser Breslau which had previously escaped the British Navy; bring aid to the hard-pressed Russians; and bring countries like Greece and Italy into the war on the Allied side.

The Army Chiefs of Staff, especially Kitchener, were not at all keen on Winston's idea, despite the fact that the Allies had already suffered a million casualties in the first three months of the war. They held—though without enthusiasm—to the textbook rule that there should be no division of forces, until, that is, the Russian Grand Duke Nicholas made a personal appeal to Kitchener to make some demonstration which would bring hope at least to the Russians locked in battle with the Turks in the Caucasus. Backed up by Lloyd George, who had ceased to be a pacifist, and Maurice Hankey, Secretary to the War Council, Winston urged his colleagues to adopt the hopeful new strategy.

Deeply impressed now by his convincing arguments, the War Council agreed. None of them really relished the current theory that only by killing Germans at a greater rate than they killed Allied troops, could victory be won in the trenches.

A naval force of old battleships was got together, all that could be spared. It was however also agreed that the Queen Elizabeth, the super-Dreadnought which had just been completed and was scheduled to fire her fifteen-inch guns on trials in the Mediterranean anyway, could join the armada to find instead some real targets to aim at. Accordingly, on the 19th February 1915 a long-range naval bombardment of the Turkish outer-defences took place. Outranged, the unfortunate Turks could not even reply to the fire. By afternoon the battleships had closed in and silenced the forts on the Gallipoli peninsula, on the Western side of the Dardanelles and, before darkness, all but one on the Eastern side. Bad weather intervened, but a few days later on the 25th the attack began again, this time wiping out all resistance. The Turks and their German advisers having fled during the night, parties of marines and sailors landed on both sides of the Straits the following day and blew up what was left of the guns and forts.

Kitchener and Fisher, who had both expressed doubts about the enterprise, were now convinced believers. Troops who could consolidate the expected naval victory were suddenly made available–the Anzac Army Corps, the Royal Naval Division, a French Division, a promise of three Greek Divisions, the Russian Army Corps at Batoum; and if success seemed assured, Bulgaria, Rumania and Italy would join the war on the Allies side.

The attempt to run the gauntlet of the narrow waters began on March the 18th. In brilliant sunshine on a calm sea the fourteen British and four French battleships entered the Dardanelles and opened up a terrific bombardment of the inner forts, and, by the afternoon, silenced almost all opposition. Though the French battleship Bouvet, hit in the magazine by a plunging shell, sank with nearly all hands, the makeshift minesweeping force of North sea fishing trawlers, manned by civilian crews, were ordered forward; and struggling against the fierce Dardanelle's current succeeded in exploding six mines. Confident that the way was now clear, the line of warships advanced in their wake. Shortly after 4 p.m. however, the Inflexible and Irresistible reported they had encountered an unsuspected row of mines and were hit below the water line. At 5 p.m. de Robeck, the Naval Commander-in-Chief, gave orders for a general retirement, and as that took place the battleship Ocean struck another mine and she and the Irresistible sank. The Inflexible and the French battleship Gaulois, both badly damaged by gunfire, reached safety, but de Robeck was shattered when he counted his losses. Out of nine battleships engaged in the attack six had been sunk or crippled. Fearing that he would be replaced and accused of incompetence, it was a tragedy that he failed to realise he was within a hairsbreadth of success. Roger Keyes, de Robeck's second-in-command, had no doubt that they were on the verge of victory. That night he got permission to re-enter the Straits with a destroyer to try to salvage or torpedo the Irresistible and the Ocean. Describing in his memoirs the eery stillness and silence of the battlefield, fitfully illuminated by Turkish searchlights, he wrote how he experienced "A most indelible impression that we were in the presence of a beaten foe. I thought he was beaten at 4 p.m. and at midnight I knew with still greater certainty that he was absolutely beaten; and it only remained for us to organise a proper sweeping force and devise some means of dealing with drifting mines to reap the fruits of our efforts."

Winston was in no way put out when the news reached him. Only sixty-one men had been killed or wounded and after all, the three old battleships which had been sunk were due for scrap in any case. Hastening to reassure de Robeck that he still enjoyed their confidence, Winston and Fisher promised him four more battleships, a fleet of destroyers equipped with minesweeping apparatus and an aircraft squadron for spotting the enemy's guns. The Turks in fact had almost exhausted their ammunition, and the minefields, thinly spread, seemed a greater obstacle than they were.

De Robeck's nerve, however, failed to recover, and he replied saying that he didn't think he could continue without the assistance of the Army. As troops were not yet immediately available this meant a hold-up of three weeks. Winston was horrified and immediately drafted an answer to de Robeck pointing out the dangers of delay through submarine attack and the possible heavy cost in human lives of a military operation, ordering him to renew the attack at the first favourable opportunity. Submitting this telegram for the approval of Lord Fisher and the Admiralty, Winston was astonished that neither they nor Asquith were prepared to overrule the Admiral on the spot, and as a consequence it was never sent.

Fatefully, everyone responsible drifted into a new scheme which had never been envisaged. When Winston told the War Cabinet that the Admiralty had refused to continue the all-naval attack, Kitchener boldly declared that he would carry the plan through by military force, though the troops were stll not ready and by now any chance of surprise had been thrown away. Only two Turkish Divisions were at the Straits when the preliminary bombardment had taken place, but within a month these were increased to four and again to six by the time Ian Hamilton, Winston's friend from his days as a young officer on the North West Frontier, was at last able to attempt a landing.

Beginning at daybreak on April the 25th the Gallipoli Peninsula was pounded by an immense naval bombardment. The Turks made no reply. After an hour the un-natural stillness gave rise to hopes that the enemy were either dead or absent. The 'River Clyde,' a merchantman with two thousand men on board, surrounded by twenty smaller craft, approached the shore in calm seas. When they grounded within a few yards of the beach the Turks leaped from their trenches and poured a devastating fire at close range into the densely crowded masses of men sitting packed like sardines in the boats. They died there in hundreds. Some dived into the sea and tried to swim for the shore and reaching it were mown down. Only two hundred ever succeeded in reaching the pitiful shelter of the cliffs. Commander Samson of the Air Squadron flying over the scene reported that, "The calm blue sea was absolutely red with blood for a distance of fifty yards from the shore . . . " Night came at last, and under cover of darkness the River Clyde landed her remaining men, and at daybreak, under cover from a renewed naval bombardment, Hamilton's shattered Army regrouped and was able to advance to capture the high ground and move forward unopposed for some miles.

A foothold had been won but the problems of supply were enormous because the Turks still held the commanding heights and were able to bring up their almost inexhaustable reserves of man-power. Here, as in France, the stagnation of trench warfare was to set in. Kitchener was complacent but Winston was deeply disturbed by the tremendous losses which had been incurred, and, joined by Lord Fisher, pleaded with him to send immediate reinforcements from Egypt. But too little was given too late; while at the same time, by slow degrees, the Allied committment was to grow out of all proportion with a casualty figure by May, of twenty thousand.

In London there was increasing and bitter disappointment with the whole affair, for on the Western Front the war for the Allies was also going badly; three battles of Aubers in March, the second battle of Ypres in April, and Festubert in May, had resulted in heavy casualties and no gains. The Germans had also opened up unrestricted U-boat warfare by sinking the Cunard passenger ship 'Lusitania'. And, there was a chronic shortage of shells, more of which had been fired by the British alone in the first three months of this war than had been fired in the whole of the Boer War. Winston was distraught but could not bring himself to recommend a with-drawal from Gallipoli. Even de Robeck, touched by the suffering and sacrifices of the Army, offered to do now what he would not do at the beginning. This Fisher opposed until the Army had occupied the shores of the Narrows. Then, on the night of May the 12th, after the Goliath was torpedoed in the Dardanelles by a Turkish destroyer, Fisher immediately demanded the recall of the Queen Elizabeth. Kitchener protested furiously at this desertion of the Army in their hour of need, but Fisher replied, "Either the Queen Elizabeth leaves the Dardanelles tonight or I leave the Admiralty tonight." It was a fortnight later before his judgment was vindicated when a dummy Queen Elizabeth, which had taken the place of the original, was torpedoed. Three days later Fisher made a statement at the War Council that, "He was against the Dardanelles and had been all along . . . "

That night Winston wrote to Asquith complaining of how Fisher until then had agreed in writing with all the decisions that had been made. Immediately afterwards, Winston visited Fisher in his room and frankly told him how he felt. Fisher looked at him in an odd sort of way and said, "I think you are right–it isn't fair." Though they parted amicably, Fisher boiled below the surface. How dare Winston, a mere civilian politician touch *his* Navy, the perfect creation of his Nelsonian genius. He shut himself up in the First Sea Lord's house adjoining the Admiralty and pulled down the blinds in a monstrous huff. He sent Winston a note saying he was off to Scotland, and to Asquith he tendered his resignation. Asquith, greatly alarmed, wrote back immediately, "Lord Fisher,–In the King's name I order you to remain at your post."

But it was too late, Fisher would not come back and he plunged the Government into a political crisis. With the negotiations which were to bring Italy with her million-strong Army into the war having reached a delicate stage, Asquith hastened to consult with Balfour and Bonar Law, the Tory leaders. Their conditions for not rocking the boat were simple; Winston must be removed from the Admiralty; Haldane, who had once expressed an admiration for German culture, must be removed from the War Office; and Cabinet representation must be made for prominent Tories. Asquith had no alternative but to accept and called for all his Ministers to tender their resignations. Forming a National Coalition, he kept with great skill all the key posts in Liberal hands, with the exception of the Admiralty; and even for that, Balfour was in fact, Winston's own choice. Despite Tory hatred, Asquith refused to part with Winston altogether and managed to get him the Chancellorship of the Duchy of Lancaster, a Ministry without any designated responsibility which would at least give him a seat in the Cabinet. Such consolation, however, could not assuage Winston's despondency. Violet Asquith records how she met him soon afterwards in a passage in the House of Commons:

"He took me into his room and sat down on a chair–silent, despairing–as I have never seen him. He seemed to have no rebellion or even anger left. He did not even abuse Fisher, but simply said, 'I am finished.' I poured out contradictions, protestations–but he waved them aside. 'No–I am done. What I want of all things is to take some active part in beating the Germans. But I can't–it's been taken from me. I'd go out to the Front at once–but these soldiers are so stuffy–they wouldn't like my being given anything of a command. No–I am finished.' "

He was very nearly right, for as he wrote of the cavalry charge at Omdurman comparing it philosophically to the hazards of civilian life:

"So long as you are all right, firmly in the saddle, your horse in hand, and well armed, lots of enemies will give you a wide berth. But if you have lost a stirrup, have a rein cut, have dropped a weapon, are wounded, or your horse is wounded; then is the moment when from all quarters enemies rush upon you."

Richmond, the Irish leader, now a Member of the Cabinet, described him as 'A shouting amateur,' whose 'personal vanity occupies so large a place in the arrangements that the operation is either a fiasco or is most wasteful in lives or material–or both.' Admiral Beatty wrote venomously without a trace of gratitude: "The Navy breathes freer now it is rid of the succubus Churchill." Admiral Jellicoe described him as "A public danger to the Empire." The King said he was "Impossible." And Margot Asquith, wife of the Prime Minister, speaking on behalf of many Liberals, ascribed the destruction of the Liberal Government to: "The man whom I always said would smash it."

Although still a member of the Dardanelles Committee, Winston was now a solitary voice; alone among its twelve members he pleaded for speedy and massive reinforcements for the troops on the peninsula, dying in their hundreds from Turkish bullets and disease. He argued against squandering Britain's new armies in frantic and sterile efforts to pierce the German lines on the plains of Flanders. "Through the narrows of the Dardanelles and across the ridges of the Gallipoli Peninsula," he claimed before his constituents in Dundee, "lie some of the shortest paths to a triumphant peace." In June, he pointed out that Joffre's May offensive on the Western Front had cost two hundred and twenty thousand casualties and that since the 22nd of April the British had suffered a hundred thousand, and that out of the 19,500 square miles of France and Belgium in German hands the Allies, by that prodigious effort, had recovered only 8 square miles!

The Committee impressed at last by these arguments, decided to send five of Kitchener's new Divisions, but much precious time had slipped away and by the beginning of August the Gallipoli campaign reached its terrible climax. All the errors of the original landing were faithfully repeated and less than three weeks later Hamilton, after one last brave attempt to break through at Sulva Bay, had to report that he had lost in dead and wounded over forty thousand men.

All but Winston now accepted the campaign as a disasterous failure. Hamilton was replaced on the 14th of October by Sir Charles Monroe, a general who was convinced that the war could only be won on the Western Front by a process of attrition. On the 11th of November the Dardanelles Committee was replaced by a War Committee from which Winston was excluded. Giving up his £4,000 a year post, he wrote a few days later to Asquith saying he did not "feel able in times like these to remain in well paid inactivity" and concluded, "I therefore ask you to submit my resignation to the King. I am an officer, and I place myself unreservedly at the disposal of the military authorities, observing that my regiment is in France. I have a clear conscience which enables me to bear my responsibility for past events with composure."

In the prevailing countrywide mood of gathering despair his farewell speech of hope to the House of Commons turned out, by a curious irony, to be a triumph.

"There is no reason," he declared, "to be disheartened about the progress of the war. We are passing through a bad time now, and it will probably be worse before it is better, but that it will be better, if we only endure and persevere, I have no doubt whatever. The old wars were decided by their episodes rather than by their tendencies. In this war the tendencies are far more important than the episodes."

He defended his own part in the course of the war and made it clear to the House that the naval attack on the Dardanelles was:

"A naval plan, made by naval authorities on the spot, approved by naval experts in the Admiralty, assented to by the First Sea Lord, and executed on the spot by Admirals who at every stage believed in the operation . . . I will not have it said that this was a civilian plan foisted by a political amateur upon reluctant officers and experts."

He declared himself finally as an unabashed Easterner:

"All through this year I have offered the same counsel to the Government: Undertake no operation in the West which is more costly to us in lives than to the enemy. In the East, take Constantinople. Take it by ships if you can. Take it by soldiers if you must.

Take it by whichever plan, military or naval, commends itself to your military experts. But take it; take it soon, take it while time remains."

On sitting down he received an ovation from the whole House and Asquith rose to pay him tribute saying, "I have always found him a wise counsellor, a brilliant colleague and a faithful friend." Kitchener paid Winston perhaps the greatest compliment when he said: "The Fleet was ready: they cannot take that away." Even Bonar Law, who had rejected him, conceded grudgingly: "He has the defects of his qualities, and as his qualities are large the shadow they throw is pretty large also. But I say, deliberately, that in mental power and vital force he is one of the foremost men in our country."

Nothing however could disguise the fact that Winston was now a man of yesterday. He was to write thirty years later, "I was ruined for the time being over the Dardanelles and a supreme exercise was cast away, through my trying to carry out a major and combined operation of war from a subordinate position. Men are ill-advised to try such ventures."

One month after he went to the Front the Gallipoli Peninsula was evacuated, and for the rest of his life Winston's name was to be linked directly in the public mind with the thirty-four thousand lost lives.

Sir John French, the British Commander-in-Chief of the Expeditionary Force, hearing of Winston's decision to return to the Army offered him the command of a brigade. Winston declined saying, "I am a professional soldier who knows war, but not this kind of war. 'Colonel' yes; 'Brigadier-General' no, until I have learnt my job." French gave him a battalion in the Grenadier Guards with the promise of early promotion after he had had experience in the line. Accordingly, four or five weeks later, all was arranged for him to take over the command of a brigade of the 19th Division. A dinner was even planned at Divisional Headquarters to mark the occasion. Then French was suddenly recalled to London to be told he had been superseded by General Douglas Haig. Winston's promotion was discussed; and though Haig himself made no objection, Asquith, fearing another political storm, refused to confirm the appointment. French, though hurt and disappointed at his own dismissal, broke the news to Winston himself.

Instead, therefore, of the hoped-for command, he was transferred to a Colonelcy in the 6th Royal Scots Fusiliers which had distinguished itself in the battle of Loos. Many soldiers in the regiment had been miners in the Ayrshire coalfields and a Captain Gibb, who wrote a little book on the episode, recorded how the men grew mutinous when they heard the rumour of Winston's appointment.

Winston found on his arrival that his Battalion Headquarters consisted of a tumbledown farmhouse, a thousand yards from a sector of the front line called Plug Street (Ploegsteerk); and in the front line itself officers and men stood guard, in verminous clogging wetness, separated from the enemy by a mere 300 yards of crater-torn mud and barbed wire. According to Winston it made little difference whether one was in or out of the trenches, for the same number of men lost their lives through the continuous shellfire.

The first thing he did was to set about knowing his officers and, first scrutinising them, "silently and intently from head to foot" said: "War is declared, gentlemen, on the lice . . . !" Hot irons were pressed into service and after four days relentless attack victory was won when the 6th Royal Scots Fusilliers achieved the remarkable front line distinction of being lice-less. He encouraged, with admittedly only marginal success, his soldiers to sing on the march, and the Plug Street farmhouse became for every kind of new idea, the centre for discussion. All he had learned of the theories of defensive warfare in Sandhurst days came back and he found himself fascinated with the techniques of laying sandbags, the building of parapets, traverses and parados; the devising of shelters, scarps and counter scarps, dug-outs, half-moons and ravelins.

"Early and late he was on the line," wrote Captain Gibb, "just as the enemy field guns began, the Colonel (Winston) came along to our trench and suggested a view over the parapet. As we stood up on the firestep we felt the wind and swish of several whizz-bangs flying past our heads which, as it always did, horrified me."

"Do you like war?" Winston asked Gibb in a dreamy faraway voice.

"The only thing to do was to pretend not to hear him" wrote Gibb. "At that moment I profoundly hated war. But at that and every moment I believe Winston Churchill revelled in it. There was no such thing as fear in him . . .

"No Commanding Officer ever was more interested in or more attentive to his wounded. On the one hand he was utterly impervious to all feelings of aversion from the unpleasant sights of war and I have seen him . . . sitting calmly discussing questions of state with 'Archie' (Sir Archibald Sinclair his Second-in-Command) in blood saturated surroundings but on the other he was always first on the scene of misfortune and did all in his power to help and comfort and cheer."

Winston's hard work and genuine concern for his men won over even those of them who had started off by being most doubtful about a Colonel who was 'a damned politician'. The troops also admired his impudence. On one occasion a very pompous and unpopular military personage visited Battalion Headquarters after it had been badly damaged by shelling. Sent for, Winston was told that he ought to get something more effective done for the protection of the men. 'You know it's dangerous' said the General, 'it's positively dangerous.' "Yes sir," replied Winston, "but you know this is a very dangerous war."

"War is a game to be played with a smiling face" was Winston's motto. But, he felt frustrated. Men at home were hard at work undoing much of what he had effected. News of the evacuation of Gallipoli hit him especially hard; it was soon after announced that the Royal Naval Battalion on which he had grown so keen was also to be disbanded; and Balfour had given up all but one of the prototype land-ship developments. Besides, although he genuinely enjoyed the danger and comradeship of the front line, for a man so fastidious that he could only sleep in silk pyjamas the filth of trench life was an obscenity hardly to be borne.

Due some leave, Winston returned to London on March the 2nd, and fell into a nest of political intrigue. Invited to lunch one day with his mother, were also a number of discontented and influential Tories and Liberals, among them F. E. Smith, Sir Edward Carson and the editors of the Observer and the Manchester Guardian newspapers. Together they persuaded him – and he required little persuading–that he was the man of the moment–the only one, who could save the rapidly deteriorating war situation. They urged him to take the initiative and lead an Opposition in Parliament against the Coalition. The naval estimates were to be debated on the 7th of March and these Winston thought could be fashioned into a stout stick to beat the Government. But it was not in his nature to be a true conspirator and on the 6th he invited Asquith and his wife round to dinner. They both tried to dissuade him from speaking in Parliament and warned him against his ill-found friends. Margot Asquith reminded him of his recent farewell speech to the Commons and of his fine gesture in giving up money, position, and influence and risking his life for his country in the trenches. "Don't go" she pleaded "and spoil it all." Clementine, too, felt a deep sense of unease, for one recent luncheon had been attended by Lord Fisher. As with many another of her husband's eccentric friendships, she neither liked nor trusted Fisher and with a rudeness matching her anxiety told him "Hands off my husband. You have all but ruined him once. Leave him alone now."

In the House of Commons Arthur Balfour opened the debate and Winston followed. In a speech notable only for its lack of substance, he charged the Board of Admiralty with lack of drive and energy, threw doubt upon the strength of the Fleet, and concluded with the astonishing proposal that Lord Fisher be recalled as First Sea Lord! Balfour was devastating in his reply. With the facts, all the figures and careful argument he refuted every one of the charges and reserved for his own, more subtle, brand of merciless scorn Winston's supposed solution to the imaginary problem:

"I do not imagine" he said, "that there was a single person who heard my Right Honourable friend's speech who did not listen to this latter part of it with profound stupefaction. My Right Honourable friend has often astonished the House, but I do not think he ever astonished it so much as when he came down to explain that the remedy for all our ills, so far as the Navy is concerned, is to get rid of Sir Henry Jackson and to put in his place Lord Fisher. My Right Honourable friend has never made the smallest concealment, either in public or in private, of what he thought of Lord Fisher . . . What did he say when he made what at the time he thought was his farewell speech, when he exchanged a political for a military career? He told us that the First Sea Lord, Lord Fisher, did not give him, when he was serving in the same Admiralty with him either the clear guidance before the event or the firm support after it which he was entitled to expect . . . My Right Honourable friend had six months in which to meditate his relations with Lord Fisher before he made that considered judgment, and anybody who knows my Right Honourable friend is aware that when he makes one of these great speeches *they are not the unpremeditated effusions of a hasty moment . . .* "

Violet Asquith, married the previous November to Maurice Bonham-Carter, remembers how the day afterwards, having asked especially to see her, she found Winston alone at his mother's house in Mayfair:

"He looked pale, defiant, on the defensive. I shall never forget the pain of the talk which followed. I knew better than to criticise, reproach or even ask the question that gnawed at me, 'What possessed you? Why did you do it?' I saw at once that, whatever his motive, he realised that he had hopelessly failed to accomplish what he had set out to do. His lance was broken. What he had conceived as a great gesture of magnanimity–the forgiveness of the wrong Fisher had done to him, for the sake of a greater aim, our naval supremacy–had not been interpreted as such."

All of his other real friends were disconsolate too, for apart from their personal misgivings of the role he had played, with the exception of course of the Observer and Guardian, the remainder of the press and his other enemies were already interpreting his speech as the clumsy maneouvre for office of an unprincipled self-seeker.

He sent a letter to Kitchener asking. "To be relieved of my command in order to grapple with the political situation at home." Asquith told Kitchener not to make a reply for the moment and summoning Winston to No. 10 Downing Street, reminded him of the self-same ruin Lord Randolph had brought on his career and advised him to return to the Front. Only for the moment was he persuaded because censure, however well-intentioned, weighed less with Winston than praise. Alone among the newspapers, the Manchester Guardian assured its readers that "Mr Churchill can best serve his country in his old character of a Parliamentarian." That was good enough for Winston. His resignation was not withdrawn, though Kitchener made the condition that Winston would not apply for military service again.

If 1915 had seen the war go badly for the Allies, 1916 was to see it go worse, and for the remainder of that year Asquith's Ministry had to contend with an avalanche of troubles in comparison with which Winston's personal and political affairs could be swept aside into insignificance.

In February the Germans began their onslaught on the fortified French town of Verdun which was the key to the entire French defence. In the four months until July they sacrificed five hundred thousand men to take it and almost as many French casualties to keep it. The British line had been spared from that shambles but Douglas Haig planned his own.

The British Army had been increased by voluntary methods to five hundred thousand men, but now only a trickle of recruits came forward to serve in a war which was already known to bring almost certain mutilation of death. Kitchener estimated his weekly manpower requirements as something in the order of thirty six thousand men and the only way it seemed possible to get them was by compulsory conscription. Every Liberal shrank from such a betrayal of their principles. Asquith steeled himself to deliver the fatal blow which he knew must destroy his Party. Four Liberals and three Labour members of the Cabinet resigned but with the support of Bonar Law and Lloyd George the Government held together and the Bill was passed conscripting all men between the ages of eighteen and twenty one. Winston, who had always been in favour of conscription, applauded it.

In April rebellion broke out in Ireland. A German ship carrying arms was captured; Sir Roger Casement, an ex-British Consular official landed by a German submarine was taken prisoner, and fighting broke out in the centre of Dublin. The rebellion was suppressed in only six days but one hundred and eighty innocent civilians had been killed and the Sinn Fein rebels, executed by shooting in Mount-Joy prison, sowed the seeds for a fresh harvest of Irish violence. Asquith attempted to bring in Home Rule immediately, with Lloyd George as a conciliator, but despite Redmond's Republican support and, surprisingly, that of Sir Edward Carson, F.E. Smith and the other Ulster Loyalists, the settlement was wrecked by Lord Landsdowne in the House of Lords. Though a hundred and fifty thousand Irishmen were serving as volunteers in the British Army, the Government now dared not implement the new conscription laws in Ireland for fear of fresh insurrection.

Within a week of the Irish Rebellion on the 1st of June the long awaited battle on blue water took place between the British and German Grand fleets off Jutland on the Danish coast. The Admiralty had been forewarned, by the now routine interception of the enemy code, that the Germans were venturing out at last, but heavy mist shrouded the North Sea, delaying the encounter. By the time the British battle fleet had time to come up the approach of night made it difficult to sight their guns at the German ships strung out low on the horizon, and two days after the action on June 3rd the Admiralty was forced to announce the heavy loss of three battle cruisers, three armoured cruisers and eight destroyers. The Germans, with only one battle cruiser, some light cruisers and destroyers missing, despite their opponents two to one strength, slipped back safely behind the mine-sown German coastline. There, they jubilantly announced their victory to the neutral world. It could not be known then, that although Jellico's caution had won the British no Trafalgar, the next time the German Navy was due to venture into the North Sea again would be to surrender intact at Scapa Flow at the end of the war.

A mere three days after the battle the nation suffered almost as great a psychological shock when the news was announced that Lord Kitchener, on his way to assess the situation in Russia, had been drowned when the ship in which he had been travelling struck a mine off Orkney.

Winston, in the meantime, almost recovered from his discomfiture and desperate to give advice poured a stream of memoranda which he circulated through the medium of his friends F. E. Smith and Sir Max Aitken, later Lord Beaverbrook. He pressed for the formation of a separate Air Ministry and busied himself with the preparation of the evidence he would have to give before the Dardanelles Committee, appointed to look into the disaster. Oddly enough he was also specially commissioned by Asquith and the Cabinet to prepare for circulation in the press of the neutral countries a British version of the battle of Jutland which was to undo much of the propaganda success the Germans had gained.

On July 1st 1916 the first battle of the Somme began, Sir Douglas Haig's long prepared first great offensive. After a fierce artillery bombardment along an eighteen mile front the fresh young blood of Kitchener's new Army scrambled over the trench parapets and advanced on the German lines. When the Germans, who had been sitting out the British barrage in comparative safety deep in their re-inforced dugouts, heard the lull in fire they swarmed up to the shell-torn surface, manned their machine guns and cut down with a scything fire the advancing harvest of khaki uniforms. At the same time, the German gun batteries far in the rear laid down a barrage behind the British, not only cutting off retreat but preventing fresh reserves from coming up. On that first day British casualties totalled 60,000 (including 20,000 killed) and day after day afterwards the slaughter went on.

Winston wrote and circulated a memorandum on the offensive which brought to the attention of the Cabinet Army Headquarters in France a considered criticism of their strategy:

"This is the danger into which we are now drifting," he warned. "We are using up division after division not only those originally concentrated for the attack but many taken from all parts of the line. After being put through the mill, and losing perhaps half their infantry and two-thirds of their infantry officers, these shattered divisions will take several months to recover, especially if they will, in many cases, have to go into the trenches once more. Thus the energies of the Army are being dissipated, and if the process is allowed to go on the enemy will not be in the need of keeping so many troops on one front as heretofore, but will then be able to restore or sustain the situation against Russia."

Though his colleagues were furious, Haig himself was unmoved, and with wooden impassivity continued to organise with even greater efficiency the mechanics of slaughter till by the end of the year with the help of the French and using some of the new tanks, whose development Winston had encouraged, a great wedge of nine miles deep had been driven into the German line, at a cost in casualties of 418,654 British, 194,451 French, the Germans losing 650,000 men. Ironically, Winston had been against the use of tanks in this way, fearing the Germans would quickly copy the idea, losing the British the surprise advantage of a secret weapon. He wanted the tank held back until the moment when it could be revealed in overwhelming force, and it was fortunate that this, their premature use at the battle of Thiepval, attracted little attention from the enemy.

As frustrated now, as Winston was at the conduct of the war, Lloyd George, holding the new post of Minister of Munitions since the death of Kitchener, prepared the way for Asquith's downfall.

Carefully toadying to Lord Northcliffe, the newspaper owner, whose egotistical personal opinions were purveyed daily for the consumption of the masses, Lloyd George was beginning to emerge in the public mind as the dominant figure in the Government and the man most likely to lead them to victory. After a great deal of intrigue, Lloyd George gained the tacit support of Bonar Law and Sir Edward Carson and impudently offered Asquith the choice of staying on as Prime Minister provided he surrendered to himself the whole direction of the policy of the war.

Asquith was astonished but suspecting nothing, refused the dishonourable contract and Lloyd George resigned. In order to form a new Government Asquith followed with his own resignation but when the King sent for the advice of Bonar Law the latter urged that Lloyd George and not Asquith should be the new Prime Minister.

Like Winston, Lloyd George, too, had at first resisted strongly calls from the Tory opposition for military aggrandisement, and it had generally been expected that he would resign office when war broke out after Belgium was invaded. It was a complete surprise when he condemned Germany's aggression straight away and came out solidly behind the war party. As Chancellor, shelving his social policies, Lloyd George then set out to gain the confidence of banking and landed interests, hitherto his most bitter enemies, in order to raise funds for the war effort–his "silver bullets" as he called them. The first to realise that German industrial power was outstripping Britain in the production of shells, after the formation of the Coalition, his dynamism at the Ministry of Munitions made sure that the British Army was soon as well equipped as the German in armaments. Having now seized the Premiership, he gathered together a team of professional men, not all of them politicians, and gave new energy to the war. He rallied the fainthearted, discouraged by the enormous losses in men and materials, and stood out against any talk of a "peace by compromise."

CHAPTER IV

THE WARMONGER

WINSTON BELIEVED AT FIRST that Lloyd George would immediately bring him into his administration, but for a time he had to restrain his impatience. There were too many difficulties. Bonar Law remained intransigent, claiming he would rather have Winston against him than for him: The Dardanelles Committee was still sitting, apportioning degrees of blame: And above all, Northcliffe, owner of the Daily Mail and the London Evening News, who had never liked Winston, nursed his hostility in print. However, on the 10th of May the following year, 1917, Winston outshone Lloyd George in debate at a special session in the House of Commons which was called to consider the course of the war, and in a speech which made an immense impression Winston pleaded again for the adoption of the principles of his Somme memorandum, written all these lives and long agonising months ago. He argued once more that no more lives should be wastefully sacrificed on "killing Germans," that the Army should save itself by practising what he called "the active defensive," and that the Navy should conquer the growing menace of submarine warfare by the adoption of the convoy system. Soon, he said, the armies of the United States would join in the conflict, and until they came, the armies of the Allies should play a waiting game.

Lloyd George, with more imagination and realism than Bonar Law, wanted Winston with him, and braving all opposition offered him the Ministry of Munitions. Tory hostility exploded in Parliament and the Press, and for a time it looked as if the Coalition might fall, but Lloyd George stood firm. Finally, Bonar Law, assured that Winston would remain merely a servant of the new administration and would not gain admittance to its inner councils, reluctantly accepted the situation. Northcliffe too was calmed down by the honour of heading a Government mission to the United States. And so, on July 16th 1917 Winston took over his new post, having been out of office for twenty months.

Winston and Sir George Ritchie, Chairman of the Dundee Liberal Association taken outside the drawing room of the Royal Hotel during the 1917 election. It had been Sir George back in 1908 who had said to his colleagues in the Party "We must get that brilliant young man to represent the city and put Dundee on the map."

But just as he had once had to do nine years before, on being promoted to the Cabinet, Winston had to submit himself to his constituents for re-election. It was thought at first he would be unopposed, for all three parties had agreed to a truce for the duration of the war. It was true there was one declared candidate, the Hon. Stewart Erskine of Mar, who stood for Scottish Home Rule; but it was generally expected that he would stand down. And although Mr Edwin Scrymgeour, the Prohibitionist, who had now also become a Pacifist, remained unrelentingly critical of both Winston and Lloyd George's War Government, he too was not expected to fight the seat as it was most unlikely he would be able to raise sufficient money at such short notice–the Returning Officer's expenses being fixed at £500, payable by the candidates.

Winston, however, had no desire to leave anything to chance, and, a week after taking up his duties at the Ministry of Munitions, travelled up to Dundee for the weekend, accompanied by Clementine. He addressed one public meeting, consulted Sir George Ritchie, and speeding south again left the still problematical campaign in the hands of his two friends, Glaswegian John W. Pratt, Liberal M.P. for Linlithgow and the Party's Scottish Whip, a Mr A. MacCallum Scott, M.P., who, as long ago as 1905, had written Winston's biography.

It was well he took these precautions, for by Wednesday the following week Scrymgeour's nomination papers were lodged making a contest inevitable.

Edwin Scrymgeour, 51 years old, married but childless, had inherited from his Methodist father and mother an evangelical approach to life, a zeal for total abstinence, and a loving care for those less fortunate than himself. He had left school at fifteen to work as a clerk in a Dundee office. From there he went to work in London, but returned soon after to find employment in the office of the Caledonian Railway and later in the same capacity with an Ironmerchant. These boring ill-rewarded jobs brought him no satisfaction and his active spirit craved to play a more positive part in bringing closer to reality his ideal of the Kingdom of God. He had been brought up with strict conventionality to accept and, when possible, try to ameliorate the existing nature of things; but forced to the conclusion that christian charity alone was powerless to wipe out the appalling hardship he saw around him, he became convinced that only by struggling to transform the social order itself could a Christian be true to himself, though he did not, and was never to, join the Labour Party. In 1898, after being elected to the Parish Council, Scrymgeour gave up regular employment and six years later was firmly established as the founder and organising secretary of the new National Prohibition Party and the full-time editor of its journal 'The Prohibitionist,' which had in Scotland a circulation of more than 10,000 copies. Totally sincere, armed with the best of motives, Scrymgeour felt himself annointed by God, and, elected to the City Council in 1905, earned an unenviable reputation as a 'muckraker' prepared to expose on any occasion abuses, real or imaginary. Forcibly ejected from the City Chambers for making slanderous remarks during his first attendance along with his friend and lieutenant Bob Stewart, his Council colleagues mocked him as 'the white star of purity'. Ridicule only strengthened his resolve, and Scrymgeour entered the Parliamentary contest of 1908 solely because no other candidate would support total abolition of the liquor traffic from which flowed, he believed, most of the manifold miseries of mankind.

Scrymgeour's greatest tactical weakness was undoubtedly his rejection of official Labour Party support–his handbills read: HAVE DONE WITH BOGUS LABOUR REPRESENTATION AND GO IN FOR SOCIALISM–and as a lone voice, his was inevitably an uphill struggle. It was a paradoxical irony, which was not wasted upon him, that a goodly proportion of those selfsame people who listened approving of his tirades against the evils of drunkenness were themselves at the time actually drunk; and after his defeat, in the General Election of January 1910, he wrote bitterly in The Prohibitionist of his fellow working class that they "contained a pack of craven cowards selfishly settled down to the present conditions so long as the majority of them can succeed in obtaining sufficient means of existence with occasional fits of what they are pleased to call recreation." Later that year the Dundee "Advertiser" referred to his "mawkish self-righteousness, ill-nature, suspicion-mania and crankism", and even Bob Stewart, who finally broke with him, was constrained to remark, sarcastically: "He dwelt too much on religion. He had a great advantage over all the other candidates because he had a mandate from God."

These detractors failed to see, however, the strong element of compassion which more than outweighed the harsh intolerance of Scrymgeour's words.

As time passed he mellowed a little, but when war came and with it the advent of conscription his tough uncompromising brand of courage found him, an avowed Pacifist, at every military tribunal in Dundee and district, standing four square in the defence of those young men, vilified as cowards, whose principles would not allow them to kill their fellow creatures. Scrymgeour's attitude in this respect and to the War in general was, to say the least, extremely unpopular, but the carnage had raged now for nearly three years and the enormous sacrifices and the manifold injustices were bringing a number of people to share with him a sense of disillusion and despair.

In every belligerent country other voices were also at this time being raised in the cause of peace. Emperor Franz Joseph had died at last and a new regime in Austria appeared to offer an opportunity to break the deadlock of carnage. A Socialist peace resolution was passed in the German Reichstag. A flood of Pacifist propoganda circulated in France. In Italy the Pope tried to mediate as morale at home and at the front wavered. Russia was dissolving into the first stage of her anarchic Revolution.

Britain by comparison still stood strong in her resolve to bring the war to a conclusion by a military victory though nineteen Members of Parliament pressed the British Government to sue for a "just peace" with the Central Powers.

These hopes were in fact delusive. Ludendorff, now virtual dictator of Germany, behind the Kaiser's blustering facade, allowed talk of peace merely to weaken Allied determination. Even President Wilson of the United States, who was an incurable optimist, was forced reluctantly to face the fact that Germany still wanted to win the war at all costs, and provoked by the resumption of the unrestricted U-boat campaign gave up any thought of mediating a 'peace without victory'.

Delusive or not, to those who were war weary, the sweet voice of peace beckoned seductively and Scrymgeour found himself, for once in his life, standing as a candidate with a far greater platform than merely the prohibition of the sale and consumption of alcohol. The whole world, and especially those hard grey men in the German High Command, would gauge with studied interest the outcome of that odd, slightly ludicrous process of British democracy which was soon to be enacted at Dundee.

Scrymgeour opened his campaign at the seaside and golfing town of Carnoustie on the date of his nomination, and, addressing a large crowd of Dundee holidaymakers, some among them men on leave from the trenches, spoke of the cowardice of the people in not facing the real National issues as they knew them.

A soldier shouted back, 'What about your courage?'

"Don't you think," Scrymgeour replid, "it takes a lot of courage to come down here and talk to such gallant lads as you?" (Laughter)

Returning to Dundee in the evening and addressing a meeting in the High Street, Scrymgeour was asked by a voice from the audience:

'Would you not be better to get the soldiers out of the trenches?'

"Oh, yes," he answered, "I am thoroughly for that. I am for peace by negotiation. I am prepared, if returned, to take the effectual step to encourage by direct resolution antagonism to any continuation of War Credits and to join the German Socialists in refusing to provide additional supplies for continuing the war."

That morning Scrymgeour found he had gained a welcome ally–though not for his views on the war. In a letter to the Courier, J. F. Sime, the Secretary of the Dundee and District Jute and Flax Workers Union, referring to Winston's election address, lashed out at his record as Member of Parliament for the city:

"Sir,–No doubt a large number of Dundee electors will be struck with the claims of Mr Churchill regarding the amount of labour legislation he was responsible for. During the whole time that Mr Churchill has represented Dundee there has not been any labour legislation passed that has benefited the Dundee textile workers who form a considerable percentage of the inhabitants of the city. In my opinion, founded on experience of Mr Churchill, he is one of the last men in Parliament who will do anything for the working classes unless they compel him by vigorous action to do so . . . Mr Churchill asks for 'immunity from factious criticism'. Before he asks that he should be sure whatever criticism he receives is not justified at least so far as labour is concerned."

But, almost as though in immediate response, Winston gained a number of unexpected friends.

Sir George Baxter, now Chairman of the Dundee Unionist Association, published an open letter on July 27th saying:

"I now ask you to vote for my former adversary the Rt. Hon. Winston S. Churchill. I attempt no defence of my attitude; the reason of it must be plain to you all. In the time of the country's need there must be no Party. In my view, and I hope in your view, we must be united in the face of grave peril to the State."

The same day Coalminers' leader Stephen Walsh also wrote in open letter:

"Dear Mr Churchill,–While I regret with every fairminded man that, in the discharge of your heavy responsibilities as Minister of Munitions, you are compelled to shoulder the added burden of a fight for your seat, yet I have the greatest pleasure in sending these few lines of heartfelt wishes for your success.

"For nearly twelve years I have had close knowledge of work in Parliament and no man knows better than I how valuable your services have been for the working classes, how noble a stand you have invariably taken in matters of high Statesmanship . . . I trust the citizens of Dundee, by an overwhelming majority, will show their appreciation of such a record."

Even the Dundee "Courier", hitherto Winston's most consistent detractor, had to write grudgingly:

"The Dundee Unionist Committee acted wisely yesterday in agreeing not to oppose the re-election of Mr Winston Churchill. To have done otherwise would have been to have broken the truce between the two parties and would have created useless trouble. What we have to do is to avoid party politics and personal feelings and get on with the war. The prosecution of the war requires all the strength we can command."

Clementine arrived in Dundee on the morning of Thursday, July 26th, and from her base in the Royal Hotel lent her personal appeal to the proxy cmpaign being carried on by J. W. Pratt and MacCallum Scott. That evening, in the High Street at an open-air meeting in pouring rain, she was loudly applauded by a heckling but good-humoured crowd:

"I hope very much," she said, "you are going to give my husband a very big majority–(A Voice, 'He'll be all right')–not only for his sake, although, of course, I care for that very much, but for the sake of the Government which he has been invited to join, so that a message will be sent to Germany to show them that over here we have no dissension. I wish that Dundee will give my husband a big majority, which will be a sign that we want to carry on with the war. However high-minded and however sincere the opinions of Mr Scrymgeour might be, I do not think that any sensible man or woman can say that a vote given to Mr Scrymgeour this time is a vote to carry on with the war." (Applause and a Voice–'A vote to the Kaiser')

Driving on to another meeting in the West Port, an area saturated by public houses, the crowd were more boisterous, "due in no small measure", as MacCallum Scott put it, "that among the audience Mr Scrymgeour could find excellent arguments for his prohibition campaign!" The rain continued to pour down, but undeterred Clementine mounted the driver's seat of her hackney carriage to make her speech.

'What has Mr Churchill done for Dundee?' shouted a voice.

"My husband," she replied with spirit, "while First Lord of the Admiralty, did his very best to get the Fleet ready for the war–(Hear hear)–and I know that everybody in Dundee cares very much for the Fleet . . . (Great interruptions) You are fighting for democracy," she persevered, "If Germany wins this war there will be no more democracy . . . " (Uproar) She turned for help to MacCallum Scott and as she sat down a woman's voice shouted–'Have you got to buy your sugar in pennyworths?'

MacCallum Scott, heard only by those nearest him, fared no better and in frustration remarked, "People who deny the right of free speech to anyone are enemies of democracy. We are fighting a very terrible enemy . . . "

A Voice–'In the House of Commons.' Another Voice–'And Profiteers?'

A woman with a child in her arms struggled forward and appealed to Clementine to hear her case:

'My husband had Two pounds Ten shillings a week before he joined voluntarily two years ago, and I received an allowance of Twenty five shillings a week which has been increased to only Thirty four shillings. Do you think that's right?'

Clementine–"I wish very much you could have more, but, as you all know the Army is very big, and there are a great many women in the same position. All our men are better paid than the French or German soldiers."

MacCallum Scott tried again to address the crowd but his hoarse voice could make no headway against the deafening clamour.

At this point a Mr David Stewart Robbie, D.C.M., recently discharged from active service and bearing four wound stripes on his arm, protectively mounted the dicky beside Clementine but, after appealing for order, rather spoiled his chivalrous gesture by saying: "I am not altogether in favour of Mr Churchill." Though to make amends he shook hands with Clementine immediately afterwards.

The prestige of khaki had a calming effect and for a little while MacCallum Scott was heard patiently, even for a moment capturing the crowd's imagination when handed up a soldier's biscuit. He broke a piece off and putting it in his mouth, made a valiant effort to chew upon the dry and unpalatable morsel.

'There's nae pride there,' a woman remarked amid laughter, 'whit is guid for the sojers is guid for him.'

Scrymgeour held rival open-air meetings that evening at Bell Street and the foot of the Hilltown.

"I want to know," he said, "why in the face of the fact that soldiers who have been wounded are sent back to the front, Mr Winston Churchill who, after three months experience of the war, was allowed to return to this country and accept an appointment. (Hear hear) "You will never find Mr Churchill when he is on the track of endeavouring to secure such appointments, falling into the trap and finding fault with the Government. I consider that Mr Churchill is a man of great ambition. He has considerable ability, with an element of genius, but his one concentrated goal is to secure appointments. I, however, am getting a hold of the people of the constituency and my numbers are increasing every day."

A Voice–'Why is it that practicaly all the Temperance legislation is dumped upon Scotland.'

"Because," replied Scrymgeour, "in Scotland the Government has found 'the saftest of the family' ".

A voice–'In the event of you being returned to Parliament would we, as your constituents, be permitted to call you Neddy?'

Scrymgeour–"Seeing in that event I will have the freedom of the city you too will certainly have it!" (Laughter)

Although much of the levity among certain members of the electorate was due no doubt to the fact that this election coincided with Dundee's annual holiday fortnight, everybody's attention was brought back to the serious issue facing the country when Winston arrived from London the following morning.

"What is the issue placed before the electors of Dundee?" he asked his audience that evening in Lochee West United Free Church Hall, "What is the question which those who will go to the polling booths on Monday will answer by the crosses which they put on the ballot paper?"

(A Voice–'Shells versus Booze'!) (Laughter) "I come forward as a candidate whose sole proposal to you in an untiring prosecution of the war until Prussian militarism is definitely beaten." (Loud and prolonged cheers) "My opponent on the other hand proposes to seek peace with Germany in order to suppress the liquor traffic in Scotland. (Loud Laughter)

"I would not have wished to quote my opponent in ordinary circumstances, but the doctrines which he represents, and which he seeks to tar Dundee with, are doctrines which at any rate you ought plainly to comprehend before you let the opportunity of polling day go past. Two days ago Mr Scrymgeour said at his meeting that he was prepared for peace by negotation. (A Voice 'Hear hear') He was prepared, if returned, to take the effectual step to encourage by direct resolution antagonism to any continuation of war credits and to join the German Socialists in refusing to provide additional supplies for the continuance of the war."

At this point a Mr James Reid stood up and amid a lot of interruptions protested that Winston had quoted Scrymgeour's words out of context.

"Here are the words which have been definitely used in public," Winston persisted with emphasis, "by the candidate who seeks to represent Dundee, and when I read out these words those who are the candidate's own supporters take offence. Why? Because they know they are words which ought not to have been spoken. (Loud cheers) Every vote given for Mr Scrymgeour is a vote for a shameful peace with Germany." (Loud cheers and a Voice 'There is no doubt about that.')

Going on to deal with Scrymgeour's appeal for Prohibition and interrupted once by a voice saying, 'They dinna ken whit's good for them,' Winston submitted statistics which showed a decline in the convictions for drunkenness adding, "There is no excuse for any patriotic man, in view of this decline, voting for a shameful peace in the hopes of furthering liquor prohibition. I go further, and I say on the contrary there is every justification for a sincere Prohibitionist voting against a Prohibition candidate because he is an avowed Pacifist."

"If there is mis-management," he continued, "let us try to cure it. If there is profiteering let us try to punish, but do not let it be said that in a struggle of this kind the Germans are able to endure hardship from which the Scottish race recoils. (Cheers) That is not so on the fighting front, for there is no bitter form of war in which the Scottish troops are not the master of the Prussians. (Cheers) Is this the time for us to fail or to flinch? Is this the time for you to refuse to vote for the credit in the House of Commons to carry on the war, to deny our soldiers the munitions they need, to seek to hold up our hands and cry 'Kamarad' to the Crown Prince? (Laughter) Is this the time for us to pull down the flag and slink away in cowardly surrender and is that the kind of job that Dundee, world famous, gallant Dundee, will be associated with? (A Voice, 'Never'.) Let us not suppose for a moment that if we made peace without victory with the German Socialists that would be the end of the story. Now is the time for victory–now or never–and now is the time to end war once and for all." (Cheers)

One man was not carried away by Winston's rousing oratory, and at question time asked:

'Will Mr Churchill inform the electors present what part he played in the tragedy of Antwerp when hundreds of young lads, many belonging to Dundee and not much over school age, without proper equipment, were sent across to provide a target for German guns?'

Winston–"I suppose that people now are gradually beginning to appreciate the importance of Antwerp (Hear hear) I suppose as the months have passed and the enemy submarines have come out of their nests at Ostend and Zeebruk and the enemy's aeroplanes and Zeppelins have come from Belgium to attack us, and now that we see our armies fighting to regain all this ground on the sea coast against the Germans, to regain ground which was so improvidently given away–I suppose people realise now the value and importance of Antwerp. I realised it then." (Loud cheers) Winston went on to make a full and spirited defence of all his actions there, and concluded, "There has been no subject which has been made more a parrot cry by people whose brains are smaller than those of the smallest parakeet than the subject of Antwerp. There is no word in my vocabulary that I am more proud to be associated with than the word Antwerp." (Loud cheers)

Asked if he was in favour of the nationalisation of shipping, railways, mines and the conscription of wealth, he replied:

"I have always been in favour since the beginning of the war of the state-control of shipping and have urged it from the very earliest days. A very large portion of the mines are already being controlled and the railways are being completely controlled by the state."

Questioner–'For the duration of the war?'

Winston–"I am only interested in the duration of the war. After the war we will talk of what is to happen after the war but let us get out of the war first. (Cheers) As to the conscription of wealth, we have raised nine-tenths–it is something like that at any rate–we have raised over five hundred million pounds by the conscription of wealth under the Excess Profits, Taxes, Super-Taxes, and the Income-Taxes."

Mr D. S. Robbie, D.C.M., the ex-soldier who had stood to Clementine's defence in the West Port, asked why the Government, which was to find sufficient money to carry on the war until March, could not find sufficient money to pay discharged soldiers more than four shillings and eight pence per week?

Winston–"Any man who has got four wound marks on his sleeve has a right to be saluted by any audience–(Cheers)–I don't think however that you ought to blame me for the situation as it is today."

Mr Robbie–"Not altogether."

Winston–"In other words I have not been in power and have been out of power and I have been in the same position as you have been–a private person–for the last two years, therefore if the arrangements which now prevail are not satisfactory you ought not to make that a cause of quarrel with me. Broadly speaking I will always do my best to see that the discharged soldier and his dependents and the widows and the orphans are treated as generously as this country can afford. It was due to my speech and motion in the House of Commons that the new Military Service Act was made not to apply to discharged soldiers who had been discharged through wounds. So it is not fair to pretend that I have not been a friend, as far as my influence has enabled me to be. I think the debt we owe to discharged soldiers is one we can never pay." (Cheers)

The Rt. Hon. William Brace, the Labour M.P. for South Glamorgan and Parliamentary Under-Secretary to the Home Office, followed Winston with a supporting speech:

"I come here" he said, "on behalf of the Labour members of the House of Commons to support Mr Churchill. (Loud cries of 'You do not!') It is a most extraordinary thing," retorted Brace amid laughter, "that these Pacifists are the most vocal people I have ever met," and replying to further interruptions said, "I cut coal for my living from twelve to twenty-five years of age and today I am the leader of the men with whom as a boy and a man I have worked side by side in the pit. And if I thought for one moment that this was a violation of the great principles for which I and my people stand I would not be here to support Mr Churchill. (Loud cheers) I think it would be a great calamity if Mr Churchill is not returned in this election by an enormous majority. (Hear hear and a Voice, 'That's a sure thing'.) My great complaint against my Pacifist friends is that they assume for themselves a divine attribute that others do not possess."

The following morning, in modest contrast to Winston's huge half-page advertisements in both the "Courier" and the "Advertiser", Scrymgeour set out in somewhat disorganised prose his appeal to the electors:

"The industrial victims of Capitalism," he said, "have been the soldiers subject to British martyrist torture in Mesopotamia . . . The Prussianism under which we were understood to be fighting now envelopes us completely. The U-boat menace is but a retaliation of our blockade attempting to starve out the Germans, man, woman and child. Ireland stands out as a mockery of our professed anxiety for the safeguarding of 'little nations'. What we need is Home Rule all round and Scotland must insist upon summoning her own thoroughly democratic convention."

And referring to Winston personally: "In all the bitterly galling circumstances it would be preposterous if Dundee allowed any man to continue making it be a doormat for walking again to power.

"Besides his autocratic disdain for consideration of my fellow citizens is in itself a strong reason for opposition. My fifty-first birthday being tomorrow the electors might decide on Monday to provide me with further scope for serving them. God willing, I am but 'Ready Aye Ready' ".

Winston was brought further support that morning with the arrival of a delegation of Trade Union leaders representing the Sailors and Firemens Union, who, outraged by U-boat atrocities on their members, were wholly opposed to Pacifism.

On Saturday evening Winston was loudly cheered when, speaking before an enthusiastic audience in the Kinnaird Hall he said:

"The question which every man has to answer is whether at this juncture he will give his vote to the candidate who is in favour of the prosecution of the war or to the candidate who, in the more coherent portion of his address–(Laughter)–stated, and stated plainly that he would certainly oppose the insanity of continued war. (Hear hear) No-one can escape the duty of pronouncing an opinion one way or the other at this juncture. The figures of the election will be telegraphed all over the world, and if the majority should be seriously reduced through the holidays, through a feeling of over-confidence, through all the curious circumstances of a depleted register, a war-time register, the result will undoubtedly be proclaimed and exploited by every foe and every faint heart of Britain's cause wherever they lie on either side of the fighting line all over the world, and it will everywhere be proclaimed and exploited as proof that Scotland is weakening in her determination, that her purpose is breaking, and her fighting strength and energy will soon collapse. Surely it is your duty, a sacred duty, transcending all others, and a commanding obligation laid upon the heart and spirit of every brave and faithful man to take steps which are obviously within his power to make sure that the opinion of Dundee is not misrepresented. (Cheers)

"There are in the House of Commons a small number of Members of Parliament . . . who might be called a Peace Party. (Some cheers) They hold views which are extremely unpopular (Cheers) . . . But the Prohibitionist candidate of Dundee–(Cheers) –in his election address goes far beyond the responsible leaders of this peace group in the House of Commons. He proposes, if he is returned, actually to cut off the credits on which the supply of everything necessary to our soldiers and sailors depends. And he proposes to do this in order by producing a great catastrophe on the fighting front to force a peace at any price and on any terms. (A Voice–'Never'.) He even describes the continuing of supplies to our Army as insanity–rather a dangerous word, I should have thought, to use. (Laughter) The views of the Prohibitionist candidate are not the views of Mr Ramsay MacDonald as far as I understand them. They do not find a single responsible exponent in the House of Commons."

Continuing, Winston made what was a too far-fetched comparison between Scrymgeour's own views and those of the newly prominent Bolshevist leader, Vladimir Ilyich Ulyanov Lenin, who had recently been returned to Russia by the Germans in order to wrest power from the Socialist Revolutionary Government of Prime Minister Kerensky who wanted Russia to carry on the war:

"I am not here to villify Mr Scrymgeour. I am here to deal with his opinions, and I say the opinions he has put forward in his address can only be described as Leninist opinions, the policy for which he stands for is not Pacifism even; it is Leninism. The views he puts forward are the views which have caused the utmost ruin and disorder in Russia, and which are being repressed by the extreme democratic forces of Russia. Dundee must not be tarred by these dirty and degrading doctrines." (Loud and prolonged cheers)

Immediately after the meeting Winston returned to London but left his wife behind to represent him over the Monday poll.

Scrymgeour had an opportunity to reply in the same hall on Sunday evening, though he was comparatively muted, and the most powerful attack upon Winston came, not from him, but from a Sergeant Bowman of the Discharged Soldiers and Sailors Association who described Winston as "probably the most brilliant failure produced in modern times. (Applause) Many men's lives had been lost through the absolute incompetence of Mr Churchill's actions during the war."

With probably greater impact, Clementine and her husband's supporters contented themselves by promenading in the Albert Square, stopping from time to time to speak to small groups of interested spectators.

Polling took place on Monday with none of the pre-war gaiety and enthusiasm and even at the most exciting moment, as the votes were being counted, a crowd of only 3,000 gathered outside the Sheriff Courthouse to hear the results. So few votes had been cast that as early as 10.15 p.m. the results were announced; Winston Churchill 7,302; Scrymgeour 2,036; majority 5,266 with 32 spoiled votes out of a total poll of 9,290. This meant that only 43% of the electorate on the roll had voted, or had been able to vote. Scrymgeour's 21.8% share of the poll had so far been his best result.

Mrs Churchill moved the vote of thanks to the Returning Officer saying:

"On behalf of my husband I thank all the electors of Dundee who by their votes have given this great mandate to the Government to get on with the war." And giving a special thanks to Sir George Baxter and the Unionists she concluded, with great significance, marking the beginning of her husband's drift back towards the right, "We have learned many things in this war and I think one of the greatest is that in common service we have learned to know each other better."

In reply Scrymgeour said that he considered the contest had been "thoroughly warranted by the magnificent vote which had been given against the Coalition forces in the city of Dundee," concluding as perceptively as Clementine:

"To say that a Cabinet Minister had to be dependent upon the votes of Unionism in a constituency so marked for its Liberal tendency is a stimulus to us."

On Tuesday the "Courier" noted with satisfaction:

"The electors have inflicted upon the advocate of shameful peace a defeat which will have far-reaching effects and which will show to the world the determination of the Scottish people to hold out until Prussianism is destroyed. Dundee's decision is an adequate vote of confidence in the Lloyd George Government. It is striking proof of the electors desire to get on with the war. Dundee has been true to her grand traditions."

First told of his victory by the London correspondent of the Dundee "Courier", Winston dictated an immediate address for transmission to his electors, and explaining the low poll, said:

"It was hardly possible to choose a worse moment for such a test of Scottish opinion . . . yet the result shows beyond all dispute that the leaders of the three great parties in Britain, Liberal, Unionist, and Labour–have got the overwhelming mass of Scotland behind them in insisting upon a definite and unmistakable result for this three years struggle.

"A period of intense exertion and increasing strain lies before us, but Scotland is sound as a bell, confident of victory and resolute to endure to the end. There ought to have been no contest, but the result . . . will be helpful in many ways, to the British and allied cause. The Russian Revolutionary Government will be encouraged by the pronouncement of Scottish democracy, and France should regard the result as a special message of friendship and comradeship from the United Kingdom."

Free at last to get on with the job, the post of Minister of Munitions was one Winston was well fitted for and he brought to it his inventive grasp of the machinery of war, a measure of ruthlessness, tremendous drive and a sheer capacity for hard work. The department he inherited was already a vast organisation which had grown up to meet the insatiable demands of total war. A staff of 12,000 Civil Servants grouped in fifty departments controlled enormous quantities of material and literally millions of workers. Winston decided at once that this establishment was far beyond the capacity of any one man to control and working in friendly harmony with the best business brains in the country–in stark contrast to his neurotic period with Fisher at the Admiralty–he set about the business of reorganisaton. The fifty old groups were combined into less than a dozen new ones and these were represented by a council of industrialists, similar in Winston's view to the Army Council or the Board of Admiralty but also, in his opinion, a great deal more efficient, combining the initiative and drive of manufacturing industry with the methods of the Civil Service. Each group was referred to by an initial, F. for Finance; D. for Design; S. for Steel and Iron; M. for Material; X. for Explosives; P. for Projectiles; G. for Guns; E. for Engines; A. for Ally; L. for Labour; R. for

Requirements and Statistics; W. for Trench Warfare and Inventions. These activities were co-ordinated by what he called a Clamping Committee and soon, under his leadership, the wholy mighty machine hummed with smooth efficiency.

Twelve months before, he had urged the Government to make a greater use of mechanical power in fighting the war on land, and convinced that his foster-child, the tank, had been consistently misused, presented yet another memorandum to the War Cabinet. The main obstacle, however, to an extension of the use of tanks was Sir Eric Geddes who had taken over from Balfour at the Admiralty, and who wanted for shipbuilding every steel plate being manufactured, to replace the millions of tons of merchant shipping which was being sunk by U-boats. For a time Winston was forced to allow Geddes' opinion to prevail, but as the pressure eased up and it became clear that the Navy had all but won the war at sea, he ordered the production of an additional fifteen hundred tanks. All opposition in military circles to the new weapon disappeared after the triumphant demonstration at the battle of Cambrai in November 1917 and by the beginning of March 1918 the programme was expanded to a total of nearly 5,000 tanks. But the lesson of pitting machines against machine-guns instead of men, had been hard-learned, for between July and November 1917 Douglas Haig and General Nivelle had lost between them, entombed forever in the mud of Flanders, hundreds of thousands of British and French lives.

Now that America had entered the war, Winston's task was to equip its forty eight lightly armed divisions with 72,000 medium artillery weapons and this additional burden on the straining munitions industries brought a fresh outburst of labour unrest. Outright mutiny had broken out on Clydeside in 1916 but Lloyd George had been able to conciliate the moderate majority of the workers' unofficial leaders and was only forced to withdraw immunity for call-up from a minority of those extremists who remained defiant. But in 1918, however, harrassed by labour troubles on a far greater scale, Winston affected no subtlety and countered threats of strike by announcing that he would withdraw immediately all immunity from active service, at the same time ruthlessly threatened to "proceed with the utmost rigour of the law" against the ringleaders. The strike collapsed and once again Winston had shown himself as no friend of the workers. That, however, was a political consideration which could not at the moment be allowed to cloud his judgment. The success of the Bolshevik coup in October 1917 had sealed the total collapse of the Russian Front, and over a million Germans had been released immediately for service on the Western Front. Hindenburg and Ludendorff's desperate gamble to bring Britain to its knees by unrestricted U-boat warfare, by its very failure had forced the German leaders to consider a yet more reckless course; for they knew now, that faced with the American intervention they had brought upon themselves, Germany must win the war before a single American soldier landed in France. It was a race against time Winston did not intend to lose.

Disgruntled Tories, disillusioned Radicals and of course a certain section of the Press, carped continually that the frenzied spending of his Ministry would bring financial disaster. The ghosts of Gallipoli were paraded with sickening regularity and Winston was labelled a danger to the national interests. Almost too busy to care, he replied coolly to his critics that, "His business was frightfulness," and that he had, "of set and deliberate purpose, dedicated his life to devising diabolical schemes." His present lifestyle did little to inhibit the criticism. Provided by the French Government with a delightful headquarters in France–the Chateux of Verchocq which was within the war zone and only two hours flight from Hendon–he indulged his zest for an exciting life by spending a morning at the Ministry of Munitions, following the course of a battle in the afternoon, returning to Whitehall in time for dinner, and leaving the rest of the day's work to be done in the evening.

On March 21st 1918 Hindenburg and Ludendorff like bankrupt spendthrifts, staking everything on one strong card, launched their long-prepared Great Offensive. Along every sector of the German side of the Western Front the mightiest artillery barrage in history spewed forth a maelstrom of pitiless death upon the Allied lines.

"How low the art of war had sunk," Winston was to lament, "In its supreme expression at this melancholy epoch it represented little but the massing of gigantic agencies for the slaughter of men by machinery. It was reduced to a business like the stock yards of Chicago."

At first the Germans appeared to have succeeded beyond even their greatest expectations and in a few days their troops over-ran all the territory which the British and French had captured during the previous summer pushing them back, bemused and shattered by the enormity of the onslaught, thirty five miles. By July 15th the Germans had crossed the Marne and were within only a few miles of Paris hoping to cut the French Army in two. But the energies of the German soldiers were spent. When Foch launched the Allied counter-attack they fell back in sullen exhausted retreat.

The Allies did not however expect total victory to come until the Spring of 1919, and Winston in the meantime negotiated a contract with Henry Ford of America for an additional ten thousand tanks. General Foch and Haig wished they had them now, but those they did possess were at last used in the late summer of 1918 as they ought always to have been used from the beginning. At the battle of Amiens six hundred iron monsters, the final version of Winston's landships, emerged from an artificial fog supported by low-flying aeroplanes, and within four days the long dream of breaking through the German defences was accomplished. Twenty-two thousand prisoners and four hundred guns were taken, and when the news arrived Winston got into his aeroplane and took two days 'holiday' at the battlefield with his old friend General Rawlinston with whom he had fought at Omdurman and Antwerp.

All along the line now German resistance crumbled, their troops deserting or retreating in despair and confusion. Germany's Allies, Turkey, Austria-Hungary and Bulgaria, sued for peace. The German Fleet was in mutiny. The Socialists in Beralin overthrew the Government and the Kaiser fled to Holland.

At 11 o'clock on the morning of November 11th Winston, waiting in his office at the Hotel Metropole, Charing Cross, heard with relief of the Armistice, but there was in his heart little joy. He was to write of the victory celebrations:

"These hours were brief. Their memory fleeting; they passed as suddenly as they had begun. Too much blood had been spilt. Too much life essence had been consumed. The gaps in every home were too wide and too empty. The shock of the awakening and the sense of disillusion followed swiftly on the poor rejoicing . . . "

Within a month of the Armistice Lloyd George called a General Election. A supreme realist, he knew that the harvest of victory would have to be reaped swiftly before the bitterness set in. Nearly one million British soldiers and sailors were dead and two million more suffered some degree of mutilation. One hundred and sixty thousand wives were widowed and over three hundred thousand children were fatherless. Lloyd George had believed, quite sincerely, that if he had lost the war he would have been hanged as a criminal, and although the British people and the newspapers acclaimed him now as the man who had won it, he was convinced that once everyone had time to comprehend the extent of their sacrifice he and his fellow Ministers of the Coalition would be driven ignominiously from office. He was not, however, motivated by a selfish desire to cling to power; he believed simply that he alone was the man best fitted to tackle the job of reconstruction.

The difficulties facing Britain and the world were enormous and a less extraordinary man than Lloyd George would have been forgiven if he had shrunk from the task. The empires of Germany, Austria-Hungary, Russia and Turkey were in fragments; normal trade between nations was almost at a standstill; countless ethnic groups demanded a national identity; and the newly emerged doctrine of Communism threatened to engulf the shattered self-assurance of Western Europe. At home, there was the problem of how to deal with soaring inflation, how to demobilise four million troops, how to disperse five million munition workers, how to conciliate a militant labour movement; and last, but not least, remained the question of Ireland. Lloyd George was undeterred. With the team of experts, business men, politicians and statesmen which he had forged into an instrument of war, he prepared now to enter the battle for peace. But, to have even a slight chance of success, he knew he had to have a solid vote of confidence in a General Election.

The position of Lloyd George, however, within the Liberal Party was peculiar, to say the least. In his single-mindedly ruthless and egotistical role as the War Leader, Lloyd George had drifted far from the course of orthodox Liberalism. He had brought in conscription. He had imprisoned Conscientious Objectors. He had trampled on many other old and treasured Liberal principles, and had driven Asquith, the Leader of the Party, and nearly all his former colleagues out of office. But all of that might yet have been excused if he could only effect a reconciliation with Asquith for the latter too, albeit unwillingly, had also supported many of these same measures as acts of wartime necessity, and his prestige within the Party remained high. Each attempt however was met with petty rebuff. Even when Lloyd George insisted on meeting Asquith in person to offer him the Chancellorship of the Exchequer, should a united Liberal Party win the election, Asquith's pride forbade the act of statesmanship. He still controlled the Liberal Party machinery and a gesture on his part would almost certainly have saved it from ruin, but his personal antagonism to Lloyd George overcame his common sense and he declined the offer with ill-grace. From that moment on, as the main alternative to a Conservative Government, the Liberal Party was doomed.

At the very pinnacle of his power therefore, Lloyd George was without a base. With the few remaining Labour members of the wartime Coalition already returning to their natural allegiance his position as Prime Minister of the Coalition would have been untenable if the Tories had done likewise. They did not, however, although for his Party's continuing support Bonar Law struck a hard bargain and Lloyd George was forced to accept a pact of humiliating betrayal by agreeing not to contest any Conservative safe seat and limiting the total number of official Liberal Party contestants to one hundred and fifty. The Conservative and Liberal candidates thus chosen received a seal of approval with what came to be called "the Lloyd George coupon". Bonar Law cynically stated the position exactly when he told his fellow Tories:

"By our actions we have made Lloyd George the flagbearer of the very principle upon which we shall appeal to the country. It is not his Liberal friends, but the Unionist Party which has made him Prime Minister and made it possible for him to do the great work that has been done by this Government."

Although Winston had always been attracted to the notion of a genuine Coalition or Centre Party – he had mooted the idea even as far back as 1910 at the beginning of the Irish crisis – Lloyd George's pragmatic acquiesence in the final destruction of the Liberal Party made him uneasy. As he frankly admitted:

"To this election I was a consulted and consenting party. I thought we had need of all the strength we could get to face the problems of bringing home and disbanding our Army . . . reconstructing our industry and making the Treaty of Peace . . . I therefor swam with the stream. If I had taken the opposite course, it would not have made the slightest difference in the event, but candour compels acknowledgement of this measure of responsibility."

Max Aitken, Baron Beaverbrook, owner of the "Daily Express", a Conservative, and, until three weeks before, Winston's colleague in Cabinet proffered wise warning when he said: "Speaking to you as a friend I think you are making a mistake. You have accepted the Coalition compromise as a necessary expedient for carrying on the King's Government but not from the heart. Its policy is not really to your mind. Believe me, any man makes a great mistake who compromises on great issues of principle . . . "

The Dundee "Courier", alarmed by the "rush and hush by which the election had been engineered," described Winston as a "barnacle" determined to cling to the rock of power at all costs.

Winston did admittedly manage to get several small alterations made in the Coalition's manifesto suggesting, in one case, the promise of an enquiry into war profits, but the main tenor of the document remained Tory.

In order to implement a wartime promise, but also to exact the full measure of his popular support in the country, Lloyd George made certain that the last legislation enacted by the outgoing Parliament was the Representation of the People Act, 1918. It gave the right to vote to all men, and with certain qualifications to all women over thirty years of age, and admitted to the electorate an additional eight million voters, but as the great bulk of armed servicemen were still in France and Overseas most of the new voters remained effectively disenfranchised.

Winston noted with regret, conscious again of his own measure of responsibility:

"When the election came it woefully cheapened Britain. The brave people whom nothing had daunted had suffered too much. Their unpent feelings were lashed by the popular Press into a fury. The crippled and mutilated soldiers darkened the streets. The returned prisoners told the hard tale of bond and privation. Every cottage had its empty chair, hatred of the beaten foe, thirst for his just punishment, rushed up from the hearts of the deeply injured millions . . . In my own constituency of Dundee, respectable, orthodox, lifelong Liberals demanded the sternest punishment for the broken enemy. All over the country the most bitter were the women . . . "

Feelings like these were alien to Winston; as he had felt towards the Boers, so did he now feel towards the Germans and hearing of food riots and starvation in their cities his first impulse was to provision a warship and send it to Hamburg. He knew that by showing generosity to yesterday's enemy it would be possible to ensure a lasting peace, but the voice of the people clamoured deafeningly for instant vengeance.

They made two demands: The Kaiser must be hanged, and the Germans must be made to pay for the war.

Winston realised that the Kaiser, grossly caricatured by propaganda, was no more guilty than any other German in authority — he would in fact have been content to see a continuation of the Hohenzollern monarchy rather than a Socialist regime. But he admitted, in the face of "the earnest and deep-seated demands from all classes and all parties in the city of Dundee that the Kaiser should be hanged I was constrained to support his being brought to trial." At a speech in the Kinnaird Hall on Friday, December 13th, Winston accordingly pleased his audience and brought approving remarks from the following day's "Courier" when he said:

"Do not suppose that because the enemy has laid down his arms, that our troubles and anxieties are over . . . At the Peace Conference we have got to see that the punishment for war atrocities is not confined to the humble brutes, the little brutes, the petty brutes, the squalid brutes, who have kicked or bludgeoned or butt-ended or teased our unfortunate prisoners. It should be passed, rank by rank, upwards, not diminishing in its course until it reaches those who were the source of origin of these hateful orders."

The second demand Winston knew to be wholly unsound. Germany had been beggared and he had been assured by the British Treasury that, even if given a chance to recover some of her normal peacetime capacity, Germany could not possibly be made to pay more than two thousand million pounds in total, which would go

Winston in the Kinnaird Hall at the time of the 'khaki' election in 1918 immediately after the Great War. In the front row, Sir George Ritchie stands at Mrs Churchill's right; Lady Ritchie on Winston's left and Provost Don on his right. D. J. Macdonald, Winston's fellow-candidate in the 1922 election and Sir George Baxter, Winston's opponent in the election of 1910 are 3rd and 4th respectively on Winston's left. D. C. Thomson, owner and managing editor of the Courier and Advertiser newspapers, Winston's constant critic and most persistent detractor stands 2nd from the end on the right of the picture. This, and the election campaign of 1917, were the only occasions to which he lent his tacit support and muted his opposition.

towards reclamation of the devastated areas in the war zone – and even that could only be paid in instalments. However, with tempers running so high and estimates appearing in the Press that the war had cost the Allies some forty thousand million pounds, presenting such a case would, he knew, be a delicate one.

"I held firmly to the Treasury estimate and dressed it up as well as possible," he wrote later of the speech he made in Dundee:

"We will make them pay an indemnity. (Cheers) We will make them pay a large indemnity. (Cheers) They exacted from France a large indemnity in 1870. We will make them pay ten times as much." (Prolonged cheers) (Two hundred million times ten equals two thousand million).

Everybody was delighted until the next day when the figures began to be scrutinised. Then came a hectoring telegram from the Dundee Chamber of Commerce:

"Haven't you left out a nought in your indemnity figures?"

The Dundee papers gibbered with strident claims. "Twelve thousand million, fifteen thousand million," recorded Winston in amazement, "everywhere on the lips of men and women who the day before had been quite happy with the two thousand million, and were not anyhow going to get either for themselves."

To placate further demands Winston resorted once more to rhetoric and speaking at the Kinnaird Hall on Wednesday 27th November, while praising the humanity of Liberalism he announced by sudden contrast:

"Don't suppose because I speak of these particular principles of humanity that I do not consider that stern justice should not be meted out to our German foes. (Cheers) We have won the victory, and we must see we are not robbed of its fruits." (Cheers)

"While I go the full length with those" he continued judiciously qualifying his recent remarks, "who say take everything you possibly can from the Germans, make them pay to the full for the crime they have committed and the damage they have done, yet I would not go to such a point as to break that country down to a welter of anarchy."

Lloyd George did not, unfortunately, maintain as much equanimity on the same subject. Almost howled down at one meeting of women voters because his speech trailed behind the popular demand he flung out "in the hot squalid rush" of the moment, as Winston related, the ill-chosen phrase, "they must pay to the uttermost farthing and we shall search their pockets."

"Search their pockets," became the slogan of the hour.

If Lloyd George was indiscreet on that occasion, as the election progressed Winston himself showed no less intemperance in his choice of words, especially when dealing with the rival candidates.

James S. Brown, Dundee Labour Party's first choice, was a forty three year old native of Dundee and a foreman ship-rigger in the Caledon. Sporting a large black moustache and darkly handsome with longish curly hair, he had worked at his trade in the United States of America, Australia and South Africa; and in all of these countries had been active in the Trades Union Movement. For the period of the war he had been President of Dundee Trades Council and, in a reserved occupation himself, had campaigned vigorously on behalf of the Conscientious Objector and in the cause of Pacifism. For all that he was a level-headed individual, and working voluntarily in several welfare associations in the city, had earned a large measure of respect from Dundonians.

Scrymgeour also, still undaunted, was standing again and now spoke with supreme assurance of firm policies which seemed bound to appeal to a wider spectrum of Labour sympathies, more so than in his previous more limited programme of Prohibition and Pacifism.

Now he also stood for, "production for use instead of profit, abolition of competition, the organisation of the workers as land and industrial directors for the common weal, taxation concentrated on capital, income graded in proportion thereto, international exchange of commodities, national and municipal banks, adult suffrage and referendum, national and municipal press, ratification of all international agreements subject to the approval of the House of Commons, and all round Home Rule."

On November 25th Winston hurried to Dundee, though his personal inclinations urged him to remain in London where Clementine, after a difficult confinement, was nursing their ill-fated fourth child Marigold; a daughter nicknamed by them the Duckadilly.

Though Winston felt neither Scrymgeour or Brown posed him personally any real threat he was gravely concerned of the effect they, and perhaps a third Labour candidate, would have on the chances of the re-election of his friend and helpmate, Alexander Wilkie. While Winston himself, as a Coalition candidate enjoyed the support of both the Unionist and Liberal Associations in Dundee, Wilkie, also representing Labour, found himself in an invidious position. Recognised by his national organisation he had been virtually repudiated by the local Labour Party who disliked both his support for the war and the Coalition. They had already chosen Brown to fight in the constituency, presumably against Winston, and serious moves were now being made to bring in another Labour candidate to fight him.

Winston's reception at his opening meeting in the Kinnaird Hall on Tuesday 26th of November decided the style of his approach during the rest of the campaign. The hall had been filled an hour and a half before the advertised time by intending demonstrators, pro-Bolsheviks and disillusioned ex-servicemen; and the press of people outside who had been unable to gain admittance were already sullen and angry. On the arrival of Winston's car the crowd erupted violently into a hostile mob and, struggling to the entrance-way, Sir George Ritchie was torn from Winston's side. With great agility the old man gamely turned on his assailant, seized him by the throat and succeeded in forcing him under the wheels of the car where he was only rescued from rougher treatment by Winston's friend, the more pacific Archie Sinclair. Seeing the tables turned in so violent a manner the crowd shrank back allowing them to enter the Hall. It was however the most turbulent meeting Winston had ever addressed, and he had, under a barrage of heckling, to scrap his speech entirely and trust to interruptions and rejoinders to make his points with the audience. One heckler from the rear of the Hall persistently cried out in a high-pitched whining voice 'What about Russia?' and Winston, after he had stoically borne the fourth or fifth interjection, mimicked back in an equally high-pitched whine "I am coming to Russia in a minute!" It was, he wrote to Clementine of the meeting, "the roughest I have ever seen in Dundee."

After that Winston had no hesitation in deliberately setting out to discredit both Brown and Scrymgeour by unscrupulous innuendo.

Addressing the Dundee Liberal Association in the Y.M.C.A. Hall on Wednesday while praising the record of the Black Watch, he said, by contrast:

"It is unthinkable that we should allow the glory of our victory to be filched away from us by a parcel of ne'er-do-wells and degenerates whose Pacifist defeatist doctrines would have led us to a shameful surrender in the struggle, and who now come forward boasting that they are the apostles of liberty and the trustees of truth." And, a fortnight later, at a rallying meeting of his friends and supporters just before the poll on Thursday, December 12th, he said:

"What is to be said about our opponents? (A Voice 'Nothing') I wish it could be nothing. In so far as these men had any influence at all — (laughter) — they exerted it on the side of a shameful surrender to our Hun enemies. One (Scrymgeour) has said that a Conscientious Objector is more worthy of honour than a soldier in the Black Watch who has won the D.S.O. It might be said that a Conscientious Objector is not devoid of courage. There are some Conscientious Objectors who have shown great courage, but what I want to point out to Dundee's electors is that the kind of courage he showed is not of very much use to preserve the safety of our hearths and homes. (Cheers) If that had been the only kind of courage which Scotland could put forward in those years from which we have, thank God, emerged alive and safe, I expect our Conscientious Objectors would be learning the goose-step by now. (Great laughter) Is it not a curious state of mind for a man to be in that he should be so afraid of and shocked at the shedding of blood that he would rather let his country be over-reached by the enemy than lift his hand against the foe? Show them an enemy and they say, 'Do not lay any sacrilegious hands upon his sacrilegious form.' (Laughter) Show them their fellow citizens—(Interruption)—I am afraid it is painful to some of those who are present to be subjected to an examination of their mental state. (Great laughter) Show them," Winston continued, "a fellow citizen with whom they disagree, or is perhaps more fortunately circumstanced or is perhaps a better worker or a more industrious, thrifty, or careful person, and their hearts are filled with the utmost rage and malice, and there is no act of violence or brutality that they would not enter upon." (Cheers)

Scrymgeour weathered the abuse with boundless optimism, convinced that his programme was beginning to take root at last in the minds of the electorate and on Wednesday, November 27th, mocking one of the purple flowers of Winston's rhetoric, namely: "Let us comfort the sorrowing and the broken hearted," said amidst his audience's laughter: "If you want to do that, you should vote for Scrymgeour!" (Applause)

Since his defeat in 1917 Scrymgeour had done his best to attract Dundee's estimated 16,000 Irish voters. After declaring that he was in favour of a United Republican Ireland, Mr F. O'Rourke, speaking at a meeting of the Michael Davvit Branch of the United Irish League at the Forresters Hall on December 1st, told Scrymgeour he should receive all the Irish votes in the city—"We have always" he said, "looked upon Mr Scrymgeour as our friend." (Applause) The promise was confirmed when "loyal" Irishmen read in their morning "Advertiser" (Dundee's nominally Liberal newspaper) on Monday, December 9th, that they had been recommended by the Standing Committee of the Irish National League of Great Britain to vote for Scrymgeour and Brown.

James Brown, by contrast, had from the beginning progressively wilted before Winston's onslaught. The local Labour Party, unable to gain the services of the "notorious" Pacifist E. D. Morel, had given up their idea of ousting Alexander Wilkie, so Brown was left on his own; to fight the "pure doctrine of Socialism." Obviously a moderate man, his extremist followers, whose current hero was the Soviet Consul of Glasgow, the ex-schoolteacher John McLean who had only just been released from Peterhead after serving part of a sentence for wartime sedition, were more than an embarrassment than a help to him. His voice was weakened, too, by the fact that both Winston and Lloyd George, nationally, did not confine their speeches only to Hun-bashing and personal abuse, and were vigorously imparting a vague but exciting programme of social reform. Both men made renewed appeals to Liberal radicalism and Labour found many of its new clothes displayed and worn by its opponents as if they had been a perfect fit.

Lloyd George, speaking at Wolverhampton on Saturday, November 23rd, said that the men of the fighting forces – "Are men who have made the new world possible and who are entitled to the full share of its gladness . . . it is not the Coalition, it is our comradeship. But it is a new comradeship, for all classes. I am glad of it. What is the task? It is *to make Britain a free country for heroes to live in*. There is no time to lose. We want to take advantage of this new spirit. Let us make victory the motive power and lift the old land up to such a level that it might be nearer the sunshine than it has ever been. The first thing you have to do concerns the appalling waste of human material in the country. There are millions more maimed lives through atrocious conditions than you have got in consequence of the whole of the terrors of this great war. I want to see slums and human conditions and wretchedness sailing one after the other to surrender like the Germans and be sunk at the bottom of the sea where no human eye will rest upon their degradation . . ."

To a meeting of women in the Kinnaird Hall Winston said:

"I want land to be acquired for housing and the settlement of soldiers who are suited to agricultural pursuits. I haven't any sympathy for people who have made fortunes out of the war. I consider the whole question of profiteering requires to be examined by Parliament and I will hold myself free to press for this." And, before a meeting of members of the Dundee Branch of the Federation of Discharged and Demobilised Soldiers and Sailors at the Masonic Temple on Thursday, December 5th, he announced unequivocally that he was in favour of the forty-hour week, the nationalisation of the railways, transport and the public electricity supply. Answering the demand for Irish freedom he announced before his local Liberal Association:

"As for Home Rule, the Irish can have it when they wish, for all Ireland, except one small corner who at present distrusts it. Let Irishmen come forward to take up their responsibilities with all the aid that all the great parties can give them. They have only got to make a success of their government for a few years to have Ulster in, proudly, and of her own free will." Winston went even further in a later speech saying he was in favour of Home Rule for Scotland,

Barefoot children in the West Port.

Ireland, Wales and four big regions in England, who along with the English-speaking countries of the Empire would someday coalesce to form a great Imperial Parliament in London.

Brown, who only two days before, had shamefacedly admitted, and only under questioning, that he was in favour of the nationalisation of land, railways and shipping, as well as a national scheme for housing felt the wind die from his sails and could only comment, "The reason why Mr Churchill is the first Member of the Government to announce a decision to nationalise the railways is because there is a possibility of him being defeated. It was Mr Churchill who, in 1908, was the first to announce the old age pension. At that time he was opposed by Labour and there was a big possibility of him being beaten. These schemes are to be put into operation (nationalisation and the eight-hour day) not because the Government is in favour of the working class but because they fear revolution of the people the same as in Russia and other countries."

Poor Brown was tactically outmatched. Alexander Wilkie at Lochee West United Free Church on Monday, 2nd December, spoke roundly and powerfully against extremism:

"Let us not be misled by the red flag and the bloody revolution. If you are, the people who will suffer will be the workers. (hear hear) You have to rise above that, the straight path of the polling booth and the narrow slit of the ballot box will be better than bayonets and you will get all you want without loss of life."

Wholly discomfited, Brown, when asked if there was any animosity in the Labour Party against Wilkie, replied weakly, "Mr Wilkie and I are both candidates who are endorsed by the National Labour Party."

By Friday, December 13th, on the eve of the poll the success of Winston's tactics was so evident that, at a meeting in the Park Street Hall he could almost gloat:

"I do not think I am being vainglorious or over optimistic if I say we are met together on the eve of victory. (Cheers) Although we cannot claim that our opponents have become our supporters, they at any rate have made great progress towards conversion. (Laughter) I notice that Mr Brown is appealing to electors to 'Vote for Brown and bury Bolshevism'. (Laughter) Why, it is only a fortnight since at his meeting in the Kinnaird Hall a demonstration of a rowdy character was made by supporters of the said Mr Brown. (Hear hear) Three cheers were raised for Trotsky, and 'What about John McLean?' Now it is 'Vote for Brown and bury Bolshevism.' Poor John McLean, the Bolshevik Consul of Glasgow has been let out of prison only to be buried. (Laughter) Why, I have been tempted to put out another placard, 'Vote against Bolshevism and bury Brown.' (Laughter)

"I notice that Mr Brown has been modifying his opinions. He held out hopes of an old age pension of £5 at fifty five. (A Voice – 'He didn't') Here is the quotation." Winston retorted, and after reading the text of Brown's statement continued, "We are bringing Mr Brown back from the wilderness of Bolshevism and the wildcat dances to which he wished us to trip to the music of Lenin and Trotsky, and at the same time, we are getting him to reduce his promises to manageable proportions." (Laughter)

Then, turning from Brown to take one last dig at Scrymgeour he said, "Mr Scrymgeour was the advocate of the Conscientious Objectors. I do not deny the courage of some of them, but many of them are humbugs and hypocrites. Why, some of them would not grow potatoes in case that should relieve the grower of potatoes for service or in case those potatoes might be used to nourish those engaged in military operations against their brother Huns . . . I am not surprised that the Germans thought Britain was effete, worn out, and weak, pusillanimous, prosperous, and flabby. They thought Britain consisted of Browns and Scrymgeours – (great laughter) – the Germans made a great mistake about us, and they have paid for that mistake; and they are going to pay still more . . . Why, if the Russians had not been misled by Browns and Scrymgeours they would have been in here now to share the victory, the glory, and the triumph we have gained."

Dropping these Jingoist sentiments which he had tailored carefully to match the prevailing public mood Winston concluded on a more praiseworthy note:

"I do not want to see the curse of war lay its scourge upon the human race, and for the rest of my life I will strive to avert in every way any danger of a renewal of the kind of conflict through which we have just passed."

Scrymgeour got the last (mildly disorganised) word however, and on polling day, Saturday December 14th, retorting to Winston's jibes in the letter column of the "Advertiser" said:

"His one hope of scoring by misrepresentation against opponents meantime is by the Bolshies and Conchies. This remarkable Coalition, it is hoped by Mr Churchill, will be the saving of that wonderful democratic combination now known as 'the old firm' – Churchill and Wilkie. In order to tighten this up my name is unscrupulously associated by Mr Churchill with disparagement of the Black Watch . . . I have paid sincere tribute to the value of our soldiers in action. But it would be an insult to Mr Churchill's intelligence if I suggested that he did not know the elementary principle of Christianity that where men and women clear-brained stand in spiritual and moral strength for God's purposes against the wretched aims of Mammon pursued by means of militarism, they occupy eventually in word and deed the seats of the mighty to all eternity."!

Voting was slow to begin with, mainly due to Saturday being an ordinary working day, and also because a number of the first time voters were strange to the procedure of the ballot. Under the impression that the candidates received their votes in person, one old lady enquired seriously for "Mr Churchill's office"! Winston, accompanied by Alexander Wilkie, was given a rousing reception at each of the polling stations and another old soul who had never seen him before announced he would get her vote because "he wis sic a wise-lookin' chiel." Winston's handbills spoke with thunderous authority: "Vote for Churchill and steady work, good wages and happy homes." And: "Let those who won the war make the peace. Vote for Churchill. Your vote for Churchill counts for success and prosperity. The ballot is your bullet to finish the war right. Vote for Churchill."

Much less effectively and with only a motor bike and sidecar to carry their voters to the poll, Brown's Labour supporters cried, "Vote for Labour. Solid Vote for Brown and keep down the rents."

Some of Scrymgeour's Prohibition enthusiasts had chalked the pavements on Friday evening but their slogans, washed out by the rain, were hurriedly replaced by some of the shipyard workers to read in parody, "Vote for Scrymgeour and no beer." Alexander Wilkie's handbills appealed to the voters in bad doggerel, "Along the line the signal ran; Vote for Wilkie he's the man."

Time had to be given to allow the postal votes to come in and both candidates and electors were to endure the suspense for nearly a fortnight. Winston accordingly, long before polling had finished, left for London on the 2.47 p.m. train.

The results were declared on December 29th. Winston S. Churchill, 25,788; Alexander Wilkie, 24,822; Edwin Scrymgeour, 10,423; J. S. Brown, 7,769.

Winston's majority of 15,365 was his most impressive electoral victory to date and a record, as it was not exceeded by any other member of the Coalition. However, out of a total roll of 83,767 only 39,296 – minus 271 spoiled votes – had voted, about 47% of the electorate. The lowness of the poll was obviously due to the fact that just 6,000 of the Dundee voters on naval and military service had returned their papers out of 29,990 such voters on the roll. There were also some curious combinations of voting: Churchill and Wilkie, 20,752; Churchill and Scrymgeour 955; Churchill and Brown, 601; Wilkie and Scrymgeour, 959; Wilkie and Brown, 1,885, Scrymgeour and Brown 4,625. This last figure must have come as a considerable disappointment to the Irish National League who had thought they had the 16,000 Dundee Irish votes at their disposal.

The Dundee "Advertiser's" editorial announced with satisfaction that Scrymgeour, "who is now we think able to boast himself as the most defeated candidate in Britain is further from the goal of his ambitions than ever he was and poor Mr Brown who esteemed himself pre-eminently as a people's man finds himself treated with the contempt of the people which must be hard to bear."

As it was in Dundee, so it was in the country as a whole, and Lloyd George's political instincts proved that, however distasteful his tactics, they and his timing, as far as the electorate was concerned, were correct. He and his coupon candidates had won an overwhelming victory. But though the Coalition candidates had attracted over five million votes and now mustered a total of 484 Members of Parliament only 18 Asquithian Liberals had been returned with Asquith himself defeated. In his triumph, Lloyd George held a position of singular insecurity. The Government he was about to form was supported by 338 Conservatives and only 136 National Liberals. Time would tell if he and Winston would not have done better to heed the warning in the Dundee "Advertiser" given at the very beginning of the election campaign:

"We deplore" said the Editor, "both the manner and the circumstance of the Lloyd George election and the whole engineering of it bears an ominous resemblance of the khaki election of 1900 . . . He denies that he is asking a blank cheque, and the thing is flagrantly obvious in every statement of himself and his lieutenant . . . Thus is the character of the letter Winston Churchill read to the Dundee Liberals last night . . . Mr Churchill gives us aspirations expressed in rolling sentences . . . The country's part is to return them to power on the basis of their unlimited good intentions, and afterwards observe admiringly how they will act. That may be the way in such a time as this to get the confidence of the country but it is certainly not the way to keep it. The disappointments will accumulate when the soldiers come home and prove, as they must, that a march has been stolen on them."

The election demonstrated two other significant factors. Only 59 Labour M.P.'s had been elected but the Labour Party as a whole had attracted nearly two and a half million votes, over a quarter of the electorate, which meant that they as a Party, were coming close to the crucial $33\frac{1}{3}\%$ which, if achieved, would enable them to break through the hitherto impregnable two-party system. In Ireland, ominously the old Parliamentary Republican Party was swept away and Sinn Fein (Ourselves Alone) M.P.'s, led by Arthur Griffith, gave notice that they would not come to Westminster.

Winston with eldest daughter Diana aged 11 attending the Trooping of the Colour in Hyde Park, 5th June, 1920. Then Minister of War and Air, Winston caught off-guard by the photographer reveals in his expression the toll taken by the stress and strain of years in public life.

In the new Government, Winston was first offered the Admiralty along with the Air Ministry, which he willingly accepted; but within twenty four hours increasing unrest in the Army forced Lloyd George to change his mind and Winston was asked to take over the War Office instead. Eager as ever to solve problems others dared not touch, he accepted with enthusiasm.

Winston immediately identified the cause of the discontent. Before the war ended a demobilization scheme had been prepared, designed to prevent massive unemployment and prepare the way for a smooth transition to peacetime working with so-called key-men being released first. The trouble was that most of these men had only been called up after March 1918 when the Army's man-power demands had become desperate. As Winston noted, " . . . the ordinary soldier without these advantages saw his lately joined comrades going home to take his job or somebody's job in England while he, after years of perils and privations on a soldier's pay, wounded, and sent back to the carnage sometimes four times, was to be left until all the plums at home had been picked up and every vacancy filled."

He therefore scrapped his predecessor's plan and within days announced a completely new policy. Men with three or more wound stripes were to be released immediately and those who had served longest at the front were put first on the queue for demobilization. Army pay was doubled, and, to maintain Britain's armed strength until the Peace Treaties were sealed, a new Conscription Bill was rushed through Parliament retaining compulsorily for two years the eighty thousand trained young men who had never been on active service. Winston issued a message to the forces telling them exactly how they stood.

His swift action almost came too late. In the following week more than thirty cases of serious insubordination were reported. A full scale mutiny broke out in Calais. Luton Town Hall was burned by a mixed mob of soldiers and civilians. There were civilian riots in Glasgow and Belfast. And on February 8th three thousand angry soldiers marched on the War Office.

All of these situations Winston handled with calmness, much sympathy for the soldiers grievances, and patiently gave sufficient time for his measures to work. "Armies of nearly four million men" he wrote, "had been suddenly and consciously released from the iron discipline of war. From the inexorable compulsion of what they believed to be a righteous cause all these vast numbers had been taught for years how to kill; how to punch a bayonet into the vital organs; how to smash the brain out with a mace; how to make and throw bombs as if they were not more than snowballs . . . If these

180

Armies formed a united resolve, if they were seduced from the standards of duty and patriotism, there was no power which could even had attempted to withstand them."

As Winston had expected the trouble rapidly subsided; and over the period of the next six months ten thousand men were discharged daily into civilian life.

The next problem calling for his attention was one about which he personally entertained no doubts. At that moment Civil War raged in Russia between the Red Armies of the Bolshevik Communist Revolutionaries, led by Lenin and Trotsky, and the re-organised Armies of White Russians made up of the miscellaneous remnants of the old Czarist forces. Winston treasured a wholly unrealistic and romantic vision of Imperialist Russia; and the Bolsheviks, he was convinced, aimed at no less than the total destruction of European civilisation. He imagined that millions of patriotic Russians were willing to fight the new tyranny, and towards Lenin, whom he characterised as a "plague bacillus", he felt a fascinated repugnance. He believed, with some justice, that the Bolsheviks then represented the opinion of only a tiny fraction of the Russian people, and for a time his views were even echoed by many in the Labour Party who lamented the violent overthrow of Kerensky's Social Democrats.

Hardly anyone though, either from the right or the left, was prepared to sanction the course Winston now advocated behind the closed doors of the Cabinet Room.

After the Bolshevik's had seized power in Russia an armistice had been immediately concluded with Germany on the 7th of November 1917. The Treaty forced by the Germans appropriated large tracts of Russian territory together with vast quantities of oil and grain essential to the German war effort. Many Russians felt outraged and dishonoured, were willing to fight on, and if a front, however makeshift, could be stabilized the Germans might have been prevented from switching men and guns to the Western Front. A concerted action was accordingly carried out by the Allics and by the end of 1918 thirty thousand troops commanded by General Ironside were landed at Murmansk and Archangel along with six hundred thousand tons of munitions. Seventy thousand Czech troops seized control of the Trans-Siberian Railway assisted by Americans, French, Japanese and British troops, all of whom lent military support to the anti-Bolshevik Government of the Siberian provinces. In South Russia, General Denikin commanded an Army of thirty thousand men, and French troops occupied the Ukranian coast. British troops from Persia and Salonica occupied the Baku-Batum Railway and British men-of-war blockaded the Russian seaways in the Baltic and Crimea. The Bolsheviks were encircled.

When German resistance collapsed however and the Armistice was signed, a foreign presence on Russian soil could no longer be justified in terms of winning the Great War. And yet, though wisdom now dictated a swift evacuation, by their presence the allied troops had incurred obligations of honour, and, the allies reasoned; if the Bolsheviks were to be victorious in the Civil War, what was to be the fate of all the Russians who had remained faithful to them? It was known how the Revolutionaries, in the areas of Russia where they held power, had initiated a reign of terror and hundreds of thousands of innocents had already been massacred.

Hoping somehow that the Reds would be defeated by the Whites the Allies, for the time being, did nothing more than maintain their original commitment providing the counter-Revolutionaries with military supplies. The situation dragged on with no sign that either side would achieve a decisive result and in Britain criticism mounted in the Press, and within the ranks of the Labour movement.

Winston had had no hand whatsoever in the decisions of Government which had led up to this situation but after taking up his duties at the War Office, in an effort to establish the options open to the Government, he did circulate a Memorandum to all Army Commanders asking whether any of their men would be prepared to volunteer for service in Russia. And, at the first meeting of the War Cabinet, within which he was now allowed to sit, he set out frankly the two brutal alternatives.

The British Government could, he said, clear out and allow the Russians "to murder each other without let or hindrance" or, on the other hand, Britain and her allies could intervene "thoroughly, with large forces, abundantly supplied with mechanical appliances" and make a determined effort to crush the Bolshevik regime. Winston made no bones about which course he favoured.

In February his Army commanders replied that though the troops were prepared to serve anywhere else overseas, none were prepared to go to Russia. Winston therefore advised the Cabinet to make the decision to quit as soon as possible and "face the consequences, and tell these people to make the best terms they could with the Bolsheviks . . . " However by the early summer of 1919, though the Communists were obviously winning the Civil War, the Cabinet—Lloyd George was frequently absent at the Peace Conference in Paris—still could not make up its mind.

Winston's greatest concern now was to withdraw from Archangel and Murmansk "without disaster and without dishonour", but in May the left wing "Daily Herald" published an unsubstantiated account of an interview purporting to have taken place between Winston and a leading officer of the White Russians, who, it was alleged, had since been captured by the Red Army. Winston was supposed to have said that he hoped to send a further ten thousand volunteers to North Rusia and two thousand five hundred to Denikin in the South, while a further twenty four million pounds was to be granted to the war chest of the White Armies. Winston, making no secret of his hatred of the Bolsheviks and continuing to press insistently in the Cabinet for aid to be sent to the Whites, made a categorical denial of the accusation.

"I have explained the part I played in these events," he told the House of Commons on the 29th of July 1919, "I had no responsibility either for the original intervention or for the commitment and obligation which it entailed. Neither did it rest with me to decide whether if intervention should be continued after the Armistice or brought to an end. It was my duty, in a subordinate though important station, to try to make good the undertakings which had been entered into by Britain and to protect as far as possible those who had compromised themselves in the cause of the Allies and of Russia herself."

The affair came inevitably to its dismal end. British troops and supplies were evacuated with smooth efficiency and with no loss, but the White Russians were left to their fate.

Alone among the Cabinet, Winston felt guilt and shame at the callous decision. Thousands of refugees crowding the quaysides in the ports of the Crimea pleading for passage on the abandoning British ships were left without succour and the full extent of the deaths that came to unknown millions of Russians in the persecutions, famines and disease which followed the setting up of the Soviets will never be computed with certainty.

While Lloyd George and his advisers at the Peace Conference – he had of course completely reversed his electoral promise to execute rough and ready justice on the Germans – tried to interpose British moderation between the impractical idealism of President Wilson of the United States and the vengeful intransigence of France and Italy, trouble in Ireland reared its ugly head.

England had missed three opportunities to make a just peace with Ireland. During the latter half of the 19th century Liberal Reforms and a quiet prosperity on the land had done much to soften the old hatreds and if Gladstone's Home Rule Bill of 1886 had been accepted by the House of Commons that probably would have been the end of the age-old problem. The second chance came in 1903, when the Commons passed another Bill for Home Rule which was destroyed by the vote of the House of Lords. Finally in 1914 the third Home Rule Bill was held at bay by a defiant Ulster and although this time it did reach the statute book it had remained in suspension for the duration of the Great War.

On the outbreak of the Great War there was at first a wave of patriotism and John Redmond pledged Ireland to England's defence, but by 1916 the forces of hate in Ireland—a hate so vitriolic, in Winston's phrase that it could "eat the live steel from a rifle butt"—began to assert itself and the Easter Rising broke out. There was an attempt at German intervention but the rebellion, puny in itself, was swiftly put down and the ringleaders executed. This act of folly (or of necessity?) by Asquith's Cabinet cut off all popular support for the Irish Nationalist Parliamentary Party and from then on public opinion in Ireland found its most natural expression in the party of the extremists, Sinn Fein. At the end of the war 60,000 Irish troops still served on the Western front, but as many British garrisoned rebellious Ireland. In the election of 1918 the Nationalist Party which had represented Irish democracy for sixty years was all but swept away and in their place Sinn Feiners were elected, men of reckless but headily single-minded purpose, whose aim was, "No Crown, No Partition, Ireland Free, Independent, One, and Indivisible!" Apart from the twenty six Ulster Unionists and the six Home Rulers, the seventy three Sinn Fein Members of Parliament for Ireland refused to take their place in the Commons. On January 15th, 1919, the Sinn Fein Congress met in Dublin, read a Declaration of Independence and a week later a Republican Parliament met at the Dublin Mansion House electing a Cabinet.

There were so many other problems clamouring for attention that at first Lloyd George did nothing and it was thought, even by Winston, that matters might gradually improve of their own accord. They did not. By the end of 1919, led by the organising genius of young Michael Collins, a survivor of the Easter Rising, the Irish Republican Army had carried out seventy-seven attacks, eighteen murders had been perpetrated in cold blood, and the campaign of terror culminated in an unsuccessful assassination attempt on the Viceroy of Ireland, Lord French, on December 19th.

The British Government reacted sharply. Sinn Fein was suppressed, its Parliament banned, its members arrested and deported, and its Press voice, the "Freeman's Journal," silenced. British troops and Irish police, so far held in irksome restraint, took the law into their own hands and carried out a number of reprisals.

Lloyd George realised that something more than mere repression was required, and, under bitter protest from the Protestant North, a new Home Rule Bill—superseding the Act held in suspension—became law in December 1920 giving to the South real and important powers of self-government. But, on both sides, the outrages continued. In response, besides the large numbers of regular troops equipped with armoured cars sent to keep order,

Winston undertook to raise what he called the "Special Emergency Gendarmerie" to reinforce the Royal Irish Constabulary. These seven thousand men, raised and paid by the War Office at ten shillings a day, uniformed in surplus khaki, with black belts and the dark green caps of the Royal Irish Constabulary, arrived in Ireland and, immediately striking back at the terrorists, were swiftly dubbed the Black and Tans. Terror was met with terror as they hunted out and beat up suspected malignants at pistol point. By the end of 1920 the ranks of the Irish Secret societies were shaken and Lloyd George could report contemptuously of them to the Guild Hall Banquet on November 9th, "We have murder by the throat . . . we struck the terrorists and now the terrorists are complaining of terror."

Though demonstrably effective, the methods used generated expressions of outrage among both High Tories, Labour and Asquith Liberals, and even public opinion in American made itself felt. As a result, unauthorised action by the Black and Tans was curbed. In its place authorised reprisals against property were instituted and after an I.R.A. outrage the Special Forces were sent off in their armoured cars to burn a cottage, a policy which alienated the rural population and was wholly counterproductive as the Sinn Fein, in reprisal, would go out immediately and burn a stately home inhabited by one of the Anglo-Irish aristocracy.

By early summer the Cabinet realised the policy had failed and that to succeed with that method it would be necessary to take and shoot hostages after every incident, a procedure Winston actually considered! Another strategem Lloyd George and Winston seriously thought of was to raise a hundred thousand Special Troops, equip them with thousands of armoured cars, divide up the country with cordons of barbed wire and block houses and search and question every individual. "Some Ministers, of whom I was one," wrote Winston, "were ready to undertake the responsibility and share the exertions such a policy involved . . . " He felt however that "these drastic processes should be accompanied with the offer of the widest possible measure of self-government . . . " and was accordingly "on the side of those who wished to couple a tremendous onslaught with the fairest offer."

The Cabinet accepted the principle but not the extravagance, and Lloyd George authorised what appeared to be two mutually conflicting policies.

Signalling the first, Lord French as Viceroy was replaced by an English Catholic, and Sir James Craig, leader of the Ulster Unionists, bravely sought out the influential Sinn Fein leader, Eammon De Valera, hiding in the mists of Galway, who had only been saved from the firing squad after the Easter Rising because he was technically an American citizen. King George made a conciliatory speech in Northern Ireland and in January Winston was switched to the more appropriate appointment of Colonial Secretary. With the ground prepared, Lloyd George met De Valera and Craig at a conference in London. An end was declared to open hostilities but it soon became obvious from De Valera's pedantic hair-splitting, that little progress could be made towards a final settlement. On July 20th therefore De Valera was handed the British Government's own proposals and, as was expected, he rejected them outright. There was still an obvious desire not to see the talks break down, though letters and telegrams continued to pass backwards and forwards until September. Guerilla warfare continued despite the ceasefire, and the resulting uncertainty destroyed business confidence bringing Ireland's economy to its knees.

In Dublin, behind the closed doors of the Dail, and in the secret conclaves of Sinn Fein, De Valera and his unbending idealism lost ground. Then, while neither side moved from its original position, a formula was proposed by Britain which, in Winston's words, would ascertain "how the association of Ireland with the community of nations known as the British Empire might best be reconciled with British aspirations." Deliberately vague, the invitation was nevertheless accepted.

Meeting again in London in October, with, significantly, De Valera absent in Ireland, prepared if necessary to dissociate himself from any terms agreed by his own negotiators, the task facing the two sides seemed irreconcilable. The very characters of the men who sat round the conference table apparently ruled out any hope of mutual understanding. Michael Collins, gunman, his hands fresh stained with innocent blood; Griffith, a dedicated political agitator who had devoted his life to the cause of Irish liberty; Erskine Childers, ostensibly with the Irish delegation as a journalist, but wielding tremendous influence, an English renegade who though he had served in the Great War, felt himself an Irishman in spirit. On the British side—Lloyd George, fiery and impatient with these cousin Celts who seemed to know no logic; Chamberlain, and "Galloper" Smith who had once been prepared in the name of Ulster to plunge Ireland into Civil War—and Winston!

By a strange alchemy, some at least of these opposites discovered a mutual trust. Winston wrote of Griffith that he was "a man of great firmness of character and of high integrity and was that unusual figure, a silent Irishman; he hardly ever said a word but no word that issued from his lips in my presence did he ever unsay." Thinking of the settlement he had achieved with the Boers Winston ingenuously remarked one day to Griffith during the negotiations,

"I would like us to have beaten you beyond all question, and then to have given you freely all that we are giving you now." With droll humour Griffith replied, "I understand that, but would your countrymen?"

It was with Griffith's younger colleague, however, that Winston formed the truest understanding. "Michael Collins," he wrote in sympathetic retrospect, "had not enjoyed the same advantages in education as his elder colleague. (Griffith) But he had elemental qualities and mother wit which were in many ways remarkable. He stood far nearer to the terrible incidents of the conflict than his leader. His prestige and influence with the extreme parties in Ireland for that reason were far higher, his difficulties in his own heart and with his associates were far greater.

"I remember one night," continued Winston, "Mr Griffith and Mr Collins came to my house to meet the Prime Minister. It was at a crisis, and the negotiations seemed to hang only by a thread. Griffith went upstairs to parley with Mr Lloyd George alone. Lord Birkenhead and I were left with Michael Collins meanwhile. He was in his most difficult mood, full of reproaches and defiances, and it was very easy for everyone to lose his temper.

"You hunted me night and day," Collins exclaimed. "You put a price on my head."

"Wait a minute," Winston replied "You are not the only one." And took from his wall the framed copy of the reward offered for his recapture by the Boers. "At any rate it was a good price – £5,000. Look at me," said Winston with a twinkle in his eye, "£25 dead or alive. How would you like that?"

Collins read the paper, and as he took it in he broke into a hearty laugh. All his irritation vanished. "We had," recollected Winston, "a really serviceable conversation, and thereafter – though I must admit that deep in my heart there was a certain gulf between us – we never, to the best of my belief, lost the basis of a common understanding."

Such a man gained Winston's heart. Yet two months elapsed and still the discussions got nowhere. In breach of the truce Ireland was scarred by outrages. Every concession that the British could make had been made. Chamberlain and Birkenhead strained their enormous prestige with the Die-hard Tories and Ulster Unionists to damp down criticism while the talks limped on. On the afternoon of December 5th, 1921, the wearied Ministers faced the Irish delegates who, said Winston, "were themselves in actual desperation and knowing well that death stood at their elbows." Lloyd George, in the chair, stated bluntly that the British side could concede no further and debate was at an end. They must, he said, settle now, sign the Treaty such as it was, which embodied all that had been so far agreed between them, or else, "quit the Conference and let both sides resume whatever warfare they could wage against each other." The Irishmen gulped at the ultimatum. After a long pause Griffith, speaking in his soft voice and in his modest manner, replied, "I will give the answer of the Irish delegates at nine tonight; but, Mr Prime Minister, I personally will sign this agreement and will recommend it to my countrymen."

"Do I understand, Mr Griffith," Lloyd George returned, "that though everyone else refuses you would nevertheless agree to sign?"

"Yes, that is so, Mr Prime Minister," Griffith replied with magnificent understatement.

"Michael Collins," Winston recorded, "rose looking as if he was going to shoot someone, preferably himself; in all my life I have never seen so much passion, suffering and restraint."

It was long after midnight before the Irish delegation returned with Griffith able to report to Lloyd George that they were all willing to sign the Agreement. "Soon," Winston remembers, "we were talking busily about technicalities and verbal corrections, and holding firmly to all these lest worse should befall. But underneath this protective chatter a profound change had taken place in the spirit and atmosphere. We had become allies and associates in a common cause—the cause of the Irish Treaty and peace between two islands and two races."

"I may have signed my political death warrant tonight," remarked Lord Birkenhead after appending his signature to the document. Michael Collins replied grimly, "I may have signed my actual death warrant." It was nearly three o'clock in the morning, and as the Irishmen rose to leave, the British Ministers impulsively went round and for the first time shook hands.

The Sinn Fein delegates returned to Dublin, and although it might have been expected that De Valera would stand by them, making allowances for their difficulties, he instead repudiated them, denouncing them as traitors. Fearing for their lives two of the five signatories went over to De Valera. But Griffith was still supported by Michael Collins, to whom the principal gunmen in the Irish Secret Societies remained loyal; and although the Dail debated the Treaty for some weeks, when a vote was finally taken on January 8th, 1922, it was carried by seven votes. De Valera, refusing to accept the decision, resigned the Presidency and ostentatiously quitted the Chamber accompanied by all the hard line Republicans. Griffith was elected in his place and the Dail immediately adjourned.

As Chairman of a Cabinet Committee on Irish Affairs, Winston had two jobs to do: First, the provisional Government in the Free State had to be prevented from falling onto the chaos of Civil War, and Ulster had to be given full assurance that it could remain as long as it wished as an integral part of the United Kingdom. De Valera, with his I.R.A. henchmen, attempted to destroy both. Bloody outrages in the North were repaid with interest in the South and reprisal and counter-reprisal soon built up a foul score on both sides. Winston, in touch with Sir Michael Craig in Ulster, and Collins and Griffith in the South, struggled to prevent an open outbreak of war. In a whole series of personal letters of advice and encouragement sent to Collins and Griffith during the spring of 1922, he strove to ward off anarchy.

Collins tried at first to find an accommodaton with the I.R.A. by making a number of concessions, but the outrages grew. On the 27th June, Rory O'Connel with a band of gunmen kidnapped General O'Connel, the Chief of the Free State Army. Realising that if he did nothing there might well now be English intervention, Collins asked General Macready, the English Commander in Dublin, for the loan of two eighteen-pounder guns, and, serving the weapons himself, assisted by a small band of brave followers, made an attack on the Republicans barricaded inside the Four Courts, one of the chief Government buildings in Dublin, which they had seized in April. Though some of the I.R.A. men escaped by the rear, Rory O'Conner was captured and Cathol Brughar, a sober businessman, yet at the same time idealistic fanatic, charged out by the front door falling dead under a hail of bullets. By July 5th all the rebels actually in arms against the Provisional Government surrendered and a week later a Proclamation was issued threatening drastic reprisals against all attempts of murder. A War Council under Collins now struck back at the I.R.A. hunting down and killing men who had once been his comrades-in-arms.

"The strains and stresses upon him at times were unimaginable," wrote Winston, "threatened always with death from those whose methods he knew only too well, reproached by darkly sworn confederates with treason and perjury, the object of a dozen murder conspiracies, harrassed to the depths of his nature by the poignant choices which thrust themselves upon him, swayed by his own impulsive temperament; nevertheless he held strictly to his engagements with the Minister of a Government he had so long hated, but at last had learned to trust. He was determined that the Irish name should not be dishonoured by the breach of the Treaty made in all good faith and good will.

" 'I expect,' he said to me towards the end, 'that I shall soon be killed. It will be a help. My death will do more to make the peace than I could do by living.' "

Thus knowing he was doomed Collins died in an ambush on August the 22nd. His last words to a friend were "Tell Winston that we could never have done anything without him."

Griffith too died, of heart failure, but their places were taken by Liam Cosgrave and Kevin O'Higgins, and these men continued the struggle to maintain the Treaty forced now into using the ancient methods by which order would be restored to Ireland after two Deputies had been shot almost on the steps of Parliament House. Though only the previous year Rory O'Conner had been best man at O'Higgins' marriage, he and three of his imprisoned associates were wakened and shot without trial. By May the following year the I.R.A. had given up altogether and except for the isolated and pathetic incidents which went on down the years it had seemed (until our own time) that the major problem had been settled forever.

When Winston moved to the Colonial office in the Spring of 1921 his other job was to bring some kind of order to the Middle East. Before the Great War, the Turkish Caiph of Constantinople had ruled with brutal corruption over a ramshackle Empire which stretched from Greece to the borders of India and within whose bounds dwelt a multitude of races as diverse as Bedouin Arabs and Caucasian Europeans. With the end of the war and with it this hated overlordship, General Allenby and his British and Commonwealth troops found themselves the surprised inheritors of their defeated enemy's vast dominions. They faced an all but impossible task, for the Great War, as in Europe, had released the long pent-up aspirations of various ethnic groups for national self-determination.

Rebellion broke out in Iraq and was suppressed, but forty thousand British troops, costing thirty million pounds a year, were required to preserve order. In Palestine, which Lord Balfour in 1917 had promised as a national home for the Jews, the strife between them and the native-born Arabs threatened at any moment to explode into violence. Syria and Lebanon were under military occupation by France despite Britain's wartime promise to her Arab ally Emir Faisal, who now, robbed of the spoils of war, "lurked furious in the deserts beyond the Jordan." In Egypt, where a British Protectorate had been set up in December 1914, after nominal Ottoman suzerainty had officially come to and end, strikes and riots by nationalists demanded full independence.

"Thus," wrote Winston, after he had considered the situation, "the whole of the Middle East presented a most melancholy and alarming picture," adding, "This could not go on."

Winston and Sir George Ritchie at 'Draffens corner' in the Nethergate at the time of the opening of the Caird Hall in 1921 – Winston's plain-clothed bodyguard to the right is warily watching the photographer. The following year Winston's wife Clementine warned, "If you bring Sergeant Thomson tell him to conceal himself carefully as it would not do if the populace thought you were afraid of them. The papers (Courier and Advertiser) are so vile, they would misrepresent it and say you have brought detectives because you were afraid of the rowdy element."

He formed a new department at the Colonial Office—the nucleus of an administrative design team to whose number he wished to add the services of Colonel T. E. Lawrence. The exploits of Lawrence of Arabia had all the elements of romantic legend. How a young introverted British archaeologist, whose only apparent qualification was that he spoke fluent Arabic and loved the live and land of the desert peoples at the outset of war, armed only with British cash and promises, managed to raise the fierce Bedouin against the hated Turk: How, operating behind the enemy lines, dressed in flowing white burnous, at the head of his camel-mounted warriors, time and time again cut the slender railway which ran through hundreds of miles of blistering desert, upon which the Turkish Armies operating against British forces in Egypt depended for their supplies. And how, after disappearing for months at a time, he would mysteriously reappear at British Army headquarters to nonchalantly report with bold understatement of his incredible adventures.

Though even his friends had thought Lawrence would never work at the routine of a public office he surprisingly accepted the offer, and he and Winston, accompanied by Hubert Young from the Indian Office and Trenchard from the Air Ministry, set out for Cairo.

"We stayed there and in Palestine for about a month," Winston recorded. "We submitted the following main proposals to the Cabinet: First, we would repair the injury done to the Arabs and to the house of the Sharifs of Mecca by placing the Emir Faisal upon the throne of Iraq as King, and by entrusting the Emir Abdullah with the government of Trans-Jordania. Secondly, we would remove practically all the troops from Iraq and entrust its defence to the Royal Air Force. Thirdly, we suggested an adjustment of the immediate difficulties between the Jews and Arabs in Palestine which would serve as a foundation for the future.

Returning to Britain Winston found these proposals were meeting with tremendous opposition. The French deeply resented any favour shown to Emir Faisal who they regarded as a rebel: The War Office was shocked at the removal of troops from Iraq and predicted a blood bath: The Zionists' dismay at the recognition of native Arab rights in Palestine was only surpassed by Arab rage at the foothold given to Jews on the land they had considered theirs for fifteen hundred years. And it took, Winston noted, a year of "most difficult and anxious administration to give effect to what had been so speedily decided."

One day he said to Lawrence: "What would you like to do when all this is smoothed out? The greatest employments are open to you if you care to pursue your new career in the Colonial Service."

"In a very few months my work here will be finished," Lawrence replied, with a smile, "The job is done and it will last."

Winston pressed him further, "But what about you?" Lawrence answered. "All you will see of me is a cloud of dust on the horizon." He kept his word, gave up his salary of £1,200 a year, and became an ordinary mechanic in the Royal Air Force.

Winston's settlement in the Middle East, though largely dictated by necessity, assured Britain's oil needs for many years and a long lasting control of the lifeline to her Empire, the Suez Canal. Even the nation-states that were set up have proved surprisingly enduring, and if the tension endures the map of the Middle East remains little changed to this day. At the time, though, praise for his efforts would have been too much to expect. One newspaper cartoonist lampooned him as a cherubic little figure roped in a bosun's chair whitewashing the pyramids. Sir Henry Wilson, Army Chief of Staff, who that year was to die at the hands of the I.R.A., scathingly characterised Winston's Middle East policies as "Hot air, aeroplanes and Arabs." And harped on by the Press, public opinion was made increasingly aware of how much the cost of all these "Mesopotamian" policies was burdening the taxpayer.

Winston was inured to criticism however, and he was only hazily aware that, by the summer of 1922 Lloyd George's Coalition Government, of which he was the most prominent member, was in jeopardy. So preoccupied had he and his ministerial colleagues been by the mounting tide of day-to-day business that they had seriously neglected their roles as politicians. Admittedly Lloyd George strove to retain his popular image, continuing to curry favour with the Press Lords by handing out unearned Honours, but they did not repay his generosity, and with few exceptions they churned out daily a barrage of criticism against the Coalition. Their common cry was "Anti-waste, More Economies and Down with Germany." It seemed as if they would be content with nothing less than Lloyd George's dismissal.

But it was in Parliament itself that the Coalition found its most persistent critics.

Asquith, re-elected in Paisley, a year after his defeat in East Fife and leading the tiny remnant of Liberal M.P.'s loyal to him, pursued his personal vendetta. He proclaimed his policy to be the maintenance of an independent Liberal group, but his plans seemed virtually identical to Lloyd George's.

The Labour Party, in word at least, continued to move to the left and a spirited opposition led by Ramsay Macdonald castigated the Government for its broken promises, high unemployment and the developing economic recession.

Lord Provost Don; Sir George Ritchie; Sir Alexander Spence and Winston, standing left to right outside the partially completed doorway to the Caird Hall in 1921.

Tory backbenchers seethed with discontent, for, if Labour thought the Coalition had done too little, the Die-hard section of the Conservative Party believed they had done more than enough! Very few of the Conservative Members of Parliament had had any previous experience in politics and Stanley Baldwin, the future Prime Minister, wrote slightingly of his colleagues that they seemed composed of "Hard-faced men who look as though they had done well out of the war." And Austen Chamberlain confirmed this view by describing them as "A selfish, swollen lot." To men like these, Lloyd George's Parliamentary Bills for extending education to secondary level, providing large numbers of subsidised houses, re-organising and co-ordinating the country's transport and electricity supply and further extending the powers of the Welfare State was anathema.

In Conservative circles too, mistrust and dislike of Lloyd George was only surpassed by their continuing detestation of Winston. On one occasion Sir Archibald Salvidge, Conservative leader in Liverpool recalled how he happened to be sitting on a couch with Winston when shortly afterwards he was approached by Sir Alexander Leith, the Tory party boss for the North East of England, who, "Putting his hand upon my shoulder said – 'Salvidge, you did very well at (the 1921 Party Conference in) Liverpool, don't spoil it.' I thought his manner patronising, not to say offensive. I asked him what he meant and he replied, 'Oh, it's all right. I saw you talking to that fellow.' I said, "What fellow?" And he answered 'Churchill.' "

Despite all this dissatisfaction, and backbench Tory numerical superiority, the Coalition cabinet, containing almost every Tory notable from past administrations, seemed immovable. As Lord Birkenhead pointed out with brutal cynicism to one disgruntled Tory M.P. "Who is going to lead you to victory if you smash the Coalition? Someone like Bonar or Baldwin?"

By a strange coincidence it was again the Dardanelles, that area of Turkey adjacent to the Gallipoli peninsula, which had already had such a baleful influence on Winston's career, that was to set the scene for the final act in the life of the Coalition, and Winston's position as one of its Ministers.

After Turkey had been forced to sue for an Armistice at the end of the war the victorious Allies forced upon her the Treaty of Sevres, stripping her of all territory in Europe except a small area around Constantinople, and practically all her possessions in the Middle East; reducing her to less than a third of her original size: Worse still, the Allies, mainly Britain, occupied a neutral strip of territory on either side of the Dardanelles cutting off all free communications with the capital. The Turks burned with resentment and a nationalist revolutionary leader arose to lead the fight which would restore his country's honour.

Mustapha Kemal, one of the most able Turkish commanders to lead the resistance at Gallipoli during the War had dedicated himself to the overthrow of the corrupt Caliphate and to lead his backward countrymen into the twentieth century. Winston watched the nationalist revival with approval, believing at first that a strong and stable Turkey interposed between Bolshevik Russia and Britain's interests in the Middle East was essential to long term peace, but Lloyd George consistently refused his advice, and for a variety of reasons, which he considered sound enough at the time, promoted at the Peace Conference instead the ambitions of Greece, who wished to rule over the province of Smyrna, the Greek-speaking part of mainland Turkey.

Having won their demands at the conference table, the Greeks, with a large army, proceeded to take possession of their new dominion but Mustapha Kemal and his ragged, spirited freedom fighters stood to oppose them. By the summer of 1922 the conditions of the Greeks in the south had become desperate and thrust relentlessly towards the sea they faced annihilation in the port of Smyrna. As they desperately tried to disembark their troops and refugees, and while their rearguard temporarily held the Turks at bay from shallow trenches on the outskirts of the city, Kemal turned the bulk of his forces north towards the two Greek army divisions which had illegally entered the neutral zone of the Dardanelles and were now in the vicinity of Constantinople.

It was clear that a serious conflict in this area would be bound to lead to a whole series of repercussions. The increased hatreds caused by the war had left the Balkan states even more unstable than they had been in 1914, and if fighting spread northwards it might lead to another European war. To his credit Lloyd George immediately recognised the direction in which his pro-Greek policy had led and now wanted to reinforce the British Garrison in Constantinople against what was now known in the Cabinet as the "Greek menace." Winston too, was forced to amend his original opinions, realising that if Kemal was not stopped in time his victorious army would be tempted to liberate Turkey's lost territories in European Greece. Though the British main forces stationed at Chanak at the southern end of the Dardanelles were not strong enough to stop Kemal's formidable army, a majority in the Cabinet, including the three Chiefs of Staff, had no doubts about the necessity for intervention, and Winston wrote: "The Government might break up and we might be relieved of our burden. The nation might not support us; they could find others to advise them. The Press might howl, the Allies might bolt. We intended to force the Turk to a negotiated peace before he should set foot in Europe."

Winston was wholly opposed however to any attempt to carry out a bluff without force; but where were the additional troops to come from? With her enormous armies of the Great war disbanded, Britain could barely mobilize one division, and it was decided to call upon the French and Italians for assistance as the co-guarantors of the Treaty of Sevres. As a back up, Winston was deputed to draft a telegram to the Prime Ministers of the Dominions asking for their support. At the same time a warning was delivered to Kemal by communique, stating that British forces would prevent the Turkish Army from crossing into Europe. The effect was immediate. The Turkish advance slowed and a week later Kemal made contact with a conciliatory message.

At Chanak, however, the British garrison under General Harrington remained hemmed in by large Turkish forces. Though neither side had fired a shot the situation was on a knife edge. British intelligence had informed the Cabinet that operations against the neutral zone were to be commenced by the Turkish Army on September 30th, and so, the day before, General Harrington was ordered to notify the Turkish Commander that if his forces were not withdrawn he would have no alternative but to commence hostilities. Harrington, an intelligent and resourceful officer, had already been empowered to use his discretion if he thought the situation warranted it, and the ultimatium was, in fact, never delivered. The Turks tactfully withdrew, persuaded by Harrington's wise diplomacy, and by the 1st of October the latter was able to announce to the Cabinet that the immediate crisis appeared to be over and it had been arranged that he was to meet Kemal for talks.

A major war had undoubtedly been averted by the taking of what was obviously a *carelessly* calculated risk, but the British people, sickened of all wars, were in no mood to be involved in a new adventure which might have led to fresh sacrifices of their blood.
The countries of the Commonwealth too were astonished, especially as their Prime Ministers read of the call for their assistance in the newspapers before the official telegrams arrived. Press and public were united in condemnation of the two villains of the piece, Lloyd George and Winston. A Scottish Labour M.P. said, "There is not an interest in Asia Minor or in Europe that is worth to me a drop of blood from one of my countrymen." And Bonar Law,

emerging from his recent retirement, due to ill health, in a letter to the Times, said; "We cannot alone act as the policemen of the world."

Bonar Law's modest signal might well have been a trumpet clarion call, for all Conservatives who had a mind to see the downfall of the Coalition immediately drew together in earnest. Soon, with luck, after the Conservatives Annual Conference in November, Lloyd George and his cronies would no longer be leading them!

Lloyd George, quickly scenting a plot, determined to outwit them and asked the Tory members of the Cabinet to agree to an early election, after which, if they then so desired, he would stand down. Winston himself had earlier offered to resign, along with the other Lloyd George Liberals in the Cabinet, but it was unanimously agreed by the Tory members that some attempt should be made to coerce the rank and file members of the Tory Party behind the Coalition. As Austen Chamberlain put it, they would be told bluntly "That they must either follow our advice or do without us, in which case they must find their own chief, and form a Government at once. They would be in a damned fix."

A by-election result due to be announced at Newport in Wales was confidently expected to reveal the anti-Coalition Conservative candidate at the bottom of the poll, and Chamberlain had deliberately arranged a meeting immediately afterwards, which would determine whether the Conservative Party fought the election with the Coalition, or as a separate party.

The plan misfired dramatically. Just at the moment when the Tory rebels were trooping obediently into the Carlton Club to rubber stamp their leader's decision, news arrived from Newport that the Independent Conservative had won easily, while the Coalition candidate had come a miserable third. Despite a speech made by Chamberlain, whose previous threats were now magically transformed into pleas, Tory backbenchers decided against continued participation in the Coalition. Bonar Law, somewhat restored in health, though suffering from cancer, went along with the rebels and from then on the Coalition was dead.

Winston, under sedation in the private ward of his nursing home and being prepared for his operation, lay completely unaware that the Government had foundered. Only in the morning after he recovered consciousness did he learn the Lloyd George Government had resigned and that he had lost, as a result, not only his appendix, but his office as Secretary of State for the Dominions and Colonies!

CHAPTER V.

THE DIE-HARD

WINSTON'S DOCTORS had told him he had appendicitis and thought at first his condition would clear up with rest, a restricted diet and definitely no Government business. Characteristically Winston paid light heed to their injunctions and on Sunday, 15th October, he and Clementine gave a dinner at Sussex Place, their London residence, to such leading lights of the Coalition as Lloyd George, Lord Balfour, Austen Chamberlain and Lord Birkenhead. After dinner Winston had gone to bed feeling as well as ever but on Monday he woke early with severe internal pains. Confined to bed with his political activity reduced to the telephone, he optimistically hoped to again defy medical advice and speak at a luncheon in Bristol the following day, but Doctor Macnamara would not hear of it and permission to stir from the sick bay was firmly refused. On Wednesday Winston's condition worsened and it was decided, reluctantly, to remove his appendix, still an extremely hazardous operation – King Edward VII had undergone it; and the fight to repair the countless war-wounded had brought tremendous advances in surgery; but with crude anesthesia, no antibiotics to control infection and over 1,500 deaths yearly from acute appendicitis, the knife was still the physicians last resort. However, carried out that night, Winston went through the treatment with complete success.

Coming round from the anesthetic Winston immediately wanted to know who had won the Welsh by-election, at the same time demanding a newspaper. Both requests were peremptorily refused and he was told by the Doctor to stay quiet. However no sooner was medical supervision momentarily distracted that Winston, always a disobedient patient, was somehow or other able to satisfy his curiosity as to the fate of his government and when the Doctor returned to the room it was to find him blissfully unconscious again, under the four or five newspapers scattered on the bed.

He should have had three weeks in bed and then afterwards a convalescence period in order to make a complete recovery, but the sudden turn of events made this impossible. After Bonar Law formed his caretaker Government the King dissolved Parliament and November 3rd was appointed as nomination day, with polling day for a General Election set ten days later for November 14th.

It was patently evident that the political position of every Coalition Liberal was going to be difficult. For most, as with Lloyd George himself, their only hope was to appeal to Conservative opinion while fighting off the bitter attacks of the Asquith or Independent Liberals and, a far greater danger, the new confident, aggressive appeal of the Labour Party.

More than any of his colleagues, Winston had become associated in the public mind with the Conservative viewpoint. He had lost some of his truly Radical impulses and his public pronouncements over the last four years, indiscriminately linking together militant Trade Unionists, Labour Party members and anyone else standing on the left of politics as potential Bolshevik Revolutionaries, made final his growing estrangement with the working class. His long-sighted view of events in Russia and the rest of Europe obviously impelled him to take this stand; but, although Lenin and Trotsky had proclaimed world revolution at the Third International in 1921 Winston would have done well to remember a conversation he had once had with John Morley, his wise, old Liberal Cabinet colleague who had resigned at the outbreak of war.

"When I," Winston wrote, "one day reminded him of Lord Randolph's words, "I have never feared the English democracy' and 'Trust the People', and said I had been brought up on this, he said, 'Ah! that is quite right. The English working man is no logician, like the French 'Red', who I also know. He is not thinking of new systems, but of having fairer treatment in this one.' "

The same words might have been applied with equal force to describe the attitude of Winston's own constituents in Dundee. Like most working people everywhere, few of them were interested in Bolshevism, Communism, Socialism, or any other political creed. But, all of them were fearful of the spectre of unemployment and the rapid erosion of their precarious standard of living. When the men of Dundee had returned from the war in 1919 and 1920, they found materialised, not Lloyd George's golden promises of "a land fit for heroes to live in" but instead, had to endure all of the evils which had existed before the war, aggravated now by crushed hope. The short-lived boom which brought false promise to the rest of Britain in 1920 had hardly affected Dundee and by the time the grey mist of economic depression settled over the whole of British

"Half-timer" barefoot boys leaving Dens Works in 1908. Earning 2/6d (12½p) a week, they were employed 5 hours a day in the Jute Mill and 5 hours in the Mill School with discipline maintained at work or study by a stern mistress, whistle and leather "tawse" at her belt. Undernourished on an inadequate diet based on bread and margarine, 4½ inches shorter and a stone lighter than their counterparts in the country, Dundee boys suffered from "mill fever" brought on by inhaling jute fibre.

Winston unaccountably did nothing to relieve these conditions and some of these same boys who grew up and survived the Great War to endure a life of deprivaton on the 'dole' would not forget or forgive.

industry in 1921 there were already more than ten thousand able-bodied men in the city without work, not including the thousands of war disabled.

The danger signals should have been obvious. These men were not yet broken, and few were prepared to submit meekly to a life of deprivation.

Riots broke out. Mobs, harangued by local Communist, Bob Stewart, Scrymgeour's old election agent recently released from prison for the stand he had taken as a Conscientious Objector, smashed and looted shop windows in the city centre. For three days in Dundee the situation went so far out of control that police reinforcements had to be brought in from Glasgow and Edinburgh. Civil order had since been restored and the city remained quiet, but working class grievances mounted.

Unemployment benefit grudgingly handed out, and now derogatively called 'the dole', bore all the stigma of workhouse charity and merely alleviated a little the miserable poverty of joblessness. Those in work suffered too. In the late summer of 1922 the National Employers organisations announced wage cuts for farm workers, railwaymen, miners and shipyard workers. In Dundee on the 6th of October the Jute Trade Board, announcing the latest $3\frac{3}{4}\%$ cut in the basic wages of jute workers, which had already been reduced, noted complacently that in three months time, when the new rate came into effect, the minimum wages for men would be twenty nine shillings per week and for women twenty five shillings. The jute employers also laid before the Board proposals for a further cut of 15%.

When he visited Dundee in September 1921 Winston had seen for himself the disasterous results of the Coalition's deflationary "austere Banker's policy," and wrote indignantly to Lloyd George of the barefooted men and children who were "obviously in a savage and starving condition." And, though Winston understood little of the complexities of economics, he strove hard in the Cabinet to bring those of his colleagues responsible for Home affairs to implement any measure which could stimulate trade or ameliorate hardship. He had wanted, as he had promised his electors in 1918, to nationalise the mines and railways. He had been strongly in favour of imposing a Capital Levy (a strange irony considering what he would soon be saying of the same measure.during the coming election) to force the war profiteers to disgorge their ill-gotten gains. He also criticised severely the abandonment of the housing subsidies which Dundee so badly needed and which had left the town with prepared sites, a surfeit of labour, yet no cash to build. As usual when he wanted something done Winston circulated reams of

Cabinet papers, regularly registered his Ministerial protest over these reactionary decisions and pestered Lloyd George with letters pleading with him to exercise his experience and ingenuity to try to find a way out of the crisis. The Prime Minister, however, seemed to have lost all his earlier verve and resourcefulness and was content to leave the economic problem in the hands of the Chancellor of the Exchequer and the Treasury, pinning all his hopes for a restoration of prosperity on a successful outcome of his efforts in the international sphere at the Peace Conference.

Illustration was given of the essential problem faced by ordinary people in a letter written by a member of Dundee's Labour Club and published in the Dundee Courier on November the 1st, 1922: "Sir,—I have made painstaking efforts from personal observation, assisted by co-operative officials, private traders, and a committee of Dundee housewives and others to compile a household budget for October, 1922, and show comparative prices for July 1914 to maintain a decent standard of living for a man and wife and 3 children.

	July 1914		October 1922	
7 lbs. of Oatmeal	1/2d	(6p)	1/4d	(7p)
7 lbs. of Flour	1/2d	6p)	1/4d	(7p)
½ lb. Tea	1/-	(5p)	1/4d	(7p)
1 lb. Butter	1/3d	(6½p)	2/4d	(12p)
1 lb. Margarine	6d	(2½p)	8d	(3p)
1 lb. Bacon	11d	(4½p)	2/4d	(12p)
½ dozen Eggs	7d	(3p)	1/3d	(6½p)
Fish	2/9d	(14½p)	4/-	(20p)
17½ lbs. Potatoes	7½d	(3p)	7½d	(3p)
6 loaves of Bread	3/-	(15p)	4/6d	(22½p)
Milk	3/4d	(17p)	6/-	(30p)
Vegetables	1/4d	(7p)	2/-	(10p)
Barley, Lentils, Peas, Rice	10½d	(4p)	1/4d	(7p)
Butcher meat	5/6d	(27½p)	7/9d	(38½p)
2 lbs. Jam	9d	(3½p)	1/10d	(9p)
2 lbs. Tin Syrup	6½d	(2½p)	1/4d	(7p)
1 lb. Cheese	9d	(3½p)	1/2d	(6p)
½ lb. Currants	2½d	(1p)	5d	(2p)
½ lb. Raisins	4d	(2p)	9½d	(4p)
4 lbs. Sugar	10d	(4p)	2/-	(10p)
Sundries	1/1d	(5½p)	1/7½d	(8p)
Coat 1 met. of 1/16th of 8 lbs.	2/2d	(11p)	4/4d	(22p)

Gas and mantles	1/9d	(8½p)	2/9d	(13½p)
Clothing, weekly average	5/3d	(26p)	8/-	(40p)
Boots including repairs	2/10d	(14p)	4/8d	(23p)
Rent and Rates	5/-	(25p)	7/9d	(38p)
Soap and Cleansing materials	9d	(3½p)	1/1½d	(6p)
	46/3d	**(£2.31p)**	**74/7d**	**(£3.72½p**

"No account is taken in the above budget of such necessary expenditure as renewal of furniture, dishes, cutlery, or other domestic utensils, or for repairing materials; nor for church, charity, health, unemployment or other insurances; nor for trade union fees, holidays, recreation, or children's school books; neither is mention made of expenditure on newspapers, tobacco or liquor — I am etc. Labour Club, Murraygate, Dundee. J. G. Fraser."

Working men struggling to maintain their standard of living and the unemployed, existing on or below the bread line, were hardly likely to award Winston any credit for merely making ineffectual protests. In any case, as these took place behind the closed doors of the Cabinet they could know nothing about them. Winston, to them, was anti-Labour.

Middle class Liberals, too, in Dundee were perplexed by Winston's ambivalent public attitudes. His obvious friendships with prominent right wing members of the Tory Party, like Lord Birkenhead, and his uncompromising and vicious attacks against the Labour movement aroused disquiet. After all, for many years there had been the comfortable arrangement with the Labour Party for a Lib-Lab representaton. And though Labour now repudiated any suggestion of an electoral pact, local loyalties lingered on. For these reasons Winston seemed less and less to represent truly Liberal values. So, while nominally remaining faithful to Winston personally, the Liberal Association decided for the first time since 1906 to field an additional Liberal candidate for the coming election, a Mr D. J. Macdonald, while a sizeable splinter group calling themselves the Liberal Committee even went so far as to introduce the candidature of an Asquith Liberal, a Mr R. R. Pilkington, K.C.

Inevitably the sudden fall of the Coalition brought a flurry of speculation.

"Mr Churchill's position is extremely problematical," wrote the Dundee Courier, "the Liberal Association is simply waiting on the Senior Member for the city declaring his intentions." A Liberal Association spokesman announced, "No intimation has yet been received from the Senior Member and . . . the Liberal Association could not possibly support anyone except a candidate who is solely upholding the Liberal principles. Should Mr Churchill declare himself Liberal, then, of course, it is all plain sailing . . . ''

It took two days for Winston to make up his mind and come up with a platform which would carry some credibility with his sceptical electors. In a telegram to Mr James C. Robertson, President of the Dundee Liberal Association, he announced, "I propose to stand as a Liberal and Free Trader, but, (adding significantly by way of qualification) I shall ask the electors to authorise me *to co-operate freely with sober-minded and progressive Conservatives in defending the lasting and central interests of this Realm and its wide Empire against the very dangerous attacks now about to be levelled upon them by Socialist, Communist forces,* as well as from the almost equally serious menace of downright reaction from the opposite quarter. I shall appeal to the Liberals and Conservatives of Dundee to stand shoulder to shoulder against the Labour Communist candidates . . . if they should once again honour me with the right to speak in their name in the new Parliament 'Country before Party' shall be my guiding rule.''

Official Liberal reaction to Winston's statement was firm, though unenthusiastic, "The definite statement by Mr Churchill," said the spokesman, "that he is to stand as a Liberal and a Free Trader should dispose of Mr Pilkington's candidature. And I do not think there is any necessity for a division in the Liberal ranks in the city.''

The Unionists, who again stood unprepared for an election with no candidate of their own, displayed by contrast a marked interest in Winston's overtures, their President admitting "I see nothing in the telegram to which we need raise any objections providing that when Mr Churchill speaks as a Free Trader (innocent of any contradiction in terms!) he is still in favour of the Safeguarding of Industries Bill.''

On Thursday October 26th Lord Wodehouse, Winston's Private Secretary, wealthy Norfolk landowner, ex-Liberal M.P. with a distinguished war record, arrived in Dundee. He was well known to many citizens, having often assisted Winston in showing parties of them over the Houses of Parliament during the midsummer recess. His main purpose on this occasion was, undoubtedly, besides making arrangements for Winston's campaign by proxy, to finalise an agreement for Unionist support. In this he was immediately successful, for the following day the Unionist Association announced that they were willing to support both Winston and the other official Liberal Party candidate D. J. Macdonald.

In the case of Winston's electoral organisation Wodehouse faced a more intractable task. As Clementine wrote from Dundee a few days afterwards to Winston, "We must put in some time and work here and re-organise the whole organisation which was in chaos." General Spiers, an unopposed Coalition-Liberal for Loughborough, helped Wodehouse to organise Winston's committee rooms, distribute his manifesto and arrange visiting speakers. Spiers was later to recall ruefully, "I knew nothing about politics. Jack Wodehouse knew nothing about politics. There we were—rivals only in ignorance."

For Winston however, still physically immobilized since his operation, a start had been made and he could now regard with a little more confidence the final run up of the quite extraordinary campaign in Dundee (there were not more than two candidates in most of the other sixty eight Scottish constituencies) where six candidates were to battle it out for the two Parliamentary seats.

D. J. Macdonald, Winston's Liberal running-mate, was a local Motor Manufacturing Engineer, one of the best known in Scotland and well-liked by his fellow citizens. His record of public and charitable service on behalf of his fellow townsmen was impressive: Director of Lord Roberts Memorial Workshop; Assessor of the General Tribunal; member of Dundee Veterans Garden City Association; Chairman of Dundee Juvenile Advisory Committee; Chairman of the Scottish Committee for the training of discharged and disabled officers and men. Sixty four years old, of stolid and prosaic character, Macdonald had originally been chosen by the Liberal Association as a genuine Liberal alternative who would compensate in some degree for Winston's Tory tendencies. Hearing of the plot in time, however, Winston invited Macdonald down to London and the latter had fallen completely under the influence of the 'great man.' Self-conscious and with no appetite at all for the rough and tumble of electioneering, Macdonald was taken aback by the number of outspoken criticisms which had appeared in the local press against himself and the man he now admired.

"Let me dispel any idea that I am in leading strings or following the lead of anyone which it is my proud privilege to stand today," he was forced to protest shamefacedly and with slight incoherence to his supporters. "I have formed and will continue to form an independent judgment on every matter and every course of action . . . But I wish it to be clearly understood that it is not to be interpreted as antagonism to Mr Churchill. If I am returned to Parliament as a local man, the full power of my local knowledge and every detail of Dundee's industries and wants might be nullified unless my powerful colleague Mr Churchill is returned along with me."

Mr Robert R. Pilkington, K.C., thanks to the Liberal Association's decision to accept Winston and D. J. Macdonald's joint
candidature, lost all hope of any official backing discounting, except
that is, the purely moral support from what was left of the old
Liberal Party Headquarters organisation in London since coman-
deered by the Asquithians. Nevertheless, this tall, impressively
good-looking, genial and highly articulate Irish-born Australian
barrister, the choice of the breakaway group of young Liberals, had
been campaigning in the city for some weeks and to some extent had
established himself in the public eye. Hoping to link his progressive
brand of Liberalism with the moderate Socialism of the one official
Labour Party candidate and thus offer to the electors an unofficial
version of the old Lib-Lab alliance, Pilkington early on made overtures towards the left.

"I think," he told his Dundee audiences, pouring disbelief upon
Winston's allegations that Labour in power would mean Bolshevik
tyranny, "I have had an advantage that no present Member of the
Government has had. I have had the experience of living for a good
many years from time to time under a Labour Government in
Australia. The same prophesies of dreadful disaster were made
there when the Labour Party got into power but these disasters did
not occur. I am not saying that the Labour Party were very good but
neither were the Government that had gone before. It is as certain
as it is that the sun will rise tomorrow morning, that before many
years are over the Labour Party will be in power in this country, and
that is a fact which all of us face and recognise."

Just as in 1918, the Dundee Labour Party had been unable to
agree on the choice of a second candidate but Alexander Wilkie this
time had given notice that he wished to retire and would not re-
contest his seat, so in line with the countrywide left-wing trend the
choice of their selection committee fell on the candidate who had
first been asked to stand at the previous election.

Edmund Dean Morel, or as he had been baptised George Eduard
Pierre Achille Morel de Ville was, in some ways, as remarkable a
man as Winston Churchill, and had at one time been almost as
famous for his part in exposing the ghastly atrocities in the Belgian
Congo.

Born in Paris on July 10th 1873 his father was French and his
mother English. When he was four, his father, a cultured and
talented civil servant died prematurely from the privations he had
suffered as a soldier at the siege of Paris during the Franco-Prussian
war of 1870—a fact which was to assume great significance in the life
and thoughts of his son. Morel's mother, Emeline, determined to
give her son an English education, supplemented her small income

E. D. Morel and his wife, the official Labour Party candidate and Winston's principal opponent in the 1922 election. World famous for his exposure of the Congo atrocities, Morel had afterwards won notoriety when he was jailed as a pacifist during the Great War. Subjected to a personal smear campaign by Winston and his wife and by the controversial Lord Birkenhead, Morel's studied dignity and moderation gained him much support from uncommitted voters. He was to die tragically after a suicide attempt while holding ministerial office in the first Labour Government in 1924.

by giving lessons in English and Morel was sent to a private school in Eastbourne in 1881 where he spent five happy years, returning to Paris for holidays. In prose reminiscent of some of Winston's own passages Morel, in his unpublished autobiography, painted a charming picture of those early days: "Great memories some of these! Memories of luxurious swims from the sands of Berling Gap, of elastic turf, and golden scented gorse, long swelling downs, spinneys redolent in spring with sweet violets . . . "

Five years later he entered Bedford Modern School, boarding with the Rev. H. W. Evans. He later admitted that, despite his perfect command of French, he gained no distinction whatever in any particular subject and, like Winston, with the exception of cricket, he avoided games. Morel shared also with Winston a love of insects and indulged by his kindly housemaster, Morel collected and studied beetles, caterpillars and butterflies.

His mother's increasing ill-health cut short his schooldays and Morel had to return to Paris. There she got him a job with an American Banking House where he worked for a year until he realised one day that his mother, too, was longing for England and home. With the help of his employers he managed to obtain a job as a clerk in the Liverpool shipping office of Elder Dempster and Co., and mother and son set sail from France without regret. They rented a small house at Blundell Sands, near Liverpool, and to supplement his £60 a year salary Morel taught French in the evenings. Looking for a more rewarding spare-time activity his mother suggested that he write. But what should he write about?

"The office I was employed in" he wrote later, "was the centre of West African interests in Liverpool and indeed in England and West Africa . . . There was something very huge and serious about the whole subject which exercised an increasing fascination in my mind . . . To watch a steamer unload her endless barrels of palm oil, bags of kernels, bags and casks of rubber, elephant tusks, huge mahogany logs and so on always sent a thrill of excitement down my back. Everything that came from West Africa seemed impregnated with a wonderful pungent smell."

With the help of books and maps, Morel studied every aspect of life in equatorial Africa, and noted: "The more I read the more interested I grew and the more clearly it seemed to me that international rivalry and administrative problems were forcing West Africa to the front of national interest. Secondly, that the newspapers seemed extraordinarily ignorant of the whole subject."

Here, therefore, was his topic. His first article was published in the Pall Mall Gazette when he was twenty and from that day on his work appeared regularly in the Press.

Still nominally a French subject, Morel that year was called up for military service but was rejected after a medical examination—he had always been delicate and ill-health was to dog him all his life. He became engaged at twenty three to Mary Florence Richardson and marrying the same year adopted British nationality.

For the next three years he worked freelance with the "Daily Chronicle", captured world attention by exposing a plot to assassinate Clemenceau, the French Prime Minister, and by 1900 was able to live entirely from his writing. In 1903 he founded his own newspaper "The African Mail"—a journal upon whose pages Winston was a frequent contributor.

But it was while he was still working with Elder Dempster, after he had been promoted and put in charge of their Congo department, working from Brussels and Antwerp, that Morel was to stumble across the most startling journalistic expose of the century—the true character of the Congo Free State.

The origin of the scandal began after the European powers had finally agreed on how to carve up Africa for Colonial exploitation, when at the Berlin Conference in 1884, Belgium had been appointed Trustee over the area known as the Congo. Unscrupulously betraying their fine words, King Leopold and his associates, instead of fairly administering the territory, treated the whole region as their own private property, banned all foreign traders and reduced the native population to virtual slavery. Morel's worst fears were confirmed in 1897 when Slobblom, a Swedish missionary, made startling allegations against Leopold's Congolese officials, charging them with the most fiendish atrocities. "If the rubber does not reach the full amount required," he said, "the sentinels attack the natives, they kill some and bring the hands to the Commissary; two or three days after a fight a dead mother was found with two of her children. The mother was shot and the right hand taken off. On one side was the elder child, also shot, and the right hand also taken off. On the other side was the younger child with the right hand cut off but the child, still living, was resting against the dead mother's breast. A sentinel passed by the mission station and a woman accompanied him carrying a basket of hands; we counted eighteen right hands, smoked; they belonged to men, women and even children. One of the soldiers told me that 'the Commissary has promised us if we bring plenty of hands we will shorten our service. I have brought in plenty of hands already and I expect my time of service will soon be finished.' "

Morel started to dig deeper. He read a book called "The Fall on the Congo Arabs" written by a British Officer temporarily in King Leopold's service, containing the appalling allegation that

European officers commanding Leopold's levies in the campaign against the Arabs of the Upper Congo, had commanded an Army which had been fed for long periods by organised cannibalism. Stories came out that the Congolese officials had even murdered Englishmen. The truth, however, was so monstrous that for a time hardly anyone in the world at large could bring themselves to believe it.

Morel examined the Congo's trading statistics. He knew that with legitimate trading, exports from any area had normally to be paid for by imports, and, if the Congo statistics showed that there was no such exchange of goods – that valuable commodities were being exported from the Congo with nothing sent back in exchange – then there was, at very least, a case to answer that the natives were being robbed and exploited. The facts confirmed his worst suspicions. £7,000,000 worth of exports were being paid for by only £900,000 worth of imports, and the horrible fact emerged that the bulk of these were in the form of man-killing ball cartridge and rifles.

Morel began his crusade; and in a series of books and newspaper articles over the next two years strove to rouse public opinion, but, even after a report prepared by the British Foreign Office had more than confirmed all Morel's allegatons of atrocities, King Leopold refused to co-operate in any investigations. To apply more pressure Morel formed the Congo Reform Association, went to America, met Present Theodore Roosevelt, enlisted the help of Mark Twain, the novelist, and by 1907 had so organised world public opinion that the worst abuses ceased and three years afterwards the Belgian Government itself took over most of the Congo administration.

When Leopold died in 1910 Morel knew he had triumphed, and for his long, almost single-handed struggle, he was accorded world-wide acclaim. He travelled to Nigeria as special correspondent of "The Times." "The Daily News" said he would find "An enduring place among the great deliverers of mankind." And, the "Evening Standard" wrote, "His name should go down to posterity with that of Wilberforce."

Amid the acclamation of well-wishes Morel was already engaged in his next crusade. During his efforts to get justice in the Congo, he had observed at close quarters the so-called "secret diplomacy" then carried on between nations and saw – long before Winston had done – that the great European powers were moving inexorably towards a world war.

After the German gun boat incident at Agadir, Morel wrote a book, published in 1912, called "Morrocco in Diplomacy" revealing the dangerous web of international intrigue. But while Winston, realising the same danger, thought only of rearmament and girding the loins of the nation for war, Morel, an international-ist, was convinced that the problems and rivalries between Germany, France and Britain could be resolved easily through open and honest discussion. He believed Germany's ambitions were dictated, not by greed for Empire, but by a desperate shortage of trade outlets for her expanding industries, and he attacked the transformation of the Entente Cordiale between Britain and France into a war-like alliance directed against her.

In October 1912 Morel became the prospective Liberal candidate for Birkenhead, and in his adoption speech he defined with eloquent rhetoric the principles for which he stood, principles with which at that time, Winston himself would have been in full accord: "What after all is the social phenomenon of our age?" he demanded. "Wealth, piling up more and more every year, more and more concentrated; luxury more and more pronounced; and, beside that wealth and luxury a vast increasing uncharted depth of human discomfort and distress. A more equitable distribution—gradually brought about—of socially produced wealth should be, must be, the ultimate, constant, perpetual aim of Liberalism if it is to retain its virility, maintain its hold upon the masses, justify its existence, and safeguard the state from violent and perhaps fatal disturbance."

Winston, too, not so long before would have applauded Morel when he went on to speak of: "The horror and folly of Europe who after two thousand years of Christianity is spending four hundred million pounds and training five million of the flower of her man-hood not to improve society, not to insure a more equitable distri-bution of socially earned wealth, not to fight poverty and prevent-able disease, but to kill men and to break the hearts of women."

However, just when Morel's views were gaining him public support, war was declared, and his work was blown away, along with his supporters. That same night he sat down and wrote a letter to the Chairman of the Birkenhead Liberal Association, recalling the numerous warnings he had given as to the character of British foreign policy as pursued by the Cabinet, severely indicting the secret diplomacy which Sir Edward Grey had revealed to the House of Commons on the preceding night. Urged not to publicise his views Morel nevertheless, in a letter signed also by Ramsay MacDonald, Charles Trevelayan and Lord Montagle, to the "Morning Post," made a violent attack on the Liberal Cabinet and, resigning from the Party, said, "I cannot play the hypocrite among you." With these few friends of like mind Morel founded the Union of Democratic Control whose main object was to bring the war to an end by a just peace.

Even above his colleagues Morel was singled out for a storm of abuse. All that he had achieved in the Congo was forgotten – some newspapers went so far as to say that he had invented the whole thing! "Tool of the Kaiser" – "In German Pay", cried the people. The experience of mob hatred made Morel fanatically defiant: "You think you are living in a palace of truth" he declared at public meetings. "You are not; you and the people of Germany also, and the people of all the countries concerned, are imprisoned in a dungeon of lies, and the truth is kept from you all. It shall be my task to show you the truth as I am able to discover it, however unpalatable and however surprising it might be."

To the Government, in the third year of war, struggling to maintain the public's weary morale, such a man was a menace; and at last on Friday, August 31st, 1917 fate caught up with him. At the instigation of the Foreign Office, Morel was arrested and charged at Bow Street for contravening one of the Defence of the Realm regulations. The charge was obviously contrived on a pure technicality, for all he had done was send four copies of an anti-war pamphlet he had written to his friend Romain Roland, a Frenchman living in Switzerland. What is more, although it was no crime to send a pamphlet from France to Switzerland, or, to send a pamphlet from Britain to Switzerland, it was an offence to send a pamphlet via France to Switzerland!

He was refused bail, spent Saturday, Sunday and Monday in a police cell without legal assistance, and finally appearing before a Magistrate, found to his astonishment that the Counsel assigned to him by the Court had, without any previous consultation pleaded guilty to the charge on his behalf and he was summarily sentenced to six months imprisonment.

Although his treatment aroused the greatest indignation, even amongst men who had disagreed strongly with his views, and questions were raised in the House of Commons, Morel served his full sentence, only being released in March 1918.

The same month he joined the Labour Party. He continued to speak up and down the country for the Pacifist cause but the Dundee Labour Party's offer of nomination to fight the 1918 election came too late. Since then, however, although given the opportunity of a number of other possibly more attractive constituencies to fight, Morel, just as Winston had done in 1908, deliberately chose Dundee and with the help of J. F. Sime, the Jute Workers Union official, a long-standing critic of Winston, he had become a well-known figure in the city. Appreciating, probably more than any of the other candidates, the importance of the female vote, Morel went out of his way from the very beginning to win their support.

"The Labour Party," he said, speaking in the Broughty Ferry Y.M.C.A. Hall on Tuesday, 31st October, "has a concrete and definite way of working for the improvement of conditions of the poorer sections of the community. Many women might say–'What is the good of voting?'–in the poorer sections of the community I know quite well the worries and troubles women have, but that is a wrong point of view to take up. Politics play a vital part in your lives and you must know how the country is governed. The Labour Party, if it comes into power, will settle the conditions of your housing, the question of your health, and how to educate your children, but the two most important questions which it will have to tackle are the conditions of the slums and the prevention of another war."

Also claiming to represent Labour, the fifth candidate fighting in the constituency stood boldly and unashamedly as a Socialist; and although, unlike Morel, had been refused official Labour Party support, the life of William Gallacher was more typical of the young and thrusting aspirations of the Scottish working class.

Born in Paisley in 1891 Gallacher was the middle member of a family of seven children. His father was Irish, spent most of his small pay as a builder's labourer in the public house and died of drink and ill-health when Gallacher was seven. His mother, a Gaelic-speaking Hebriddean from Islay was forced to go out washing every day to maintain her children in abject poverty. At ten Gallacher was delivering milk morning and evening for one shilling and sixpence a week (7½p). At twelve he left school, worked with a grocer and two years later became an apprentice brass finisher in a sanitary engineering works. Life improved a little as he and his brothers and sisters brought home their small earnings and his mother was eventually able to give up washing other people's clothes.

His father's miserable end made Gallacher a lifelong teetotaler, and, instead of the pub, he haunted the book shops, the stalls, and the barrows looking for copies of Burns, Scott, the Brontes and Dickens. Oliver Twist made the greatest impression upon him. He joined the Independent Order of Good Templars where he took the 'pledge,' played in the Christopher North cricket team, sang in the Templars' choir and attended the bible class of the Calvinistic Reverend Rene Caird. He graduated to the choir of the Wall Neuk Mission, a Sunday morning bible meeting sponsored by Peter Coates the millionaire thread manufacturer. Then, around 1903, hearing and reading about the Boer War, Gallacher experienced a restlessness of mind which could not be satisfied with these safe and innocent pursuits.

One by one he dropped the friends of his childhood and began to attend big open-air political meetings in Paisley and Glasgow. At Glasgow Green, Alexandria Park, Bellahousten Park, he listened, conversed and argued with other young men equally interested in the political and social issues of the day. He particularly remembered being impressed by Lloyd George exposing the imperialist character of the Boer War as "A war for loot, for gold and diamonds."

Once he bought a ticket for a meeting in the Diamond Hall addressed by John Redmond, the leader of the Irish Parliamentary Party. "What a meeting that was!" he remembered, "did you ever hear The Boys Of Wexford' sung by about a thousand Irishmen packed into every corner of a moderately-sized hall? Jesus! But the Irish blood in me leapt as I listened to them!" And, coming away from that meeting, he recalled how, when he was about six years old, his father liked to put him up to sing 'The Irish Patriots.'

> God Save Ireland, cried the heroes,
> Save Ireland say we all,
> Whether on the scaffold high or on the battlefield we die
> What matters if for Erin dear we fall.

He joined the Independent Labour Party in 1905 but left after several months and joined instead a small militant group calling themselves The Social and Democratic Federation who met occasionally—like true revolutionaries—in a shoe repairers shop after closing hours.

Though a good worker, Gallacher was becoming more and more outspoken, and in 1909 was finally given the sack. He served briefly then as a steward in the Merchant Navy but went ashore again and worked as a milling-header with Babcock and Wilcox in their wrought iron department. This back-breaking toil he said later was the nearest thing to manslaughter he ever experienced. He stuck it for three months then got a job in the Argyll Motor Works in Alexandria as a lathe operator, and from there went to the Albion Motor Works where he remained until 1916.

In the meantime Gallacher married and gained experience in public speaking by touring up and down Scotland at the weekends. At the beginning of 1914 he was elected by his workmates as a delegate to the Allied Trades Committee, an unofficial body representing the principle Engineering Unions on the Clyde, which was demanding an extra twopence an hour from the employers.

At the outbreak of War, Gallacher condemned Britain's participation and, as prices rose rapidly, he and his colleagues' original wage demand appeared to them more and more modest.

The employers, expressing a different view, offered only a half-penny; and with no agreement reached it was the end of January 1915 before they were prepared to meet the Unions again. Then, calling for a common spirit of sacrifice and reminded of "the boys at the front" the delegates were offered an extra farthing.

Gallacher's blood boiled: "You," he shouted, pointing to one of the comfortable and complacent Glasgow business men, "You talk about sacrifices when you know there are three guns lying there at Greenlaw Goods Station and your firm won't touch them until the Government gives you a higher profit! Not one of you but will have bigger and ever bigger profits every day the war goes on. Will you accept our demand or else—?"

His outburst was futile and ruined the very real possibility that the employers might have settled in the end for a penny an hour, and the talks broke down. Workers on the Clyde continued to labour a 54-hour week for eight pence an hour.

The War shattered Labour solidarity. The majority of workers and their Trade Union leaders supported the war effort and the minority of left-wing Pacifists were picked off one by one and silenced. In January 1916, fighting the Conscription Bill, Gallacher and a number of other activists published the first edition of 'The Worker.' It had only one issue. He got home one evening to find his pregnant wife in a state of shock after his house had been raided by the police, and immediately afterwards the paper was seized and Gallacher was arrested and sentenced at Edinburgh High Court in April 1916 to twelve months imprisonment. When he was released in 1917 though it was with the euphoric knowledge that the revolution which had broken out in Russia had also been paralleled by a workers' revolt on the Clyde, his hope that Revolution would break out all over Scotland was soon disappointed, and although active in a number of industrial disputes, Gallacher's efforts never seriously endangered the war effort, nor brought any nearer the civil disorder necessary to the birth of a Bolshevik State.

After Armistice Day Gallacher attended the one day Labour Party Conference in London which was intended to heal the breaches brought about by the war. He records how G. R. Clyne, a Labour member of the Coalition Cabinet, attended bearing a message from Lloyd George appealing for continued Labour Party participation in the Coalition and remembered approvingly how George Bernard Shaw, another of the delegates, after ridiculing the Prime Minister's shifty character, concluded by pointing his finger at Clyne exclaiming "Go back and tell Lloyd George, nothing doing!" Attacking in turn G. H. Thomas, another of the Labour ministers in the Coalition, Gallacher said, "It's all right for Jimmy Thomas to plead for peaceful revolution but he'll find when we get to that stage the strongest argument will be a six-inch Howitzer and the man at the business end of it is going to win the argument."

Neither his views, nor those of the other members of the newly formed Communist Party, gained any acceptance. Their application for affiliation to the Labour Party was refused.

Clinging to the idea of violence as a political weapon he helped to organise a confrontation with police and strikers in 1919. As planned, a riot broke out, the police made a baton charge and Gallacher struck with his fist Glasgow's Chief Constable. In Court, however, ingenuously admitting most of the blame for the fracas, he made such a favourable impression upon the Judge, Lord Scott-Dixon, that he got off lightly with a sentence of three months. His comrade in conspiracy, but hardly in arms, Manny Shinwell, later Lord Shinwell, the Labour peer who had made an elaborate defence, was by contrast awarded a stiff five months.

By 1920 Gallacher had become a professional agitator supported by the contributions of sympathisers and his wife's earnings as a Manageress in a Co-operative shop. That year the Second Congress of the Communist International was due to open at Leningrad in July. Possessing only the clothes he had on, he stowed away from Newcastle in a ship bound for Bergen. After a number of adventures on a journey made hazardous by the Civil War Gallacher reached Leningrad only to be told that the Conference, because the White Russian forces were so close, had been switched to Moscow,. He made this last lap of the journey by train, fearing at any moment that marauding Cossacks might cut off the line, but after several false alarms reached Moscow safely. At the Conference he was introduced to Lenin:

"Lenin held out his hand and said: "Welcome to our country, Comrade Gallacher!" "I said something about being happy to be there, and we chatted for a moment or two about the situation in Britain, which at that moment was of particular interest, with Churchill mouthing fire and brimstone like an inebriated dragon."

Later the following evening, invited into the privilege of Lenin's private sitting-room, Gallacher was asked whether he was prepared to work with the Labour Party and replied without enthusiasm, "I don't like it but I'll accept it."

"That is not enough," lectured Lenin, "you have got to believe in it."

Protesting that every working-class representative who had ever gone to Parliament had been corrupted, Gallacher pointed to the various members of the Labour Party who had served in the Coalition.

"Comrade Gallacher," Lenin interrupted, "I know all about people. I have no illusions about them. But if the workers sent you to represent them in Parliament would you become corrupt?"

"That's not a fair question."

"It is a fair question," Lenin urged; "I want you to answer it. Would you become corrupt?"

Gallacher recorded how he sat and looked at Lenin for a moment then answered: "No, I'm sure that under no circumstances could the bourgeoisie corrupt me."

"Well then, Comrade Gallacher," Lenin smiled, "You get the workers to send you to Parliament and show them how a revolutionary can make use of it."

Gallacher got back to Newcastle after more adventures, helped to found the British Communist Party, carried on his agitation and did another spell in prison. Then he took a hand in the Irish troubles.

Tipped off by Erskine Childers that the Treaty was about to be signed, the Communist Party Executive in London empowered Gallacher to take the night boat to Dublin and make contact with Cathol Brughar, the Defence Minister. Gallacher told him that a Treaty partitioning Ulster from the South had been drawn up ready for signature by Churchill and Lloyd George and pleaded for an alliance between Labour and Sinn Fein. Brughar refused to believe him. Pressed then to arrest Griffith and Collins as soon as they landed in Ireland, Cathol Brughar declared steadfastly, "I won't be the man responsible for shedding Irishmen's blood."

This rebuff seems to have been the occasion which finally decided Gallacher to give up his dreams of bloody revolution and take the more prosaic road Lenin had advised towards a Socialist state in Britain.

Gallacher was to find the expected humdrum process quite exhilarating. His arrival in Dundee for the campaign was greeted by an enthusiastic multitude organised by Bob Stewart, and he was escorted to the local Party Headquarters with the belligerent strains of a pipe band ringing in his ears.

Old Neddy Scrymgeour, the sixth candidate, was entering the fray for this, his sixth attempt. Gallacher called him a "freak" and Winston had dismissed him patronisingly as "quaint" but Neddy's bouyant faith in a new and better world armoured him with the certainty of ultimate victory. His voting figures over the years alone brought him a quiet confidence, and although he could point to no crushing majorities like Winston's, he could survey with honest pride the way his personal following had grown from just over six hundred votes in 1908 to over ten thousand in 1918. And Prohibition, the central issue in his programme of social reform which he had advocated so steadfastly, was no longer regarded by the world at large as the panacea of a crank. In America and Canada, state-legislators hoping to cure one of the greatest social evils of the day were seriously debating similar measures, and in Dundee, especially with the womenfolk, the subject was not to be lightly dismissed. Besides, though Scrymgeour in previous elections had been unsupported by any of the usual structure of a political party he had now, in every mill and jute factory in Dundee, election committees manned by dedicated and willing crusaders, sharing the cause in which he believed.

With the battle lines drawn, Winston, in his sick bed in London, opened the offensive on Saturday, October 28th, 1922. Addressing himself to the Unionist and Liberal electors by means of an open letter to the President of the Dundee Liberal Association, he began:

"My dear Mr Robertson—The outstanding fact of the political situation is that a purely Conservative Government is now in power. Such a government has not been since 1885 . . . What is my attitude towards this administration? It is absurd to suppose that Mr Bonar Law has vitality, resourcefulness or constructive capacity superior to that with which Mr Lloyd George was endowed," and "how far the new administration is equipped with parliamentary and popular figures (thinking no doubt of himself!) well known in the homes of the people and long established in the life of the nation, you will be able to judge for yourselves . . . When I think of the gravity of the hour, of its formidable problems, of its measureless uncertainties, I marvel at the temerity and presumption which have squandered so many friendly forces and stripped the state of much serviceable experience and power."

This criticism was hardly more than desultory in comparison with the broadside Winston then directed upon Morel and Gallacher—Scrymgeour he ignored as insignificant.

"When we turn our eyes from this newly fledged administration to the formidable Socialist attack which is gathering in the opposite quarter, we must see how great is the need for patriotic men and for men of sincere goodwill to stand together. We cannot afford to be divided on minor issues when the whole accumulated greatness of Britain is under challenge. Her (Labour's) predatory and confiscatory programme, fatal to the reviving prosperity of the country inspired by class jealousy and the doctrines of envy, hatred, and malice, is appropriately championed in Dundee by two candidates, both of whom had to be shut up during the late war in order to prevent them from further hampering the national defence. It is, indeed, a wrong to the patriotic workers who followed Mr Wilkie in unswerving support of the national cause that their votes should be marshalled in support of candidates to whom the greatness of Britain is nought but an odious mockery and 'Scotland For Ever' only a barbaric cry."

Defending his own record Winston stressed the great savings he had made in the Middle East; rejoiced in his participation in the Irish Peace Treaty and declared proudly that the part he had played in the Chanak crises was one of the greatest honours of his long official life.

"I take my stand by Mr Lloyd George," he continued, speaking up defiantly for his fallen chief, "I was his friend before he was famous. I was with him when all were at his feet. and now, today, when men who fawned upon him, have praised even his errors, have climbed into place in Parliament upon his shoulders, have cast him aside . . . I am still his friend and lieutenant . . . I am sure among the broad masses of the faithful, millions of toiling, Britain-loving men and women who he led to victory, there will still be left a few to wish him well.

"And now," Winston ended on a contrived note of pathos, "I have to make a most melancholy confession. At the time being I am helpless, I cannot stir a yard to defend myself and the causes about which I care, and must trust my fortunes to the Liberal Association of Dundee as you have sustained me all these years when I have been your representative in the Council of Nations; and indeed I may say of the Empire. Now, at this moment of peculiar crisis and difficulty, I still rely on you. You must do with me as you please."

The Dundee "Courier" of the same date was unimpressed. "Mr Lloyd George and Mr Winston Churchill" it censured, "have for years posed as the champions of the masses; now they are absolutely terrified of Labour. They would rather combine with the Progressive Conservatives than with the progressive working man."

In the same edition, a correspondent calling himself Consistency" catalogued with high emotion the list of Winston's crimes". "How any responsible politician, more particularly an ex-Cabinet Minister can have the effrontery to pose as a true Liberal after holding high office for so many years in a Tory administration simply passes the wit of man. But the public memory is not short after all, and the remarkable achievements of this political acrobat stand out absolutely unrivalled in the annals of foreign policy . . . Mr Churchill's parliamentary record during his tenure of office has been a costly one to the nation and ghastly in many details. Witness for example his dramatic failures at the Admiralty—the Antwerp bungle, the Gallipoli tragedy, the Russian scandal, involving the loss of one hundred million pounds to the British Exchequer; and last, but not least, the horrors of the Mesopotamian campaign, all of which go to prove that whatever degree of statesmanship he may claim to possess he is first and foremost a colossal blunderer and should he by any mischance happen to be returned to the House of Commons as one of the city's representatives such a regrettable result would put a sad commentary on the intelligence of the electorate."

Scrymgeour, adding to the chorus of condemnation, labelled Winston as "The most dangerous man in the ranks of the 'enemy' and utterly unsuited to represent a great industrial centre like Dundee . . . "

On the following Monday the Dundee "Advertiser" published a statement by E. D. Morel refuting Winston's allegations. "Mr Churchill," he said, fastidiously divorcing himself from Gallacher, "makes a personal attack upon me. In the first place he persists in bracketing me with another candidate as a representative of the British Labour Party. The tactic is obvious. It has already been officially and publicly stated by the Dundee Labour Party that they have only one candidate in the field—myself . . . I am unalterably opposed to Communism, the central doctrine of which, as I understand it, is dictatorship of the proletariat, imposed, if necessary by force. I have no use for dictatorship of any kind. I stand for democracy."

After explaining the circumstances which had led up to his imprisonment Morel concluded: "As between Churchill and myself, it simply comes to this, I was working for peace before the War. He was working for war before the War. I tried to shorten its duration, not by peace at any price, but by conference.

"He was for prosecuting it at any price. I have worked for reconstruction and reconciliation since the War. He has promoted fresh war. Let Britain and the world bear witness as to who saw the clearest."

By Wednesday when the election battle opened in earnest with all but one of the candidates facing the electors, it was clear that Winston in his absence was getting the worst of it. Even D. J. Macdonald, as Winston's ally, was proving himself more of a hindrance than a help.

Subjected to a lively attack by hecklers at a crowded meeting in the Blackness Hall, Macdonald explained the nature of his partnership:

"The reason why Mr Churchill is voluntarily my colleague is because Mr Churchill is the only candidate in the field who has the personality, the power, and the experience to give sufficient force to my local knowledge, and to carry through the reforms that are wanted." Asked if he could not find a more "humane" companion he answered lamely, "I am choosing Mr Churchill as the best of all the candidates, and not as the best man in the world."

Robert Pilkington, in St. Mary's Hall in the Hilltown district of the city, denouncing the extravagance of the Coalition, advocated a policy of sound finance and threw a common sense measure of cold water on Winston's wilder allegations against Morel. "There is a close connection," he said, "between the mentality of those who are guilty of wild extravagance and those who are guilty of wild adventures. The Coalition is guilty of both. Mr Lloyd George has called himself a pugnacious animal and I think the same might be said of Mr Churchill . . . In his manifesto Mr Churchill has attacked the Labour programme. I am no Labour man; I am opposed to Socialism—but I recognise that Mr Churcill's description of the Labour programme is a gross and shameless caricature."

In his second speech of the day, Morel, addressing a meeting in the Forresters Hall declared passionately, "The war has torn the bandages off the wounds in our social system . . . They might shout 'Bolshevism, Confiscation, Revolution' that is unwisdom. They can, however, look the evils of the society they have created squarely in the face—evils which have been long with them, and to whose extent and significance they have been blinded by the deadly paralysis of habit. That is wisdom. (Applause)

"What is to be done? The Prime Minister, Mr Bonar Law, is in effect saying, 'Why nothing.' The ex-Prime Minister, Mr Chamberlain, and Mr Churchill say, 'Abuse the Labour Party'—the only party which has produced a constructive constitutional social programme to deal with evils which can no longer endure if Britain is to live—(Applause) . . . I say to these men, 'You are smoking cigars on a powder magazine. You are trifling with the country with your comic opera politics, empty rehetoric, your contemptible personal quarrels.' " (Applause)

Blaming the unemployment problem on the European Peace Treaties and the Coalition's foreign and trade policies Morel questioned:

"How is the nation going to live? In view of the oratorical fireworks which Mr Churchill is constantly exploding from his bedside, it is no longer possible to refrain on account of his illness from criticising him." (Laughter) "The Russian war has been an ignominious failure, like all Mr Churchill's pet military adventures. (hear, hear) The Blockade of Russia carried starvation and disease into millions of peasant homes in Russia; it has brought wretchedness into thousands of Dundee homes by putting Dundee off from the Russian market. It is a curious irony of fate that the man chiefly responsible for blocking every attempt to restore normal relations with Russia—the policy which I have uged for three years, the policy for which big city bankers and business men are now clamouring."

"It is conceivable," he concluded on a humourous note, "that later the careful historian of these recent years will find little difficulty in arriving at the conclusion that the Government in 1917 left the wrong man at liberty. It might have been more profitable for the country as a whole, and for Dundee in particular, that the Senior Member for Dundee, not the future member, had been locked up." (Laughter and applause)

William Gallacher, caught like the other candidates in the double vote dilemma, declared before a packed audience in the Lochee West United Free Church Hall:

"Neither Mr Morel nor the Labour Party can repudiate me. I am a member of the Labour Party, and represent Labour. I am not concerned one little bit about anyone other than the working class. I am standing definitely as a working class representative. I am not out to serve the community. I am out to give whatever energy I have on behalf of the class to which I belong. (Applause) And," he concluded before his mainly Irish listeners, "if I am returned I will give my support to the Irish Republicans."

At a meeting in Dens Road School, Scrymgeour breezily announced:

"Candidly, I am going in this, the sixth time. I have been kicked out often, but I am like a ball—I keep 'stotting' back. Some day I will get into goal." (Laughter) Ridiculing all the other candidates with the significant exception of Morel, Scrymgeour saved his best sally for D. J. Macdonald who was, he said, "Like a blind man in the House of Commons crying out, 'I have lost Churchill.' "

Forced to remain well behind the lines and to endure impatiently the sounds of small arms fire from these distant skirmishes, Winston had no intention of remaining hors de combat. Each day he thundered forth long range artillery fire in the shape of telegrams, letters and statements, all designed to gain him maximum Press publicity.

"In laying down my official responsibilities towards the government of the Irish Free State," he telegrammed Liam Cosgrave the Irish Prime Minister, "I take the opportunity of expressing to you and your colleagues in the Irish Government, as well as to your principal military commanders, my most earnest and abiding good wishes, and my sure confidence that success will not be denied you . . . "

Cosgrave's reply to this communication, coming the same day, and appearing side by side with Winston's telegram in the newspapers was no doubt gratifying:

"The valedictory message which you have sent us on vacating office touches many chords . . . we are not concerned with party issues in Great Britain, and we know nothing of the merits of the domestic question on which your Ministry has quitted office but we do know that in our regard your Ministry represents a combination of vision and boldness and statesmanship unparalleled in the relationships of our two countries, and that you have done a big thing too close to us yet to be truly valued . . . "

Mr Robertson, the President of the Dundee Liberal Association, a Chartered Accountant, who had pioneered investment trusts in Britain, the U.S.A. and Canada, and whose business acumen had swelled both Liberal Party funds and given him the job of Dundee's City Treasurer, was treated to another long and extremely boring letter from Winston on the subject of government economy and expenditure, the substance of which was a fresh reference to the savings he had made in Palestine and Mesopotamia:

"It is very easy," Winston explained tenaciously, "to talk about economy, and very hard to effect it, and I assure you that I have had to cudgel my brains continuously to find ways of effecting this great saving."

He drew attention to the way he personally had pruned hard, and how, by invidious comparison, Baldwin, the new Chancellor of the Exchequer had been unable to announce any prospect of a further reduction in taxation and who would have great difficulty in balancing the budget:

"I do not think we ought to be satisfied at all," Winston concluded critically, "with this kind of loose and superficial view. As a member of the Finance Committee of the Cabinet I had formed the opinion that if proper measures were taken, real efforts and real ingenuity used, it should have been possible to have given the taxpayer a further relief in the course of the present year, and I think I should be authorised by the electors to press strongly for it."

The postage stamp had hardly dried upon the envelope on its way post-haste to Robertson before Winston followed it up with a telegram saying, "I very much regret to see Mr Bonar Law's proposal to abolish the Ministry of Pensions and I cannot undertake to support the measures he declares he will introduce for this purpose." It was certainly true that by transferring the payment of pensions from the direct control of a Government Minister who had great powers of discretion, to the bureaucratic administraton of Treasury civil servants, many pensioners were bound to suffer hardship. As Winston observed: officials, however competent, can only administer rigid rules in a spirit of routine and red tape.

His fellow candidates were in the meantime warming to their work.

In answer to a question why he was now "creeping about with Churchill," while at the beginning of the year he had been running down the Government, D. J. Macdonald replied with greater self-assurance but with fading loyalty to his chief, "In the first place Mr Churchill isn't the Government, and in the second place I have chosen the second best candidate." (Laughter) Positive but hardly more helpful support came for Winston at the same meeting when Matt. Terrel from North Shields, and George Reid from London, officials of the National Seamen's and Firemen's Union, who had supported Winston in the 1917 election, stated that they had come to Dundee this time in an effort to combat the "Red" menace.

Since his invitation for an unofficial alliance had been ignored by Morel, Pilkington had shifted his ground to the right and in reply to a heckler said:

"I believe I can do as much for the worker as Mr Morel. Mr Morel believes in a system of Socialism which I do not believe in. (Applause) I do not believe that Socialism will bring prosperity to the workers. I think the Independent Liberal programme more likely to do so. I am not in favour of the nationalisation of mines and railways."

Annie S. Swan, the well-known romantic novelist and a regular contributor to the publications of D. C. Thomson & Co Ltd., the owners of the "Courier" and "Advertiser" newspapers, ranged her considerable influence on his behalf. "Mr Pilkington is a lover of peace," she exorted her female readers, "and will further all the economy and reform we need. He is a true man. You can trust him. Give him your vote."

Addressing an audience of ex-Servicemen in the British Legion, Morel made a spirited defence against Winston's continued innuendoes upon his war record:

"I have no defence to make," he stoutly told his listeners, "I will not repudiate a word which I have used in the last four years . . . when war broke out I was 32 years of age. I have testified at least to the sincerity of my convictions by throwing up my Parliamentary candidate. I could have retired altogether from public life until the war was over, following the example of the two men who in their public life have been called honest—John Morley and John Burns . . . It would have been easy for me to have got a 'cushy billet' and swaggered about in Khaki. That did not suit my ideas."

At the Y.M.C.A. Gallacher, stubbornly re-asserting his claim to official Labour Party recognition said, "I merely stand for one form of organised Labour and Mr Morel for another: Mr Morel and the Independent Labour Party welcomed me cordially at one time, but are now repudiating me in the hope of getting a few respectable votes."

Scrymgeour, harking back to his old muck-raking days, addressed a meeting in the Downfield Hall and hinting of dark secrets yet to be revealed said: "I have read the programme of the Communists, and I possess information that will enable me to smash Mr Gallacher and keep him or anyone else from opening their mouths. I have books showing certain agreements and plans that have been made to accomplish a great upheaval."

Gallacher, in shart ripost, later in the week said: "Mr Morel and I alone represent organised Labour . . . if Mr Scrymgeour aspires to further working class interests he ought to come into the Labour movement. Mr Scrymgeour has said he has books which will close my mouth; well, Mr Scrymgeour ought to hand over the documents to Scotland Yard and make a fortune." And, that problem disposed of, Gallacher returned to his main theme: "I am an extremist and proud of my extremism. I do not consider any class of any value other than the working class. Mr Churchill is the bitterest enemy of that class."

Winston in the meantime fretted restively, kept in touch with events by means only of newspaper reports and long expensive telephone calls from Lord Wodehouse. The political correspondent for the Glasgow Herald observed on Friday, November 3rd:

"Mr Churchill has suffered one of the greatest disappointments of his life in being forced by illness to be a spectator of the fight. He has certainly been busy with his pen, but that modest, though in his hand, powerful weapon, is an insufficient outlet for his combatitiveness. Happily, he is making a rapid recovery, and should his convalescence proceed satisfactorily, as is expected, he will yet be seen in the field. He cannot, as he would have liked, roam at large over the battlefield; but is is his firm intention, unless his doctor intervenes, to visit Dundee on Saturday, 11th inst., to deliver a speech to his constituents."

Until then, therefore, Winston intended to keep the pot boiling. In a letter to the "Manchester Guardian," Saturday 4th November, he virtually accused Pilkington of lying when the latter claimed to be paying his own election expenses. "Can you really suppose" asked Winston rhetorically, "that the funds for Mr Pilkington's candidatature are not being supplied directly or indirectly from the Abingdon Street fund? (The Liberal Party National Headquarters in London) Can you really suppose that Mr Hogg, the Whip of the Independent Liberal Party is not behind it, or that Mr Asquith in a neighbouring constituency is not aware of it, and is not approving of it? I assert all three propositions, and I challenge any denial."

These accusations re-published in the Dundee "Courier" met with an immediate and indignant reaction from the Independent Liberal camp:

"Mr Winston Churchill," wrote Garnet Wilson furiously, their 37 year old leader and proprietor manager of one of the city's largest departmental stores," is the latest of political Rip van Winkles. He seems to have been asleep for months, or his advisers in Dundee have been. He has now awakened from his long sleep, and becomes suddenly aware that he is being opposed in Dundee by a genuine Liberal in the person of Mr R. R. Pilkington, and that the electors are rallying to Mr Pilkington's support."

Refuting absolutely all Winston's accusations — Pilkington had as a matter of fact placed a bond of £1,100 for his expenses and was prepared to pay finally up to £1,300 — Garnet Wilson continued, "Mr Pilkington was brought to Dundee by the committee of Liberal stalwarts who had for long recognised the falsity of Mr Churchill's pretensions to Liberalism — whatever other merits he possessed — and were determined to have no more of them.

"The test of a true and genuine Liberal today lies in the electors knowing that — when such a one describes himself as a Liberal, he is also a Free Trader and other high principled things as well. The necessity is not imposed on a true Liberal like Mr Pilkington to say, 'I am a Liberal and a Free Trader.' The first includes the second. But the necessity is imposed on Mr Churchill, for Mr Churchill is neither Liberal nor Free Trader. He says he is, but his political record confounds his statements."

Pilkington himself, shocked by the gravity of Winston's charges, confined himself to a brief denial, the depth of his feelings indicated in his final paragraph:

"The imputation against me personally is of so offensive a character that I have found it difficult to express myself with restraint. I have no doubt however that the electors of all parties will accept my assurance that it is without a shadow of foundation."

On Monday the 6th as the controversy raged Clementine, accompanied by her infant daughter Mary, her fifth child, born only a few weeks before and not yet baptised, arrived in Dundee. (Her fourth child, 3½ year old Marigold, had died tragically of a septic throat in August of the previous year, to her and Winston's deep distress).

Staying with friends she lost no time in getting to work addressing a meeting of lady Liberals and Unionists in the Liberal Rooms in Reform Street that evening.

"My husband," she said rather disjointedly in her opening remarks, "sends a message to say he is very much better. I think that undoubtedly he will be in Dundee this weekend and be able to take, not his usual part in the election, though he will be able to address some of his constituents at least once, and perhaps several times before the poll. (Applause)

"I want to appeal first to the Liberal women because my husband is a Liberal, and the Liberal causes which are dear and sacred to all Liberals, are causes which he has fought for ever since he was a young man. (Applause) He has spoken and written and worked for Free trade, and during these last two years the Irish Settlement. (Applause) That, I think, is the reason why every Liberal in Dundee should vote for my husband. (Applause) He has not only spoken for it, he has put in a great deal of hard departmental work. I think that is indeed an irony of fate that the Irish Settlement which has been brought into being by a joint Government of Liberals and Conservatives, will finally be ratified by a purely Conservative Government."

Appealing to her listeners to canvass among those "moderate" women who normally voted Labour she continued:

"I think it is a sad thing to think that those moderate Labour votes which, in normal circumstances, would have gone as in the past to a splendid man like Mr Wilkie, should be devoted to men who preached such extreme socialistic doctrines as were put forward in the manifesto issued about a fortnight ago by the Labour Party." (Applause)

Ending on a warmly domestic note she said: "My husband came to Dundee just before we were married. It was just before he proposed to me. (Laughter) During these fourteen years he has fought six elections, and they have always returned him at the top of the poll. Now he is on his back and not able to fight for himself, I am sure you will do it again." (Applause)

Later the same evening, however, Clementine received a more robust reception at a public meeting in the Larch Street Hall, situated in one of the more deprived areas of the city. As in 1917 she was supported by John Pratt, Liberal M.P. for Cathcart, since then the ex-Parliamentary Under-Secretary for Scotland in the Coalition who had been promised a knighthood in the forthcoming Honours List.

Almost from beginning to end the meeting was in a state of uproar and in a choking atmosphere made almost impenetrable by a thousand puffing cigarettes and pipes, the Chairman's opening remarks were drowned in an epidemic of coughing and sneezing suitably encouraged by a practical joker who had discharged into the air a nasal irritant called 'electric snuff'!

"I am afraid the atmosphere has been artificially treated," the Chairman remarked superfluously and referring to Winston's unavoidable absence was met with the comments: 'Don't apologise for him' and 'I wish I was as comfortable as he is.'

The atmosphere became slightly more breathable after a member of the audience appealed to the others not to smoke, but the whole of Pratt's opening address was subjected to an unceasing barrage of interruptions:

"If," he complained, "a cause is so poor that it can't hear the other side, then it will meet with nothing but disaster in the polls. The great mass of the people of Dundee are not going to be won over to one side or the other by efforts to stop free speech, and I for one am quite prepared to make the best effort I can to tell you, in my opinion, why you should return Mr Churchill and Mr Macdonald." (Uproar and cries of 'Out with it' and 'Shame' and 'He's a disgrace to Dundee' and 'We have had enough of him').

One brave member of the audience stood up in the sea of hostile faces and, appealing for order, said:
'Give Mr Pratt a chance.'
"I am sure Mr Churchill would be the man to hope . . . " Pratt tried to continue in the brief lull.
A Voice – 'How's the baby?' (Laughter)
Pratt – "I am glad to say the baby is very well indeed, and I have no doubt the Dundee air will do the baby a great deal of good." (Renewed laughter)
A Voice – 'Dundee Margarine.' (Laughter)

Further interruptions followed, and Pratt retorted, "If you are determined not to hear me I am quite prepared to sit down."
'Cheers for De Valera.'

Just then, amid renewed uproar, Clementine entered the Hall accompanied by D. J. Macdonald and took her seat on the platform.

Several interruptors, obviously Gallacher's supporters, drew attention to the Irish situation again and again, and led a large section of the audience in making three cheers for De Valera.
A Voice – 'Give Mr Macdonald a chance. He will talk to us about finance.' (Laughter)

Answering a query as to whether Winston worked for his money, Pratt replied: "Mr Churchill is one of the hardest workers the country has ever known." (Ironical cheers and cries of 'Good old Gallacher')

A woman – referring to the recent publicity surrounding the engagement and marriage of the exiled German Emperor to a young Dutch princess – scolded 'Churchill was going to hang the Kaiser, but he was married yesterday.' (Loud laughter)

In comparison to Pratt, Clementine was better received and matching the rumbustious spirit of the proceedings said: "I am pleased to see you are all alive and kicking in Dundee . . . "
A Voice – 'It's a good job we're living.'

"I only wish my husband," she smiled, "had not been prevented through his illness from coming to this meeting. He has been very ill but if he had been better I would not be in Dundee. He will, I hope, be in Dundee before the end of the week. Although he has been prevented from coming to Dundee, I feel confident that the great majority of the men and women of Dundee will not take advantage of that, and I will not be a bit surprised if he got a much bigger majority at this election. (Uproar) I would not like to feel that after all these years when he had been able to come to Dundee and fight, you should take advantage because he is not able now to come to Dundee."

A woman – 'Play the game, Mrs Churchill, play the game. Don't use that sentimental argument about your man being ill.' (Loud laughter)

Clementine – "Whatever you may think, you know jolly well that he is an energetic strong man and I am quite certain that the great majority of the electors of Dundee will vote for him."

A woman – 'Let him be a sport like his father and stick to the point.' (Laughter)

A Voice – 'Will Mr Pratt assure the electors of Dundee that Mr Churchill will speak to everybody and not only to those who have tickets?'

"I will answer that," returned Clementine spiritedly. "Do you think this is a good advertisement for an open meeting? It is not. Mr Pratt has come all the way from Italy to speak on behalf of my husband, and you have refused to hear him."

She resumed her seat and D. J. Macdonald rose. Blundering into his speech he remarked: "I have been asked to say what I think of Mr Churchill." (A Voice – 'Keep it to yourself' followed by laughter in which Clementine joined)

Continuing he said "You are going to return a local candidate to Parliament." (A Voice – 'Scrymgeour')

"There is not a single man of the whole of the candidates with the power needed behind your local candidate to carry through the reform needed except Mr Churchill." (Ironical cheers)

Praising Winston's efforts to have the Canadian cattle embargo removed – a protectionist measure prohibiting the importation of surplus Canadian beef cattle which had kept shop prices high – Macdonald was jeered: 'Beef's no use without work.'

Surrendering to the uproar Macdonald sat down too. Pratt was called to answer further questions but refused to respond and above the noise of the barracking audience a voice was heard – 'The man's fed up.' (Laughter) The Chairman thanked the speakers and declared the meeting closed. This did not, however, diminish the uproar; a banner was hoisted and "The Soldiers Song" and other Irish Republican airs were sung with gusto.

Leaving the hall Clementine went over to one of the women hecklers and shook hands with her. Another who stood by remarked – 'Oh, but ah'll shak hands wi' yi',' and on leaving by car Clementine was given a rousing cheer.

The following morning, Tuesday November 7th, Winston's election address was published.

"Ladies and gentlemen, electors of Dundee," he boomed forth with much smoke but uncertain fire, "This is the first time during the fourteen years which I have had the honour to represent you that I have presented myself for election freed from the burden of official responsibilities and in a private station . . . I shall be able to devote my energies more fully to the care of your interests, to be more often among you . . .

"We are now confronted with two opposite dangers both of which challenge and menace the fundamental principles of Liberalism . . . The policy which has been announced by the new Prime Minister carries us back almost into the Middle Ages . . . Such a message of negation will strike a knell of despair in the heart of every earnest social worker and every striver after social justice . . . I will never stifle myself within such a moral and intellectual sepulchre. Over the portals of No. 10 Downing Street the new Prime Minister has inscribed the words – 'All hope abandon ye who enter here . . . ' I will not take back one word I have spoken in favour of active and earnest effort in social reform . . . I will accept no policy of negation.

"What do we see when we look in the opposite direction? Apart from our old friend, Mr Scrymgeour, and our new friend, Mr Pilkington, who may be safely left to expound their doctrines to their particular sectaries, we are confronted with a very serious and formidable attack in the two Socialist and Communist candidates. I observe that they are abusing and repudiating each other with a heartiness which does full justice to their high-minded profession about the universal brotherhood of men. I observe with surprise that the more prosperous socialist looks down with contempt upon his poor and more violent brother. I see no distinction between them. They have both done the best they could against this country which has nourished them, choosing its most difficult moments and employing whichever weapon they dared to use. Britain's difficulty has been their opportunity. Britain's triumph has been their mortification. Britain's downfall is their supreme objective. *Mr Gallacher is only Mr Morel with the courage of his convictions,*

Trotsky is only Mr Gallacher with the power to murder those whom he cannot convince. I view with great regret the fact that the votes of so many of those patriotic Trade Unionists and Labour men who Mr Wilkie represented so worthily during all these years should be perverted to the support of *this pair of dangerous and dismal revolutionaries.*"

The Dundee "Advertiser" received this appeal with marked hostility:

"Mr Churchill's election address is published today, but no new idea or turn of criticism will be found in it. There is a reference to the malicious intrigues of the Die-hard and Wee Free faction. Malicious intrigue, we suppose, is Mr Churchill's way of characterising a refusal to admire himself as a statesman. The contemptuous reference to the Wee Free faction is indiscreet. If we were in the way of betting we would take heavy odds on it that ten days hence Mr Churchill's faction will be the wee one, that will have undesired freedom thrust upon it."

Commenting also upon Winston's personal attack upon Pilkington, the Editor went on: "Looking upon Dundee apparently as a sort of personal estate of his own, Mr Churchill regards Mr R. R. Pilkington's appearance on the scene as a sort of impudent invasion and trespass contrived by the Independent Liberal leaders out of spite . . . The public may be left to put its own estimate on a mentality which without a vestige of ground for it, flings out aspersions of the kind in question."

That evening Clementine and her fellow campaigners addressed a meeting where the audience's belligerence paled their experience of the previous night into insignificance.

Recently completed, the Caird Hall, prestigious gift to the city of the jute magnate Sir James Caird, was already packed when they arrived—it had a seating capacity of over 3,000—and yet the doors had to be closed against a waiting queue stretching from Castle Street to Shore Terrace, a distance of about three or four hundred yards. Clementine, wearing a string of pearls bright against her dark dress arrived last on the platform amid a deafening uproar from the audience, leaning on the arm of James Robertson. Opening the proceedings Robertson said, "Nothing could have prevented me coming to do my duty and do what I can for our great representative Mr Winston Churchill." (Cries of Oh!)

Pausing to produce blown-up photographs of Robert Pilkington and William Gallacher, prolonged uproar gave way at the mention of Gallacher's name to clamourous cheering.

"Righto for Gallacher" retorted Robertson.

(A Voice—'Three cheers for Scrymgeour')

The noise continued, led by several women with infants in their arms who looked down from the left-hand balcony.

Straining to be heard Robertson attempted to denigrate the rival candidates in turn but to cries of 'Sit down' his oratory was reduced in the end to threatening the women in the balcony: "We will get someone to put you out unless you behave yourself."

When Clementine rose to speak she was by contrast, in recognition of her personal popularity, greeted with enthusiasm although intermingled in the applause came cries again from the left gallery. One woman among the group had a voice which was particularly hectoring and Clementine was seen to eye her impatiently. The catcalls continued and Robertson finally intervened saying: "I am afraid I will have to ask the steward to put you out."

A man bobbed up from the main floor of the hall but he was quickly back in his seat again after Robertson told him he was keeping Mrs Churchill standing.

Endeavouring to begin her speech Clementine chose by mischance the exact moment as the steward approached the woman. Attacked verbally by the harpies the steward was browbeaten into embarrassed retreat while their persistant noise forced Clementine to resume her seat again. After a moment or two however she tried once more to get her speech under way and this time with more success.

"A great many people," she said, "in the country – and I am told that some of them live in Dundee – think and say that unemployment and the distress in the country, and in Dundee, is caused by the shortcomings and wrongdoings of the Government. And, as my husband was a member of that much abused Government and he is the only member of the Government they in Dundee can get at, some people say, 'It is all Churchill's fault. Let us put him out.' (A Voice – 'So we will')

"Is the unemployment and distress not caused in great measure by men who profess to lead the working men of this country but who often give them bad advice causing the unemployment and distress? I object to the Socialist party calling themselves the Labour Party. The great proportion of the electors of Dundee are working men and women, and up to now I am glad to say they have put at the top of the poll a Liberal member and a Liberal-Labour member, Mr Wilkie. So I do not see why the name Labour should be adopted and clung to by one party more than another." Meeting a ripple of interruptions with a smile, or brushing them aside with her light attractive laugh, she asked: "Are you really going to vote for any of the three Socialist candidates? You must realise that these are men, however sincere and honest they might be, who approve of turning the country upside down just when it is emerging from its life and death struggle of the Great War."

A Voice – 'Does your bairn live on a shilling?'

"Mr Pilkington," she said, ignoring the remark, "is splitting the good Liberal vote. You might as well vote for Mr Morel or Mr Scrymgeour (Cheers, and cries of 'Good old Scrimmy') – or even for Mr Gallacher." (Applause, mainly from the left gallery)

A woman – 'Mrs Churchill ought to be ashamed to be on that platform.'

"The only result of voting for Mr Pilkington," said Clementine not to be deflected, "would be, perhaps without meaning to, let Mr Morel in by the side door. I do not think Mr Pilkington ought to stand for Dundee. I and my husband are both Liberals and what use is there in Liberals fighting against each other. My husband has represented Dundee for fourteen years and Mr Pilkington has only just arrived. If Mr Pilkington had been here first, my husband would not have opposed him and run the risk of letting a Socialist in."

Concluding with an appeal to the audience to vote for Winston and D. J. Macdonald she was greeted with a mixture of boos and applause.

A Voice – (with insight) – 'Macdonald is only there to split the vote.'

"I am sure," she continued, "that if you return them –

A Voice – 'They will be a rare pair.'

Dundee will never regret it." (Applause)

When Clementine took her seat all semblance of order departed from the meeting and neither John Pratt, MacCallum Scott or D. J. Macdonald were given a proper hearing. Afterwards, on leaving the Hall, Clementine was spat on in the crowd, and General Speirs, a member of the entourage, commented admiringly "Clemmie's bearing was magnificent – like an aristocrat going to the guillotine in a tumbril."

The stuff of which heroines are made, Clementine kept up her busy schedule the following day and addressed four separate meetings. The first in the afternoon, replacing D. J. Macdonald who had retired ignominiously from the fray with bronchial cattarh, must have been a welcome relief but marked the first of two self-inflicted injuries on Winston's cause. Asking her audience of seventy ladies not to vote for Mr Pilkington, split the Liberal vote and let the Labour candidate it, she said, perhaps with just a degree of misgiving as she introduced the next stage of Winston's smear campaign and asking:

"Mr Morel is a good speaker, but is far more insidious and dangerous than Mr Gallacher. *He is really Mr Gallacher in a refined and respectable form.*

"I put the following questions to Mr Morel and I hope he can answer them.

"Is it a fact that Mr Morel is not an Englishman but was born a Frenchman?

"Is it true that he became an Englishman to avoid military service in the land of his birth?

"Did he, during the war, render any service to Britain . . . ?"

For Clementine to descend to these tactics was not only a clumsy error upon which Morel would capitalize, but one her noble spirit must have regretted later.

"I observe," replied Morel on Thursday, at meetings crowded out now by Clementine's gratuitous publicity, "that Mrs Churchill has been paying me some very pretty compliments, and regarding me as a very dangerous man. I agree that I am a dangerous man to her husband, but I am not such a dangerous man to Mr Churchill as Mr Churchill is to the British people.

"At the rate the Churchill faction is going in its enquiry into my personal affairs I will not be surprised if it finds itself one of these days in a very unpleasant position. If it comes to raking up family history there are far more curious things in the history of the Churchills than in the historical records of the Morels. (Applause)

"But regarding Mrs Churchill's questions, I am always willing to oblige a lady. My father was a Frenchman, my mother an English-woman, and I was born in Paris. We do not select our parents or our place of birth. *I am no more responsible for the fact that my father was French than Mr Churchill is responsible for the fact that his mother was an American.* What has all this to do with the issues before the country? My father died when I was an infant. My mother sent me to school in England when I was eight. In England I have lived, with an interval of two years which I spent in Paris, ever since. Very clever of me to come over here when I was eight in order to escape military service, wasn't it? – a kind of juvenile precocity of a remarkable kind. (Laughter)

"Thirty six years ago I married an English lady of Scottish extraction who has given me a daughter and four sons.

"There is no doubt that the Churchill faction is alarmed. Their pocket-edition of Napoleon seems to see before him a future Waterloo. (Laughter)

"I have been asked what I did in the war. I will not go into the question at length, but will wait until Mr Churchill himself comes along with the blacking brush."

Clementine however had already realised her mistake in mounting personal attacks against Morel and, writing home the previous night on the 8th, she advised Winston that Morel's election address had just come out "very moderate and in favour of only constitutional methods. So we cannot compare him with Gallacher." And she added, touched deeply by the visible signs of poverty in Dundee: "My darling the misery here is appalling. Some of the people look absolutely starving."

Winston's blundering sledgehammer blows, against his rivals, until then delivered by bulletin, wife and smaller fry, were however to be given one last powerful and destructive impetus from an unexpected and extraordinary source. F. E. Smith, Baron Birkenhead, the Coalition's ex-Lord Chancellor, was to come to Dundee to speak on Winston's behalf.

Almost a self-made man—he always in later life exaggerated his humble origins—Frederick Edwin Smith was, in the opinion of the working class, a true-blue arch-Tory dyed through and through. A brilliant scholar, within five years of leaving Oxford earning £6,000 a year as a barrister, Smith was one of the few Tory newcomers returned to the back benches in the House of Commons after the 1906 Liberal landslide. His maiden speech, a masterpiece of cutting wit, might have ruined him—like later pronouncements he went too far—but it turned out a tremendous success and made his Parliamentary reputation and Tim Healey, the Irish Nationalist, a master of invective himself and one of the most brilliant debaters in the House, passed a scribbled note along the benches as Smith sat down amidst a storm of cheering saying, "I am old, and you are young, but you have beaten me at my own game."

Because Smith held a grudge against him for leaving the Tory Party, for some time neither he nor Winston exchanged a word, but when the two young men did finally meet they made an instant rapport. Winston wrote:

"Our friendship was perfect. It was one of my most precious possessions . . . he had all the canine virtues to a remarkable degree—courage, fidelity, vigilance, love of the chase."

Through Winston's influence, Asquith made F. E. Smith a Privy Councillor in 1911 but, the rising hope of his party, he led the Ulstermen along with Garson in their fight against the Home Rule bill earning the nickname "Galloper" for his outrageous and provocative speeches. When war broke out Smith fought on active service in France until appointed Solicitor General in 1915, and after Lloyd George seized the Premiership he was made Attorney General. He remained a staunch member of the Coalition becoming Lord Chancellor in 1919 taking the title Baron Birkenhead. Defiantly proud that he had swallowed many of his own principles he, like Winston, considered the Irish Settlement his finest achievement.

For him, Winston's admiration was unreserved and illustrating the power of his merciless wit, Winston, unfeeling of the tragic implications of the story, later told of the interchange which took place between Smith and Judge Willis in the Suffolk County court over the case of a boy claiming damages who had been run over and blinded in a tramway accident.

"Poor boy, poor boy!" the judge exclaimed, allowing human sympathy to outrun his discretion as a magistrate. "Blind! Put him on a chair so that the jury can see him."

Retained by the Tramway Company, this weighed the scales of justice too far for Smith, who suggested sarcastically:

"Perhaps your Honour would like to have the boy passed round the jury box."

"That is a most improper remark," exclaimed Judge Willis.

"It was provoked by a most improper suggestion" was Smith's impudent reply.

Thinking hard for a long interval Judge Willis tried to come up with a decisive retort and at last announced:

"Mr Smith, have you ever heard of a saying by Bacon—the great Bacon—that youth and discretion are ill-wedded companions?"

"Yes, I have" was Smith's instant ripost. "And have you ever heard of a saying by Bacon—the great Bacon—that a much talking judge is like an ill-tuned cymbal?"

"You are extremely offensive, young man" exclaimed the judge.

"As a matter of fact," said Smith, "we both are; but I am trying to be, you can't help it."

Winston did not record the final result of the interchange but it is to be hoped Judge Willis's baiting resulted in generous compensation for the blind child.

Birkenhead, noted Winston, did not confine "the entangling net and unexpected trident" of his skill with words only to the Law courts or the House of Commons, but also included in his armoury of dialectical expertise the "bludgeon for the platform."

The latter method Birkenhead was to exercise with indiscriminate vigour in Dundee.

On Thursday evening, 9th November, the Caird Hall was packed. F. I. Oakley, who had already given Winston his support as President of the Dundee Unionist Association, was in the Chair, and the platform party included Mrs Churchill and such dignatories as Sir George and Lady Baxter; Lord Provost Spence and Mrs Spence; Col. W. H. Ferguson; ex-Lord Provost Longair and a great many others.

Birkenhead, spare, trim, wearing a greyish tweed suit and looking positively boyish came on in "fumbling style." He had been liberally entertained all afternoon at that sanctuary for Dundee high Tories, the Eastern Club—and owlishly surveyed the vast audience.

"We have present," Oakley said, introducing him, "one of Britain's greatest legal authorities—(Applause)—one of our greatest Conservatives and he is here to speak in support of one of our greatest Liberals. It is a splendid sign that patriotic Britishers in time of need can still forget the minor claims of party." (Applause)

"I hope," said Birkenhead, introducing himself and attempting to explain contradiction of his position, "I will not be misunderstood by the Liberals present if I make it quite plain that I am here as a Conservative. (Applause) . . . A near and dear friend of mine has been your brilliant Member for many years. (Applause) He cannot at this moment effectively fight his own battle, though no man in England—
A Voice—'Britain'.
—could fight his own battle better or as well. (Applause) . . . My advice is that every Unionist man and every Unionist woman who has a vote in Dundee should give that vote to Mr Churchill and Mr Macdonald. (Applause) . . .

"Who are the candidates who are in the field? I will not speak at any length at all of Mr Gallacher. I honestly do not feel as much hostility to Mr Gallacher on reading his address and his speeches as I feel to another of the candidates. Mr Gallacher, after all, is an impulsive and ill-educated revolutionary and he is young enough to learn. (Applause)

"But Mr Gallacher is associated, if I might use the expression, because it requires qualification, with another gentleman, Mr George Eduard Pierre Achille Morel de Ville. You will hardly conclude from this long description that is the true and original name of the gentleman who is trying to creep into the favour of Dundee under the name of Mr Morel. That is really the name of this gentleman. He was a French citizen before the war. France is a very great country and on the whole I like a man to stick to the country, particularly if it is a great one, in which he was born. (Applause)

"Many years ago Mr George Eduard Pierre Achille Morel de Ville (loud laughter) decided to do us a great favour by becoming a citizen of this country. He then began to exhibit an extraordinary and unintelligible series of activities, just about the same time that the great Sir Roger Casemen (hanged for treason in the Irish Rebellion of Easter 1916 and at one time British Consul for the Congo) was writing about Belgian atrocities, real or supposed. At that very time Mr George Eduard Pierre Achille Morel de Ville (laughter) began to publish books dealing with the same subject.

What his object was I do not know. It might have been very humanitarian, but the one thing that attracted my attention was that at the very same time there was going on an intensive German propaganda which had as its object the purpose of showing that Belgium was utterly unfit to administer the Congo. There is no-one listening to me now who is not aware since the German invasion of Belgium that had that invasion succeeded the first result in the wider world of German victory would have been German appropriation of the Belgian Congo. (Applause)

"In July 1914 George Eduard Pierre Achille Morel de Ville (diminished laughter) was a Liberal candidate for Birkenhead. When the war came the Liberals in Birkenhead looked at him, his record, his speeches, and they cast him out. They said–'The Liberals of Birkenhead are true and loyal Englishmen and they want none of you.' (Applause) Mr George Eduard Pierre Achille Morel de Ville–(some laughter, but many now joined in an embarrassed silence)–finding that the Liberal party in this country had no use for a man of that class, has now become a Socialist.

"I have not the slightest doubt that when the result of the Dundee elections puts him where he ought to be put he will come out at the next election as a Communist.

"Mr Morel, like Mr Gallacher, in the course of the war was put in jail. He was put in jail because he was impeding the success of British arms and undermining the attempt which at the supreme crisis was Great Britain's very existence.

"What is quite certain about both of them is that if any great crisis comes at which those who believe in Britain are wanted, Mr Gallacher and Mr George Eduard Pierre Achille Morel de Ville would both be in jail. That is not much good to Dundee. And you do not want a Member of Parliament who will be in jail."

Birkenhead's intervention wrought on Winston's cause incalculable damage. Clementine, angry and embarrassed after the speech remarked coldly, "He was no use at all, he was drunk." The Dundee "Courier" editorial condemning it said: "These Coalition apologists have remarkable affrontery . . . The electors know how to apportion the responsibilities." And the correspondence of both Dundee newspapers revealed a considerable number of well-wishers willing to set pen to paper in Morel's defence.

A past master himself in the art of publicity Morel required little assistance. Knowing that Winston would now definitely speak before an invited audience on Saturday afternoon, 11th November, he timed a speech on the evening before which was carefully calculated to dampen the powder of the 'big gun.' Birkenhead's speech he dismissed as "A third-rate music hall performance . . .

inspired by the unbalanced and violent individual (Winston) who will no doubt refute it when he speaks tomorrow, and who is filled with a fury of resentment at being opposed in his stronghold by a man who is determined to expose the ineptitude of his policy and the monstrous usurpations of public right of which he has been guilty—I am a man who cares nothing for his diatribe. I have endeavoured to fight in Dundee a clean fight on public issues and not an unclean one on personality.''

Most informed observers in fact agreed that so far, the tactics of Winston, his wife and his friends had been almost wholly counterproductive and had merely had the effect of increasing the momentum of Morel's campaign. One factor emerged for Winston on the credit side though and that was that public interest in the other candidates—with the exception of Scrymgeour who possessed his own band of faithfuls—had diminished. True, meetings addressed by Pilkington and Gallacher remained well attended but this was due more to their natural ability as entertainers than any public ardour for their respective causes. Pilkington's ready wit, easily sparked off by an interruption, frequently led him from the point, weakened his arguments and gave his speeches an air of levity which their substance hardly deserved. Gallacher on the other hand, by his amiability and absence of true rancour revealed unconsciously, despite the virulence of his language, that there was within his character no trace of the vicious, violent, bloodthirsty revolutionary whom Winston feared. D. J. Macdonald with his at first obsequious and then half-hearted support of Winston, together with his premature retirement from the hustings had gained little credit from friend or foe; the former were too polite and loyal to say anything but the opinion of the latter was summed up by one of Pilkington's supporters who jested: "Mr Macdonald feels highly honoured at being permitted to creep under the Churchill umbrella. (Laughter) It is a case of 'Come under my plaidie; their's room in't for twa.' '' (Laughter)

Accordingly, with three of the candidates fading from the scene Winston's own position strengthened. Quick to appreciate this, Morel tacitly advised his Labour supporters to give their second vote to Scrymgeour despite the fact that Scrymgeour in contrast meanly asked his to "plump" for him. "It seems a pity," said Morel, "to throw away a vote. I have the greatest respect for Mr Scrymgeor, or any man who sticks to his principles, although I might not agree with him." Scrymgeour stubbornly refused to be wooed and taking front page advertisements in the "Courier" and in the "Advertiser" proclaimed, "Use only one of two votes to return Scrymgeour for Dundee."

For Winston this could be an opportunity to grasp. With the Labour vote split three ways and interest in Macdonald and Pilkington diminishing daily, he might, while still holding every right-wing vote, move at the same time cautiously leftwards to capture and hold the middle ground of the electorate. Clementine, with commonsense-wisdom had already written to him: "The idea against you seems to be that you are a 'War Monger', but I'm exhibiting you as a Cherub Peace Maker with little fluffy wings round your chubby face. I think the line is not so much 'Smash the Socialists' as to try with your great abilities to help in finding a solution of the Capital and Labour problem . . . "

Whether or not Winston himself would be sensitive enough to react to these changed circumstances only the morrow would show.

The London and North Eastern Railway night sleeper, its green and black livery streaked with travel, puffed wearily to a halt after its long journey from London and, steaming in the cold air of early morning, halted to discharge its passengers at the Tay Bridge Station.

Winston gazed from one of the windows of his private coach at the dreary yet familiar scene; buff, drab station buildings adorned with pre-war travel posters and shiny enamel advertising signs, and on the platform to welcome him, his wife, his younger brother Jack, ex-soldier and stockbroker, and a small group of his friends and supporters. Assisted by his private nurse and supporting himself with his cane he stepped down to be warmly greeted by Clementine. The pain from the unhealed seven-inch wound in his abdomen made his smile of greeting seem forced. He was forty eight and not for the first time in recent months Winston felt suddenly old.

Too weak to climb the steep flight of steps leading to the street, the party, with Winston in their midst, ascended by goods lift to the upper level where a car was waiting to whisk him the short journey to his suite in the Royal Hotel. For the rest of the morning he would be able to rest, make plans for the remainder of the campaign and gather his energy for the ordeal of addressing the mass meeting in the Caird Hall that afternoon.

It was Armistice Day. And some time after eleven o'clock Winston dressed ready to honour the occasion though remaining within the privacy of his suite. Sombre memories must have come to him as the muffled report of the signal gun from the Dudhope Barracks on the lower slopes of the Law heralded the two minute silence at noon. Ships in the harbour which had been sounding their sirens, the blowing bummers of the mills and factories were suddenly stilled. The electric current died in the overhead cables and the gay green and yellow tramcars stopped as one, drivers, conductors and passengers standing with bared heads. A great throng gathered in the High Street in front of the old Town House where the Lord Provost, Magistrates and Town Councillors were already assembled. Then, as the flags flew at half mast and the town pigeons wheeled agitatedly above, symbolic of troubled peace, the citizens of Dundee remembered the fallen who lay on Flanders field, on windswept Gallipoli and the other far off corners of the earth. A baby's cry and the stifled sobs of several women were the only sounds until the poignant bugle notes of the Last Post broke the stillness. Public grief merged with that of Winston's own recent bereavements, his mother Jenny after the amputation of her leg following an accident last June, and then his daughter just after her third birthday. He had written to Lord Crewe of his little Ducka-dilly, "We have suffered a very heavy and painful loss. It also seems so pitiful that this little life should have been extinguished just when it was so beautiful and so happy—just when it was so beginning."

After lunch—much lighter than he normally would have enjoyed—Winston considered the task before him. Judging from the attacks which had been made upon him that morning in the local Press, it would be a formidable one. There were a more than usual number of criticisms in the "Courier" correspondence columns and on the same page was another in the series of half-page advertisements inserted by Morel and the Labour Party attacking Winston and defending Morel's own personal record by a seemingly endless list of testimonials, from the Archbishop of Canterbury to a Major Clement Atlee, later to become Prime Minister, appropriately entitled in banner headlines "MOREL. CHURCHILL GAS ATTACK." The Dundee "Advertiser" illustrated news of Winston's award of the Companion of Honour by showing a picture of him in shiny top hat and tails—presumably to emphasise his distance from ordinary people—referring disrespectfully to the honour as one of Lloyd George's goodbye gifts. The editorial was bluntly hostile: "We venture to guess that any other of the numerous band of candidates now before Dundee would be more welcome to Bonar Law at Westminster than Mr Churchill . . . We have a strong suspicion that if the engaging Mr Gallacher and the undiscourageable Mr Scrymgeour were placed in a row before him with Mr Churchill and that if Mr Bonar Law was asked to choose the least evil from his own point of view his choice would not fall upon number three . . . Communism and Prohibition are not more than eccentricities and to say so is not to put any slight upon the genial Gallacher with his idealistic dreams of the blood of the bourgeoisie gently flowing in fertilising streams down the gutter; or the pertinacious Neddy whose unswerving tenacity has won its own measure of admiration."

Not content with that invidious comparison the editor went on to discuss the resignation honours list and to note tartly of his Companion of Honour award, "Mr Churchill becomes a C.H. so that he will not be letterless if he ceases by any unhappy accident to be an M.P."

Throughout his life Winston had had to put up with a prejudiced Press, and although up until now he had shown during this campaign more concern with the swing of working class opinion to the Left he was now bound to be worried about the effects these newspaper attacks would have upon not only Liberal but also Tory voters. Still, the Unionist Association had, in the front page of the same edition, published an advertisement advising all Unionists to vote for him and Macdonald. He knew too that he could rely on his own powers of persuasion, he had turned the tables before, and in many a time past hostile audiences had ended up eating out of his hand.

The time approached. Winston pushed aside all distracting doubt and prepared himself for the afternoon meeting. He shrugged on his black melton overcoat held ready for him, set his black homburg hat squarely upon his head and walked slowly from the hotel. His car waited at the pavement beneath the canopy and he and Clementine made themselves comfortable for the short journey to the Caird Hall one block away. Their departure from the hotel went almost unnoticed and, though a large crowd waited at the alternative entrance to the Caird Hall in Castle Street, arriving at the steps leading up from Crichton Street they were again unobserved. Still too weak and ill to surmount that obstacle Winston was transferred onto an improvised litter consisting of a wooden chair supported by two wooden battens and was carried up by four willing helpers into the Caird Hall.

Though already filled to capacity for nearly an hour, many people who possessed tickets had had to be turned away, when Winston appeared the cheering was noticeably restrained. He was assisted onto a rather precarious looking elevated platform above the stage, where, from a chair and desk covered by a Union Jack, provided with a carafe of water and a tumbler, he prepared to deliver his address.

"Ladies and Gentlemen," he began, his voice almost inaudible at first, "I ask your indulgence to speak while remaining seated because I have come suddenly into the atmosphere of the election. I have been following the fight from my bed in London, but one cannot measure and gauge the different feelings and opinions at a distance. I still have two more days in which I will endeavour by the

Winston being carried into the Caird Hall for his speech on the afternoon of 11th November, on an improvised litter consisting of a chair, supported on two battens. When word spread through the watching crowd that each bearer had been paid £1 for his services, shouts rang out with the offer, "Ah'll gie ye twa pund tae drap him."

Winston about to make his Caird Hall speech 11th November, 1922, being introduced by James Robertson, the partially blurred figure on his right, a successful financier and President of the Dundee Liberal Association.

245

strength granted to me, to meet every point and every attack that has been directed against me or those with whom I have worked in the last four years." (Loud cheers)

In glowing sentences Winston then proceeded to review the achievements of the Coalition; the abolition of conscription, success in coping with industrial unrest, restoring British credit and keeping London the financial centre of the world, the expenditure of nearly two hundred million pounds in benefits and relief works to alleviate unemployment, and the creation of the League of Nations. He defended the Coalition's refusal to repay war debts to the United States of America until similar war debts were repaid to Britain, France and Italy and full reparations had been collected from Germany.

Of the Chanak crisis he said: "That is an achievement which to my dying day I will have been proud to have participated in. (Cheers) It is an achievement which, in the face of an unpatriotic attack and abominable calumny such as has never been directed on national matters to any Government before, was gained by a small group of British public men, by a handful of British soldiers, and by the power of the British fleet. (Cheers) Someone will say to me 'Ah! but a risk was run.' Quite true, a risk was run. Risks are run every time the lifeboat goes out in a storm, but such risks never deterred men, aye, and women too, of British blood from doing their duty." (Cheers)

Discussing the Irish Treaty he observed with intuitive longsight: "I rejoice to see steady progress in Ireland. The road will be long, the process will be painful, but it is not for us to interfere. It is the Irishman's business . . . The Irishman has got to conquer himself or perish. Nobody else can do it for him. (Cheers)

"I am sure that the cause for which those Irish patriots, Mr Griffith and Mr Michael Collins, expended their lives keeping their word . . . "

A Mr Peter Swan—interrupting—"How many did they murder Mr Churchill?"

Winston—"Ah! this is no time to add up the catalogue of injury. This is the time to pass the sponge of oblivion, merciful oblivion, across the horrid past." (Hear hear)

Of his uninspiring partner he said, more in hope than confidence, "I do not care a row of buttons whether Mr Macdonald or I am at the head of the poll. I care only for the great political issue which is involved in the decision which the elector has to take. Every friend of mine, should be a friend of his." (Cheers)

Then Winston turned from platitudinous self-justification to an attack on his opponents, though this time his less virulent terminology proved he had heeded Clementine's advice—though only for the time being.

"We are opposed by two Socialist candidates, one of whom is a violent Communist. The other—

A Voice—'Be careful'

—a Socialist candidate who professes to act by constitutional means, and certainly he is a man of intellectual eminence and distinction. (Some cheers) This is a combat and issue which should be settled on broad grounds of principle; but one is entitled to show exactly the position and character of the different candidates in the field, and I say that both of these candidates, although they disown each other, or one disowns the other, did their best to prevent us from emerging victoriously and even safely from the terrors of the war. No doubt they did their best on conscientious grounds and from the most high-minded motives.

"I do not deny, that; I do not challenge that for a moment. If a man faces hardship and imprisonment for his opinions you do not deny him at all the reputation of being conscientious; but if a man is conscientiously bent on my destruction, although I may admire his methods, I resist his actions. (Loud cheers)

"It is in my mind surprising and lamentable that the patriotic self-respecting Trade Unionists who have for so long supported Mr Wilkie should be cajoled and dragooned into voting for these two anti-British gentlemen. (Cheers)

"I cannot understand what at any rate the Labour Party could not have found some solid reputable Trade Unionist identified with the interests of the city and deeply versed in its trade and industry, and who has lived the life of the people, to carry forward their flag. (Cheers) But I beg you not to under-rate the serious character of the attack you will have to meet. Everything goes to show that there will be a very heavy Labour-Socialist vote . . .

A Voice—'Have you got the wind up?'

Winston—"That is a matter which the future alone can prove—(laughter and cheers)—but there is a very good saying—'Never prophesy unless you know.' " (Laughter)

He continued: "In order to win there must be unity and concentration among you, and I hope everyone in the city will think carefully about the folly of throwing away a vote upon a candidate whose chances of success are, to say the least, very remote when that vote thrown away might influence in an adverse sense the main decision which is being fought out. Every vote given to Mr Pilkington—a very able candidate, who has made excellent speeches, and who I wish I could have followed round, but I have had to give that a miss—(Laughter)—every vote given to Mr Pilkington, no matter how well meaning the motives, is a vote given to Mr Morel.

"As for Mr Scrymgeour," and Winston paused, timing his punch phrase, "he, like the poor, is always with us. (Laughter) I admire his persistency and his fidelity to the principle which he advocates; still, a vote given to him, apart from being a testimony to the views which he holds and the opinions which he has championed for these many years, is a vote which I do not think will have any direct bearing on the great issues fought out in Dundee."

Miss "Aly May" Scrymgeour, Scrymgeour's young niece, seated in the left gallery, fumed silently at Winston's patronising words. Clementine directed Winston's attention to the fact that Scrymgeour himself was a member of the audience and Winston smiled broadly but said nothing further on the subject.

"Ah! Ladies and Gentlemen," Winston concluded, rising painfully to his feet, but his voice strong enough to thunder forth, his well-worn cliches, "Let us stand together—(cheers)—let us be united, let us tread the sober middle way amid the confusion and perplexity of the present time. Let us send forth from Dundee and the whole of Great Britain to the whole world a message of strength and conviction, of encouragement and valour, a message which will resound far beyond the limits of this small island and carry good cheer to the suffering, struggling, baffled, tortured humanity the wide world o'er." (Loud cheers)

A number of questions were then put to him but the flippancy of their general tone must have come as a disappointment, especially after all that Winston had heard from his wife and friends of the interrogatory roastings they had received. He could nevertheless feel satisfied that he had spoken for an hour and a half, had been able to marshal all his arguments without interruption and might expect to have his speech reported verbatim in Monday's newspapers. So, after being accorded a unanimous vote of confidence, Winston was helped down onto the main stage amidst enthusiastic applause, while the large crowd waiting outside greeted him and Clementine with waves and smiles.

On Sunday the Caird Hall was again in use, this time for a British Legion Service of Remembrance. Again it was packed out and the platform party included Pilkington, Morel and Scrymgeour, with Winston wearing all of his eleven medals on the breast of his overcoat. Two of the candidates were absent, D. J. Macdonald was still ill and Gallacher had no time for such bourgeous ceremonials. A request had been put to the audience prior to the arrival of the V.I.P.'s that no political demonstrations should be made, and after The Salvation Army band had led the parade the Rev. G. Kirkland

On his way to the Armistice Service held in the Caird Hall on Sunday 12th November, 1922. Winston displaying his military and civil decorations is helped up the Crichton Street steps by his private detective Sergeant Thomson. Mrs Churchill wearing a broad-brimmed hat is just behind him.

249

Cameron in his address urged the ex-servicemen to "make use of their votes . . . in making this a happier and better Britain." A Mr J. K. Robertson sang with great feeling the solo "My Task", and the service ended with the singing of the National Anthem and a two minute silence followed by the *Last Post,* sounded as on Armistice Day by Sgt. Cameron of the Black Watch. All had been observed with suitable decorum.

But in the Caird Hall that evening Scrymgeour shattered the brief truce with an election bombshell. Attacking Winston's speech on Saturday he said:

"If it had not been a breach of political etiquette I would have answered Mr Churchill's references to me there and then. I could have told Mr Churchill a fact that would have surprised him."

Scrymgeour then proceeded to tell his audience, now agog with curiosity, how he had been summoned by James Robertson, President of the Dundee Liberal Association, to come immediately to his office. Amazed, but prepared nevertheless to comply with Robertson's strange request, Scrymgeour went along, observing wryly to his supporters, who were soon rocking with laughter as he told his story: "I could not understand why I had been asked there, the Jews having no dealings with the Samaritans."!

Without any attempt at subtlety and as soon as Scrymgeour had sat down Robertson broached the subject, asking: "What are you going to do about your second vote?"

With equal baldness Scrymgeour had replied: "I am fighting for my own hand."

With just a trace of asperity Robertson patiently pursued his point: "You know that the electors have two votes?"

In droll fashion Scrymgeour replied: "Yes, I believe they do." (Laughter)

"Well," wheedled Robertson, "could you not come along and recommend that something be done our way?"

"Certainly not Sir," Scrymgeour replied hotly, in righteous indignation, "Do you suppose I have been working in this job for years, and treated as though I have been of no account to anybody, and nobody putting in a single word against this? Do you think after all these struggles I am going to take up a line such as you infer? It would simply kill Scrymgeour. Never in this world!"

With that off his chest and Robertson remaining speechless, Scrymgeour asked with beguiling concern: "But how are you doing among yourselves?—and how about Mr Macdonald."

Stunned first by his guest's vehemence and now lulled by his apparent solicitude Robertson answered unguardedly: "He (Macdonald) is away on his own. We've told him there is only one way of getting in, and that is along with Mr Churchill."

A Dundee hackney carriage: It was while standing precariously on the "dicky" seat of one of these in the pouring rain that Clementine stoutly defended her husband's political record during the Wartime elections of 1917. Taken looking east up the Nethergate, the Mercat Cross and City Churches stand on the left while the building on the right is the Royal Hotel where Winston sometimes stayed during elections.

251

"How is Mr Churchill to get in?" Scrymgeour insinuated, "And where are you?" (Laughter)

Robertson replied, betrayed into total frankness: "Well, to tell you the truth, I am not very sure where we are."

Scrymgeour's charges were of course denied but Robertson's explanation lacked credibility.

Morel too answered Winston's Saturday speech the same evening in the Independent Labour Party Hall in the Overgate, remarking, somewhat prematurely, to his large audience, "I am glad that personality has come to an end. There was a great change in Mr Churchill's speech. (Applause) That is satisfactory, but indicates rather a change of intellectual conviction than a change of heart. We are now going to fight on a broad basis. But I am glad Mr Churchill is able to be here, and I wish he had been in Dundee from the beginning. In all sincerity I hope that Mr Churchill, by entering the campaign, will not perpanently injure his health." (Applause)

Even the Dundee papers appeared to have been mollified for on Monday morning Winston must have noted with surprise that as well as reporting his Saturday speech in detail neither the "Courier" nor the "Advertiser" made any editorial comment upon it at all. Indeed, the "Courier's" political correspondent seemed merely happily intrigued that Winston himself had now entered the fray, writing generously: " . . . undoubtedly Mr Churchill's stock has appreciated since his arrival in the city yesterday morning. His presence has emboldened his supporters almost to emulate the supreme assurance of even the Labour Party enthusiasts who will have you believe the return of Mr Morel is beyond doubt. While Mr Churchill was 'still' absent, his candidature lacked the dynamic of his wonderful personality, and whatever his political opinions may be, the average Scotsman is an admirer of courage. Mr Churchill's courage in the face of a severe physical handicap has made an impression."

Nevertheless, for Winston, the suspicion must have still remained strong that Mr Thomson was reserving the adverse opinion of his newspapers for the following day when he could detonate them with maximum effect on the eve of the poll.

On Monday afternoon Winston spoke to an all-female audience at the Y.M.C.A. Hall. The meeting was so packed out that more than half an hour before it commenced some of the audience actually found themselves wedged by the crush back out onto the street again. On going in Winston and Clementine were hissed and booed by Gallacher's banner-waving pickets.

Explaining in his opening remarks how he was unable to stand for any longer than a few minutes at a time, Winston remained seated throughout. "I want to make it perfectly plain" he said, "that although Mr Macdonald and I are now conducting what is called a joint candidature, we nevertheless are indissoluble in political opinion. If I have any friend who is going to give me a vote in Dundee—and here and there you will find one—(laughter)—I hope you will not fail to give the second vote to my friend Mr Macdonald. (A Voice—'Mr Scrymgeour')

"I have been reading the address of Mr Morel, who is the Socialist candidate, the official candidate of the Labour Party. It is a very well written address and it is a very moderate address. There is nothing in the address which would lead you to suppose that Mr Morel is one of the most extreme and advanced and revolutionary political agitators in Europe.

"In his address Mr Morel makes three points. I am sure I am not describing it unfairly . . . First Mr Morel says that all this misery is due to the Coalition Government.

'Who makes the quartern loaf leaven and rise?'
'Who fills the butcher's shop with big blue flies?'
—The Government. (Laughter) Everybody puts it down to the Government. I am quite glad I am not in the Government. I remember people who were always very ready to put things down to me. When I was at the Admiralty during the war whenever a ship went down I had sunk it, unless it was a German ship; then it was the great Admiralty. (Laughter) They are always ready to put everything on to the Government, and as far as possible onto your humble servant. (Laughter)

"The second theme on which Mr Morel expatiates is that all will be put right if only the Socialists and the Labour Party are allowed to come into power." (Hear, hear—from the gallery)

Winston jibed—"There is nothing like hope. Hope, brothers, hope." (Laughter)

A woman's voice—'You are a hopeless case.' (Laughter)

Winston—"One may be hopeful and yet remain silent. (Cheers) One has the consolation that one can afford to wait until Wednesday. (Cheers)

"Why should it be supposed," he continued, brandishing the same anti-Socialist stick he had used in Dundee before the war, "that all the evils which exist in the country and in every other country can be put right by applying the doctrines of Socialism to our affairs? Socialism means that instead of having the present employers you will have a disagreeable set of men who would be appointed by the Government of the day and who will not care a row of buttons whether they give satisfaction to the people they order about or not.

"I have changed my views on the subject of nationalisation by experience. The result of state control of the railways has been that everybody was discontented. The railway service has improved enormously since it has gone back to the management of the various companies."

Winston had also changed his views on the subject of War Profits, seemingly forgetting his own recent Cabinet arguments in favour of virtual confiscation. Now disparaging the Labour Party's very similar plans he demonstrated the continual erosion of his radicalism and, incidentally, his simplistic concept of Economics.

"One of Labour's remedies is called the Capital Levy, it sounds so very attractive. The greater part of the people in this country do not possess any large share of capital, and so they do not object to taking some from those who do.

"But let us see what would happen in a Capital Levy were instituted by the Labour Party; it would mean they would say to every person with capital, 'You must give up a fifth of your capital.' What is capital? It is not gold or paper notes; it consists of houses, fields, the crops that are growing, the railways, the harbours, businesses, the goodwill of business, factories, and everything connected with them. If they took a fifth away, what would happen? Everybody would have to sell a fifth of their property, and if everybody had to sell at once, and there was nothing to buy, then everything would fall in value.

"One might be suffering, but one should not do foolish things to exaggerate the suffering. Russia, the great fertile agricultural country, one of the greatest granaries in the world, in two or three years of Socialism and Communism has been reduced to starvation." (Cries of 'Through the blockade')

Winston—"That just shows the dangers of learning only half the lesson. (Loud cheers) I said that Russia was one of the greatest granaries in the world. How, then, would the blockade make a famine there? The only effect of the blockade would be to shut in the food!

"The first thing that must be practised in public and in private life is economy . . . I have no wonderful secret to tell you. Hard and efficient work is the essential element in the recovery of our position. Meanwhile you must consider what can be done to meet the case of your unemployed fellow citizens. I was the original author of the Unemployment Insurance Scheme. (Applause) No-one can doubt that it has become an essential part of the life of this country.

"I believe that we should consider the starting of some great enterprises which will decrease unemployment. There are some great schemes of electric power, canals, etcetera, which I certainly think the Government should examine. Then we might find methods of stimulating the normal industries of the country. Far more than all that, I believe that one of the great remedies is to develop our own Empire. (Applause)

"Above all," Winston concluded, "do not let us despair. Do not let us throw up the sponge in lethargy or despair. If we hold together firmly, if we set our hands to the plough, if we follow the furrows staunchly and steadfastly the day will come when you will see better conditions established and a brighter age dawning for Britain, when you will see the fruits of the victory gathered in and the great cause for which our sons and brothers gave their lives carried to maturity." (Loud cheers)

When questions were invited, one of the hecklers in the gallery shouted:

'What about the men in the Caird Hall on Saturday? He's only talking to a puckle women. He knows there's not much in them.' (Laughter and uproar)

"That's not a question," ruled the Chairman.

Voice from the Gallery – 'Can you solve the problem of unemployment?'

Winston – "Well, I have been talking about nothing else." (Laughter)

Replying to a series of questions from Monsignor Turner, put on behalf of the Catholic community of Dundee, Winston said he was in favour of the maintenance of Catholic schools, adding in reference to the Irish Free State, "I wish it in your and their name all good fortune." (Cheers)

A woman – 'My vote depends on Mr Churchill's reply. What position does he take in regard to the reduction of pensions paid to the officials in high places, for example the Lord chancellor?' (Birkenhead)

Winston – "The Lord Chancellor gets a pension of £5,000 (shouts of 'too much') – Wait a minute, how much would he earn if he were allowed to go back to his trade? He could earn three times as much when pleading in the Law Courts but it is thought best in the public interests that the man who has been at the head of all the judges should not go back and plead in the Courts. If we don't allow a man to make a better living for himself we must give him compensation."

He then left to address an overflow meeting where after a brief speech which was interrupted by a group of women trying to sing a parody of "Oh Winnie" Winston handed over to D. J. Macdonald, now somewhat recovered from his cold.

"A great many people," Macdonald announced, making once more what had now become a habitual faux pas in regard to his relationship with Winston, "told me to drop Mr Churchill and I

255

would get their vote. If I dropped Mr Churchill against my convictions and in order to get their votes I would not be worthy of support!"

As Winston and Clementine were returning to the Hotel a young woman demonstrator threw a bundle of papers through the open window of their car. She was inmmediately placed under arrest and taken to the central police station but was later released without charge.

In the early part of the evening, speaking to ex-servicemen in the British Legion Hall in the Nethergate, Winston declared: "I put the ex-serviceman first, you can look to me as your friend and I will stand up for your legitimate rights and no-one will put me down if any of you give me your case."

Referring to Morel and Gallacher he said: "You know which side my two Socialist opponents were on in the war. It was not on our side. The Black Watch were on one side and the 'Black Guard' on the other. (Laughter) There are a certain number of intellectual people, very brainy, frightfully high-minded, who can never think of anything so humble as their own country. It is a great mistake for people to think they can skip the love of their country and support every other country and go on with vague dreams of the brotherhood of mankind." Then, discussing the attitude he would adopt in Parliament if he was re-elected: "I am for full liberty in the next Parliament in regard to the new Government. It might be a very good Government, if it is, I will support it. It might be a standstill Government. If it is, I will give it a good poke. (Laughter) It might be a reactionary Government, in which case, I will endeavour to have it dismissed from power."

At question time a burly ex-navyman with a grievance jumped up. 'In 1914 on joining the navy I was personally charged with the issue of a suit of clothes in Chatham Depot. I wrote to Mr Churchill, but my letter was ignored, and an effort was then made to incriminate me in a Court Martial for having written to Mr Churchill without permission.'

Winston–"That is the first I have heard of it."

'It cannot be,' shouted the sailor in a loud voice, 'and when you came aboard the Arethusa I asked permission to speak to you, but I was not allowed.'

"That was not my fault," Winston smiled.

At this point Captain Cumming, the Chairman intervened and pointed out that in the early stage of the war it could not be expected that the First Lord of the Admiralty would be called upon to deal personally with the suit of clothes of every individual.

The aggrieved matelot would not be placated however and cried out to Winston:

'Why did you try to incriminate me into a Court Martial?'
Winston – "Never; I never heard a word about it. Good lord we had thousands of ships at sea and a quarter of a million men."
'All right, get out of it that way.'
Winston, exasperated, – "How can I be answerable for all the administration of the Ministry?"

This outburst however was to be only the mildest foretaste of what was awaiting Winston a few minutes later in the Drill Hall at 8 p.m.

His first open meeting and well advertised in advance, Winston's appearance at the Drill Hall was bound to be of extraordinary interest to all those many working men who had until now been unable to hear him.

A queue had already formed at 5.30 and by 7 o'clock it had divided and grown into two solid columns of people stretching west and east for half a mile. Bell Street itself, outside the Drill Hall Square, was one seething mass and so great became the crush at the locked iron gates entering the Square and so threatening the demeanour of a certain portion of the crowd, that the police, fearing a break-in, drew their batons. When the gates finally opened the flood of people poured across the Square into the Hall and filled the standing room in a moment. Thousands were left outside in the street unable to gain admission.

The fortunate few who possessed admission tickets were accommodated in seats around the platform and behind them the excited throng of around 6,000 in the standing part of the Hall were packed like herrings in a barrel.

Eight o'clock came and Winston had still not arrived. 'Why the devil don't you get this show started?' came a raucous voice from the back of the Hall. 'Send for Morel', sallied another and was greeted with cheers.

Outside with every moment the crowd in Bell Street continued to grow. The pressure increased on one of the gates leading to the Drill Square padlocked again after the first onrush. It burst open and the crowd streamed towards the Hall. They were met by the line of police wielding their long night-sticks and the human wave broke and receded leaving several injured lying on the ground.

To make his way by car through that multitude would obviously have been dangerous, if not impossible, and Winston with his bearers surreptitiously entered the Hall from the rear. The platform party already assembled included Lord Wodehouse, J. W. Pratt, Brigadier General Spiers, M.P., J. C. Robertson, G. K. Smith and Professor Steggle of Dundee University College. Carried forward on his litter, and accompanied by Clementine, Winston was assisted towards the platform. Supporters cheered and the few ladies at the front waved handkerchiefs. But there was also in the huge audience, most of whom had come to be entertained, a determinedly significant faction who had come to wreck Winston's speech, and they were equally demonstrative. Many years later the memory of the occasion was still fresh in Winston's mind:

"I felt desperately weak and ill. As I was carried through the yelling crowd of Socialists . . . I was struck by the looks of passionate hatred on the faces of some of the younger men and women. Indeed but for my helpless condition I am sure they would have attacked me."

As cheers for Winston died away, louder cheers were raised to shouts of "Morel! Gallacher! Scrymgeour!"

A bouquet of flowers for Clementine was carried into the hall by Sir Charles Barrie, M.P., for Banffshire, who was to speak after Winston.

Cheers and boos broke out afresh as Winston was hoisted on to a table in a similar arrangement to the Caird Hall and beaming he waved to the audience.

The Chairman's voice could scarcely be heard as a section of the swaying crowd sang "Tell me the old old story" followed by "Three Cheers." After three minutes and appealing for fair play he managed to read out a telegram from Lloyd George to Winston saying: "You and your colleague Mr D. J. Macdonald, have my very sincere wishes for a brilliant victory in your fight for moderate councils and steady progress."

Amid a fusilade of cries Winston stood to open his address and, the ticket-holding seated part of the audience stood up with him cheering wildly while from the mass at the rear of the hall came cries of "The hero of Sidney Street", "What about Morel?", Mesopotamia", "Vote for Scrymgeour", and "Good old Gallacher."

During a partial lull, only after a considerable time had elapsed, Winston managed to begin.
"Ladies and Gentlemen . . .
'Shut up!' (in chorus)
"I ask your permission to address you sitting down . . .
(Cheers) 'Give him a hearing!' (Uproar)
"I haven't had much opportunity of prosecuting . . .
'Put a sock in it.'
"You might give me fair play . . .
'You'll get what you got in Manchester this time.' (Uproar!)
"I haven't had much opportunity of prosecuting my campaign in Dundee . . .
'Get on your feet.' (Loyalist cries of 'Shame')

"A lot of people have been criticising me and whether I deserve it or not, I have a right to make my answer. (Cheers) No man is judged unheard in Britain—(cheers)—and now that the election has been in progress for nearly three weeks, and I was only able to come here last Saturday and this is only the second great meeting I have had a chance to address. As the poll is on Wednesday . . .

'Oh! You won't get in.' (Uproar)

"If I am to be at the bottom why should you not let me have my last dying kick. (Laughter and cheers) I say I have only had three days in which to state my case to the electors of Dundee. Now it is perfectly clear that . . . (unintelligible interruptions)

Shouts of 'Let the man speak.' (Cheers!)

"when many of you I fear . . .

'You are a political failure.' (Laughter)

"are very uncomfortable and crowded together, it is perfectly clear that we canot conduct a public meeting—(interruptions)—unless everyone looks after one . . .

'Be serious.' (Laughter)

"If they do we can have an important political discussion, and if they don't, we can have a bear garden. (Uproar)

"Let me point out that my interests are not really affected in the matter. Supposing that you so disturb the meeting that I cannot make my speech, what happens is that I am able to go home to bed . . .

'Go away.'

"without having to argue a lot of political questions to my constituents or answer a lot of difficult questions to those who have a right to put them. But it matters a great deal to you, because democracy in our country operates through great public meetings, and the power to conduct great public meetings in a peaceful and orderly manner, and in a way which causes arguments to prevail, and not clamour, which raises reason on a pedestal, and leaves the whole question of the Government of this country to be fairly and freely discussed by the citizens of the country. All that is of the utmost value to you.

"Free speech is one of the greatest assets of democracy. I do not suppose it makes a great deal of difference to an individual candidate whether he is able to conduct an orderly meeting or if he is not given a hearing. I don't think so. I think he gets as much sympathy when not allowed to put his views as he would get if he put the best arguments at his disposal forward. (Cheers and discord) You see, I am not to go on longer than you will give me, I will stop anytime you feel you want me to . . .

'The time's up now!' (Laughter!) (Cheers!)

"But this I do say, as a matter of fair bargain, if you are going to let me speak at all you must let me say whatever I choose. I am not to be muzzled—to be told that I must not attack this man or that man, and that I must not say anything against this or that candidate . . .
'Get on with your speech.' (Applause)
"Not at all. If anybody has got a shrewd rejoinder to make let them make it, but let us at any rate survey broadly the situation.

"I have been severely criticised in the "Dundee Advertiser" and my complaint is that a Liberal and Conservative newspaper are produced in the same building, and owned by the same man . . . (Cries of 'Thomson')
"It is humbug for the same man to run a Conservative newspaper and a Liberal newspaper from the same office on the same day."
(Pandemonium! absolute)

Undaunted by the challenging cries from a thousand throats Winston repeated the statement.
"It is humbug for the same man to run a Conservative newspaper and a Liberal newspaper from the same office on the same day.

"What would the Labour Party say if a Tory and a Labour newspaper were run from the same office on the same day?"
(Tumult! sustained)

Winston sat back in his raised chair for a time, apparently calm and imperturbable though striving hard to catch some among the hundreds of jibes and questions hurled at the platform from all parts of the hall. It was hopeless. He waited while the row continued then suddenly Winston forgot he was an invalid. His eyes flashed, anger swelled in his throat and he shouted back:
"I am not going to attempt to put an argument before you unless I am listened to in silence."
Cat calls. 'What about the Dardanelles?" (Continued uproar)
"If about a hundred young men and women in the audience choose to spoil the whole meeting, and *if about a hundred of these young reptiles*—(Cheers and uproar)—choose to deny democracy to the masses of the people, the power to conduct great assemblies, the fault is with them, the blame is with them, and the punishment will be administered to them by the electors." A great crash of cheering greeted this indictment of the wreckers showing that if Winston had not exactly won the sympathy of the majority of his audience, he had at least marshalled their impatience against the disrupters of their evening's entertainment. Encouraged, he proceeded:
"Now you see what the Gallacher crowd are worth—(Pandemonium)—now you see the liberty you would have if the country were run by them. (Cheers and boos)
"Ah!—'boo'," Winston sneered, "no sense no brain—(uproar)—

just break up the meeting, – ('boo!') – that they would not have the wit to address. (Cheers) The electors will know how to deal with a Party whose only weapon is idiotic clamour."

(Cheers! 'Speak the truth.' Pandemonium!)

A Voice above the uproar – 'Was Miss Maloney a reptile when she interrupted a meeting? Now she has got a vote, is she still a reptile?'

(Loud cheers from the centre of the hall)

A man in a front seat rose and shouted to the interruptor, 'Put a sock in it.'

'Baby starver,' a reference to the sanctions against Soviet Russia, was a dominating accusation among a shower of interruptions directed against Winston.

Again he made an attempt to get a hearing:

"I have addressed public meetings for 25 years and I never remember having addressed one which was not willing to listen to political argument."

'Look what you have done for the ex-servicemen.'

"Perhaps you would like to hear some other speaker for the time being, in which case I will be glad to give way. I am quite willing to listen to some other speaker."

(Interruptions lasting five minutes)

A Voice – 'What about your promises at the last election – of happy homes, and the present contrasts of the dole and queues at the Parish Council?' (Cheers)

Winston waited patiently, made an expression of resignation and lent back in his chair with the remark, "I can wait." (Loud laughter and cries of 'Boo'.) "They will soon get tired," he observed in an aside to the Chairman.

'Send him home.'

"Ask them if they would like to ask questions. Obviously they don't want to hear a speech."

The Chairman, after succeeding in making his voice heard said, "You have complained that Mr Churchill would not address an open meeting and that admission was by ticket only. Here we have an open meeting, and what chance have you given Mr Churchill to speak. If you wish to put questions first, Mr Churchill is prepared to answer."

A Voice, 'We will have questions first.'

A dozen questioners fired simultaneously and the Chairman had considerable difficulty in persuading them to speak one at a time.

Question – 'Is Mr Churchill in favour of economy? If so, can he give the public any idea why £76,000 is being spent on eighteen persons in the Government at the present time while a working man has £2 per week?'

Winston-"The salaries of Ministers have been established for many, many years, and if you wish to change that, that is a matter for the new Parliament. I am quite disinterested in the matter, because I am no longer a Minister and no longer draw salary."

Question-'Are you in favour of the working man now unemployed paying for stamps to put on his Health Insurance cards to entitle him to draw sick benefit in case he needs it?'

Winston-"The working of these Insurance Acts has been most elaborately worked out, and in my opinion it would be rash for me to say I would upset the system which is interwoven, one part with the other, at this moment. I did not know that that had been a great grievance."

A man came forward and perched himself on the edge of the platform. Amid cries from the ticket holders in the front seats to take his hat off he turned sideways to Winston and asked truculently: "Weren't you one of the British Cabinet whom Lord Robert Cecil accused of giving a free hand to the Black and Tans in Ireland to beat the men and women and children down?"

Winston paused for a moment, evidently caught off his guard and having to think out his answer.

A Voice-'Come away, answer.'

Winston-"Are you going to listen to the question and not the answer? That really would not be up to the mark, would it, in Dundee? (Shouts of 'Answer') I say that when our soldiers and our policemen were shot down and murdered we had the right to strike back to defend ourselves."

(Cheers! Cries of 'Murderer.')

The man on the platform asked again, "Did the people in Ireland in 1918 vote constitutionally for freedom?"

Winston-"Haven't they got it now?"

'No!'

One questioner who had been foremost among the hecklers continued to make several attempts to have himself heard above the racket but all that reached Winston's ears was-'Are you in favour of . . .'

Winston (sarcastically)-"Give him a chance. I appeal to you; give him a look in. Don't shout him down. He is one of our little tin Socialists. Give him a chance. Let him have his go. Go on, my lad, speak up. Fair play, don't tread on him." (Laughter)

The heckler-'Are you in favour of a new Government upholding the Balfour Declaration of 1918 (the promise made by the British Government to the Zionists for a national home for the Jews in Paelstine) or do you suggest that pledge be broken?'

Winston-"I am strongly in favour of holding that Declaration." (Cheers)

All that could be heard of the next question was ' . . . we got medals for fighting. You got them for running away.'

Questions were now being shouted from all over the hall and became reduced inevitably into an incomprehensible medley of discord. The audience now degenerated into what could only be described as a howling mob. While the hecklers kept up their chorus, even those who had come to support Winston worked themselves into a state of hysterical delight cheering him wildly again and again.

As the moments passed Winston remained quietly seated watching the crowd but as there were no signs of the noise subsiding he eventually rose impatiently from his chair. With his ears ringing with the cacaphony of cheers and derisive boos he stood leaning on his stick and surveyed the heaving mass of hysterical humanity, eyes gleaming and colour mounting in his face. Raising his voice above the din until hoarse with exertion he said:

"Ladies and Gentlemen, I thank you most sincerely for the attempted hearing – (Derisive laughter) – you have given me, and I think you have indicated in a most effective manner the devotion of the Socialist Party to free speech. It has been shown very clearly that a handful of rowdies can break up a great meeting, and can prevent ten times their number from transacting their public busines. (Applause) We may be interrupted here tonight, but we will carry out our purpose at the poll. (Applause) We will not submit to be ruled. (Applause) We will stand up for the rights of British citizens, the rights and liberties of British citizens against the supporters of the Socialist candidates who, if they have their way would reduce – (Uproar) – this great country to the same bear garden to which they have reduced this great meeting." (Applause and boos)

Winston resumed his seat and in reply to several enquiries from the platform party remarked – "No, I am finished." A moment or two later he rose again, waved his hat and bowed repeatedly to all parts of the hall. He turned from his chair and, to the accompaniment of a wilder outburst of derisive shouts from the disorderly element, and cheers and handwaving from his supporters was assisted down from his raised platform. "Goodnight," he shouted with a smile and proceeding slowly on foot escorted by his friends, Winston passed through the agitated crowd towards the back of the main hall and into the smaller hall, the big separating door clanging behind him. It was still only 8.45 p.m. He had been speaking for just overy thirty five minutes.

Winston's entourage was badly shaken by the experience and as the various members relaxed from the ordeal over a champagne supper General Spiers remarked how, "Every time a cork popped we thought it was Winston being shot!'' That night it was insisted that Winston's private detective Sergeant Thomson should sleep across the door of his hotel room.

The following morning, Tuesday November 14th, was the last day of the contest before the poll and reading accounts of his discomfiture in the Drill Hall, Winston was not at all surprised that every reference he had made about the Local Press had been suppressed.

Time and time again Mr David Couper Thomson, the 61 year old tough and stocky owner of the Courier and Advertiser, had pointed out through the medium of his newspapers the one trait in the character of Winston Spencer Churchill which he found most objectionable—his greed for glory. And this was not an unnatural prejudice, though perhaps it might have been thought a little surprising in the case of a journalistic entrepreneur whose very stock-in-trade was news and newsworthiness; but D. C. Thomson himself shunned all forms of publicity and held a profound distaste for those who did. Yet modest as he undoubtedly was D. C. Thomson did share with Winston the possession of an uncompromising and individualised viewpoint upon most topics and these he had no hesitation in disseminating to his readers through the comparative anonymity of his journals.

D. C. Thomson entered the newspaper business in 1886 when his father William became sole proprietor of Charles Alexander & Co., publishers of the "Dundee Courier and Daily Argus" and other publications. The name of the firm then became W. & D. C. Thomson. In 1905 the name was changed again when D. C. Thomson with his two brothers William and Fred and their wives formed John Leng & Co. Ltd. publishers of the Liberal "Dundee Advertiser" and other publications whereby the two companies worked together under joint ownership. As a result of this the associated companies had control of the two morning newspapers, the Evening Telegraph and Post, the Sunday Post, Weekly News, People's Journal, Red Letter, etc., and the venerable Scots Magazine, in print as long ago as the Jacobite Rebellion in 1745".

The dominant member of the partnership, D. C. Thomson, was the first publisher in Britain to see that a whole new readership remained ready to be awakened and he began what was to be a singular business success by indulging the aspirations to respectable womanhood of poor but literate mill-girls who were to thrive on his wholesome and homely formula of romantic fiction, knitting patterns and cookery recipes. Later, under his guiding genius, the venture expanded to include the famous "Dandy" and "Beano"

The Thomson Publications
Combined Circulation
3½ MILLION Copies Weekly

HEAD OFFICE, DUNDEE

The "Courier" Building, Dundee, headquarters of D. C. Thomson's great journalistic empire. From these offices Winston endured more censure over 15 years than most politicians would expect in a lifetime.

265

children's comics, illustrated by that prodigy of the strip cartoon Dudley D. Watkins whose characters Oor Wullie and The Broons record for posterity the social life of an era.

As an employer D. C. Thomson was the easist man in the world to get along with, provided one knew who was boss, and his employees regarded this stubborn strong-willed autocrat with wary and deferential trepidation, allowing him to govern his domain with progressive paternalism, paying them well, providing a very generous superannuation fund and looking after them with genuine concern and solicitation if they fell ill.

A man of integrity, D. C. Thomson had no desire to join the ranks of the aristocracy with an ignobly won title, as all the other newspaper owners in the country at that time seemed passionately determined to do. He was his own man and because of that he was no respecter of rank or influence, especially when anyone challenged his authority. He exercised immense power over Dundee, and he could be an implacable enemy. Even prominent business men being afraid to oppose him in the realisation that they could be subjected to more than indirect pressures. But D. C. Thomson never allowed personal relationships to distort his sense of fair play and justice – he personally detested Scrymgeour's views, but the latter's two brothers both held high editorial posts in his organisation.

He held high principles, and reflecting these, his journals maintained the old-fashioned, peculiarly Scottish, traditional moral values; and unlike Northcliffe, Rothermere and that other disreputable apostle of the popular press shortly to be brought to book, Horatio Bottomley, with his scurrilous John Bull, D. C. Thomson said "No" to sensationalism, sex and violence.

However, although his principles and journalistic professionalism were above reproach, D. C. Thomson's political ideas lagged far behind the times and he cherished for Scottish society a Utopian vision of Arcadian order and sturdy peasant-like self-sufficiency which was unfortunately in obvious contradiction to the conditions of life which most of his fellow countrymen had to endure.

Above all though, D. C. Thomson was a man of independent mind . . . As he was to write of his beliefs to Winston in a letter of recrimination: "*I am not tied to any party or combination nor is any one of my colleagues I consult, and the papers I happen to be responsible for, of course, conform to my ideas. These ideas are perfectly simple, perfectly plain, and perfectly definite, viz: to do the best I can through these newspapers for the people of the country.*"
D. C. Thomson was in fact, in his person, complementary to Jute and Jam, Dundee's third staple.

Over the years D. C. Thomson had made it abundantly plain that he thought Winston Churchill a loud-mouthed, bullying, place-seeking show off. Winston, on the other hand, was about to reveal, with that aristocratic English arrogance, that he thought D. C. Thomson an interfering, resentful, provincial, bourgeois.

As if to signalise the open breach that now yawned between them, D. C. Thomson, for the first time, nailed all the colours of his prejudice to the mast of his Liberal "Advertiser" (his attitude in this paper had hitherto remained ambivalent but not openly antagonistic) and firing another goading broadside into the faltering Churchill battlewagon, wrote, or instructed his Editor to write: "In the case of the Coalition no member has been enraptured of self-admiration more than the attitude of that of Mr Churchill . . . The public is sick of the Coalition, and thinks that its costly administration ranks after the war among its misfortunes . . . A vote for Mr Churchill means as much more Coalition medicine as he can contrive to administer either by the agency of another Coalition Government or by its second best hope (by a Government subject to menace and threat by himself and his friends) . . . " Then, advising the electors to vote for Pilkington and McDonald, concluded: "The Liberal who supports Mr Churchill in the present situation is merely perpetuating the factionism which has sterilised his Party. The Unionist who does so is providing a sinister form of opposition for his own Chief . . . The danger ahead for Mr Bonar Law is *venom from the carcase of the late Coalition which he destroyed.*"

The "Tory" "Courier" ironically spoke in general and in milder terms than the "Advertiser" and although also advising its readers in the strongest terms to vote first for Pilkington then second-best for Macdonald did at least carry a quarter page advertisement saying "Vote for Churchill the Liberal and Anti-Socialist Candidate".

The "Advertiser" significantly carried no similar intimation and this for Winston seemed to have been the last straw. That afternoon he unburdened himself before a gathering of 300 women in the Broughty Ferry Parish Church Hall of all his opinions pertaining to the conduct of the Dundee newspapers. Referring first to the break up of the Drill Hall meeting he said:

"The blood of every free man and free women is aroused by the spectacle of a great meeting of well disposed and orderly citizens being reduced to nullity by the rowdyism of three or four hundred supporters of my rivals, Mr Morel and Mr Gallacher, who tried to substitute ignorant clamour for processes of human argument and reason, and violence and force for fair play and justice. (Applause)

"But," Winston continued, "it is not only the Communist Socialist rag, tag and bobtail which indulges in these tactics. I am sorry to say that Mr Thomson, the proprietor of the Dundee newspapers, has equally set his face against free expression of opinion. Mr Oakley, the Chairman of the Conservative and Unionist Association has just been to me this morning and told me that he wished to put an advertisement which he was willing to pay for in the columns of the Dundee paper giving advice as a Chairman of the Unionist Party, which he has an absolute right to do, to Unionist electors. He wished to put this advertisement in, quoting from Mr Bonar Law, Mr Austen Chamberlain and Lord Balfour, advising them to vote in a certain way and give their support to Mr Macdonald and me, who have received the official support of the Unionist Association, (cries of 'Shame') and this advertisement has simply been blotted out and been refused to be accepted by these newspapers—an almost unheard of episode in the annals of journalism.

"I am very glad to see the Press here, because *I have no doubt that Mr Thomson's papers will boycott every word I have said, and dare not print every word I have to say. I am sure it will only be in keeping with their conduct.* Yet it is still a free country, and words which are spoken by persons speaking in a responsible position are not suffered to be stifled by any organised boycott by the representatives of the Press. (Applause) That brings me to examine, if you will permit me, what are matters of great importance to our social life and social civil liberties. This brings me to examine the very curious positon of the Dundee newspapers. Here you have a spectacle, I think unique in British journalism.

"You have the Liberal and the Conservative newspapers owned by the same man and produced in the same office on the same day. Here is one man, Mr Thomson, selling Liberal opinions with his left hand and Conservative opinions with his right hand at the same moment. That is an extraordinary spectacle. I say that if such conduct was developed in private life or by politicians in public life every man and woman in the country would say, 'That is very double-faced. You cannot believe the two.' It would be said of a politician who made Socialist speeches in Scotland, Conservative speeches in England, and Radical speeches in Wales!—(renewed laughter)—you would say he was downright dishonest, and I am bound to say I think the Press of this country have a tradition to observe and to obey.

"A man who owns a newspaper is not simply selling apples on a stall or peddling goods across a counter, he has got a responsibility . . .

David Couper Thomson, owner of Dundee's "Liberal" Advertiser and "Conservative" Courier. A man whose fearless integrity could not be bought for any price and whose forthright criticism did most over the years to see Winston rejected by the Dundee electorate.

"Here we get in the morning the Liberal Mr Thomson through the columns of the Liberal "Dundee Advertiser" advising the Liberals of Dundee to be careful not to give a vote to Mr Churchill because his Liberalism is not quite orthodox . . . At the same time, the same moment, you have the Conservative, the 'Die-hard' Mr Thomson, through the columns of the Conservative "Dundee Courier" advising the Conservative electors of Dundee to be very careful lest in giving a vote to Mr Churchill they should run the risk of building up opposition to the new Conservative Government; and you get the same man behind these two absolutely differently served dishes, hot or cold, roast or boiled, seasoned or unseasoned, according to taste, and both brought out by the same cook in the same kitchen. (Laughter) Behind these two, I say, *you get the one single individual, a narrow, bitter unreasonable being eaten up with his own conceit, consumed with his own petty arrogance, and pursued from day to day and from year to year by an unrelenting bee in his bonnet."* (Laughter)

Winston then paused and addressing directly the reporters present said:

"Now put that down for the "Dundee Advertiser" and the "Dundee Courier!" (Laughter)

"I have had a couple of years of ceaseless detraction, spiteful, malicious detraction, anything that I have done which has been of advantage to this city, like the smashing of the cattle embargo; anything which has been in accordance with the wishes of my constituents, has been whittled away or crabbed or put in some obscure position unrelated to its importance. While anything that could be made a stick to beat me with, anything that could be worked up because I was a member of the Government and had to be responsible as a member of the Government for what was going on in the country, all that has been aggravated and pushed forward — never have I said a word. I have submitted, but it comes to the day — *it is reaching the point — when a public man has to make a stand against Press lies and Press tyrants.* I do not speak against the papers. They are ably and well conducted, but against the man behind the papers, and he is the man I hold up here in the district where he lives to the reprobation of his fellow citizens. (Applause) I remember well the balmy days of the "Dundee Advertiser", the days of John Leng and Carlo Martin, and it is with sorrow *I have seen the paper dwindling, shrinking, and rotting away in these unsympathetic and ill-intentioned hands, until we have the poor shredded rag which now appears before us.*

"I am sure," Winston concluded, "you will feel I am right to speak here quite frankly on this matter, and even though no doubt the newspapers concerned will not be allowed by their proprietor to record my words, still, they may get about, and this is not the last time I shall deal with the subject now that I have begun upon it."

Having dealt with Mr Thomson, and incidentally revealing the throbbing nerve of his wounded ego, Winston now turned his spleen upon enemy No. 2:

"Mr Morel," he said, "has put forward a testimonial by the Archbishop of Canterbury—fancy a Labour leader, pledged to the abolition of the Church and the pillage of its temporality, coming forward and saying, 'Vote for me. I have got a certificate from the Archbishop of Canterbury.' (Laughter) The certificate was obtained by Mr Morel when he was engaged in exposing the horrors of the Belgian Congo. It was certainly an exposure of an abominable crime. But it coincided with the German propaganda for eventual appropriation of the territory."

Then discussing Morel's wartime activities, and referring to him vindictively as Mr Morality, he continued, "He went as far as he dared—though he did not go as far as Gallacher; he did not go to jail so often. (Laughter) And he was not on our side—the side for which our brave boys gave their blood and lives." (Hear, hear)

He ended on an unworthy note of bigotry, "Before the war I think we were too loose in taking these foreign-minded people into our bosoms. A lot of people are trying to live *on* Britain and pretending they know our interests better than ourselves, when all the time their hearts are not with the struggling, courageous, valiant people of this little island. (Applause) They are all after some wild abstraction of an international Utopia, wherein some day they will have mastery of our affairs. Indeed I think it is very doubtful if any man not British born ought to be returned to the British Parliament." (Applause)

Morel by contrast continued this final day of the campaign as his following continued to gain confident momentum, to deal fair measure for foul. His huge audience gathered in the Caird Hall gave him a deafening reception, many of the audience rising to their feet in their enthusiasm and speaking hoarsely, likening his voice to a "wretched old raven" said:

"The fight has been instructive, five of the six candidates have fought on their programme, the sixth has concentrated on personalities, directed largely against me. I am glad that Mr Churchill has so far recovered from his illness to be able to participate in his own defence, but I cannot congratulate Mr Churchill on his methods or upon those of his friends.

"From the time of the 1st Duke of Marlborough the Churchills have always put self-interest first, their record is a record of courage certainly. It is also a record of violence and of the tramping upon the rights of the people. They have fought for domination and for themselves.

"My ancestors," continued Morel, "also fought. They fought to free the Netherlands from Philip of Spain, for freedom of conscience in Britain, and scattered along the east coast of England from Norwich to Colchester are the graves of my Quaker forebears, who fought in the cause of human liberty and the British civil rights.

"The hoardings, I observe, are placarded with bills stating that Mr Churchill is indispensable to Dundee. (Laughter)
A Voice – 'He is not.'
"Mr Churchill seems to think he has a hereditary claim to wear one of the 'Bonnets o' Bonnie Dundee.' (Laughter) On what does he found that claim? All his political life he has been a plunger, but he has plunged at other people's expense. Everything he has supported has collapsed. The stones he is constantly pushing uphill always fall down upon the toes of the people below.

"The tragedy of Mr Churchill's life is that he has failed in everything he has undertaken, and always at someone else's expense. The only people Mr Churchill benefits are the people he attacks. (Laughter) Why should he be indispensable to Dundee?"

Scrymgeour's campaign also was moving towards a crescendo and having been criticised for selfishness for telling his supporters to "plump" for him he softened sufficiently now to advise his crowded and enthusiastic audiences that if they *were* going to use their second vote they should cast it in favour of Labour, implying thus that they should vote also for Morel.

Gallacher too had a final word. "Lord Birkenhead," he said, "has remarked that there are wastrels hanging about everywhere. You can't get a greater wastrel than Churchill. He has wasted wealth and started graveyards all over the world. Churchill has referred to me as 'Trotsky without his army,' and that I want to murder him. I will not. I will give him a job. (Laughter)
"That might, of course, amount to the same thing." (Laughter)

Feeling the pressure on, Winston addressed four other meetings himself that day and at each continued to hammer away below the belt at Morel. At his final one in Lochee, a Labour stronhold where thousands failed to gain admission to the hall, Winston made the issue of free speech the main point of his argument:

"I have not had quite fair treatment," he complained, "during the three days I have been in the city but I am quite sure that in Lochee I will get a fair hearing. (Cheers and interruptions)
"I did not have fair play last night," he continued.

272

"I wanted very much to talk to 7,000 in the Drill Hall and 6,000 of that 7,000 very much wanted to hear what I had to say. Here, I see, I am going to have an opportunity of discussing public affairs."

Bringing up the subject of Soviet Russia Winston was immediately inundated by prolonged interruptions but retorted briskly, "You will interrupt when I speak of Russia. I expected that . . . "

'Good old Lenin'.

Churchill loyalist in rejoinder—'You will have to work there.'

Winston—"How do we keep ourselves going in this small island?"

'On the buroo.' (Laughter)

'What about the Dardanelles?'

Winston—"I have nothing to fear in discussing the Dardanelles . . . "

A Voice—'It is all over now.'

"All the best opinions of the world today is that if a real effort had been made to force the Dardanelles the war would have come to an end in 1915."

'Why didn't you make the effort?'

Winston—"I did my utmost. (Cheers and groans) No-one disputes or denies that was the way to go. It was my business to point that way and do my utmost." (Cheers and interruptions)

Turning then to the question of Ireland, Winston was met with cries of 'Oh!'

"Don't you like it?" he asked.

'Tell us something more about Scotland.' (Laughter) 'What about Home Rule for Scotland?'

"Do you want Home Rule?" queried Winston, and from all over the hall he was greeted resoundingly with the answer, 'Yes!'

Winston—"Then you'll have Home Rule for England too. (Laughter) Our Experience in England is that the Scots rule us. (Laughter) I see they have just put up another Scottish Prime Minister. (Cheers) You can't have Home Rule for Scotland and a Scottish Prime Minister too. (Laughter) If Scotland wants Home Rule I believe that she has only to ask for it. Nobody would oppose her. I have repeatedly said I am in favour of Scottish Home Rule if Scotland demands it, but Scotland has so far been inclined to think it is better to rule the British Empire." (Laughter)

After answering a series of questions about Mesopotamia and ex-servicemen Winston was addressed by a blind member of the audience who referred to an interview he had had with him on one of his previous visits to Dundee when Winston had promised to get him a pension. "I want to make a strong appeal," said the blind man, "to you, to see that you are going to try to do something for me. You promised me a written statement already and you have given me nothing." (Uproar)

Winston—"It is no doubt due to me that a special tribunal has already been held, and I cannot go behind the decision of the tribunal. However if you will give me a written statement I will go into it; but I do not think that we should take up the time of the meeting."

Uproar! Cries of 'Play the white man.'

Winston—"Write to me."

A Voice—'How can a blind man write?'

Winston, angrily, "What a question to ask. Are you such a selfish man that you would not write for him? I said that if I got particulars of the case I would see what could be done." In an aside to the platform party he added: "It is a very sad case."

In conclusion Winston rallied, "Give your votes tomorrow to Mr Macdonald and me . . . "

Tremendous uproar! Groaning and shouting, 'Good old Morel.'

"Make no mistake about it; we are going to win."

The meeting broke up in noisy disorder and Winston and Clementine returned to their suite in the Royal Hotel.

Polling day Wednesday the 15th of November, as on the Spring morning of Winston's first Dundee election fourteen eventful years before, dawned bright in cheerful sunshine. Winston was awake early and over breakfast in bed reviewed the contents of the morning newspapers. Though he must have had a notion his outburst of the previous day would result in some manifestation from D. C. Thomson it must nevertheless have been with mixed feelings that he saw, for all the world to see, in both the "Courier" and the "Advertiser," not only an almost complete verbatim account of his denunciations of Mr Thomson but also the whole series of private letters which had passed between them over the previous months. Under a headline entitled, "Churchill's Lies Exposed By His Own Letters" and "The Truth About The Dundee Papers" D. C. Thomson revealed all of what was alleged to have been a sordid attempt by Winston to alter the existing bias of the Dundee newspapers in his own favour by first trying to bribe D. C. Thomson with an honour and when that failed to have effect, threatening to set up a rival newspaper in the city through, no doubt, the power and influence of Lloyd George and his friends.

"In view of Mr Churchill's outburst, wrote D. C. Thomson, "on Dundee newspapers the following correspondence is of some interest."

Churchill to Thomson—6.4.22. "I shall be in Dundee until Saturday evening, and I shall be very glad to have the opportunity of meeting with you."

Thomson to Churchill—7.4.22. "I have your note of last night and should be very pleased to have a friendly chat with you here on Saturday morning although I am entirely out of sympathy with the present Coalition . . . "

Thomson to Churchill—20.4.22. "Following on your call I have had several talks with our editors. One and all they emphatically disagree that there has been anything unfair, and, on the contrary, they point out the numerous cases on which they have gone out of their way to favour you.

"Now please do not suppose any of us harbour any resentment because you complained, but it does confirm to us that too many people in London think we are living in the treetops, whereas they are living down a well . . . you remarked none of your colleagues cared what our paper said. That shows your colleagues are keeping you in the dark, for *there have been various emissaries from Coalition sources wanting me to alter our policy and sell myself for Coalition gold so as to end our criticism. But I am not for sale.*

"I have no desire to see you anything else but successful in your further career, but I see little hope as long as you stay with the present crowd in their sinking ship."

Churchill to Thomson—8.5.22. "Thank you for your letter. I am very glad to know that you and your editorial colleagues had no intention of being unfair . . . At the same time, I am sure you will let me say that it is a very serious embarrassment that both the Liberal and Conservative papers in Dundee should be uniformly directed in skilful, consistent, and calculated hostility to the present Government and to the combination of parties which support it . . . *I do not think this Coalition could indefinitely be faced with continued damaging hostility without endeavouring to the best of its ability to defend itself and secure newspaper representation in the various districts of the country which would enable its case to be stated and attacks upon it to be rebutted.* The same is true of me. I have every intention of defending myself with whatever strength and influence I can command . . . I know of no emissaries who were sent to you to suggest you being bought with Coalition gold, and am certain that no person had had any authority to make such a suggestion. If we can work with you in a friendly way we shall be delighted. But if there is nothing for it but to fight we must do our best . . .

"Many thanks for your frank letter, which I have replied to in a similar spirit."

Thomson to Churchill 23.5.22. "I am afraid, besides being kept in the dark by your friends who thought I would be as sordid as themselves and sell myself for Coalition gold, you are also under very great mis-apprehension . . .

"In this last letter of yours there is an unfortunate note of menace. This cannot possibly encourage a feeling of personal friendliness on the part of my colleagues or myself.

"To be quite candid, if you wish to discuss anything with me on friendly lines cut out all this threat nonsense, and let us discuss matters man to man, and from the State and from the point of view of the welfare of the State."

D. C. Thomson—"This last letter was never acknowledged by Mr Churchill."

In his editorial D. C. Thomson was swingeing. Under the headline "MR CHURCHILL WITH HIS CHOLER UP. THE TALE OF A LOST TEMPER", he said:

"Whatever may be his chances at the poll today there can be no doubt that Winston Churchill is in a vile temper. He has taken no pains to conceal the facts, like the disappointed man on the station platform he kicks out at anybody who happens to be near him. For those not within immediate reach he has buckets of calumny. He has sprayed Labour with invective, has sprinkled many doses of it on his rival candidates—Mr Pilkington, Mr Morel, Mr Scrymgeour and Mr Gallacher—and now he has turned the full blast of his vituperations upon the Dundee newspapers. Whose turn it will be tomorrow God only knows . . .

"We would again advise the Dundee electors to give attention to the candidature of Mr Pilkington and Mr Macdonald."

The faithful bands of tireless workers of all six candidates were out early in the field, none more so than those of the Communist and the Prohibitionist. Spaced every fifty yards down the centre of the street tramlines, slogans in favour of Gallacher saying "Don't be silly vote for Willie" and "Willie for Dundee!", were brushed on with an indelible solution of calcium carbide (used then for generating acetylene gas for car headlamps) and whitewash which would still be legible months afterwards. Scrymgeour's supporters were less destructive, chalking on the pavements, "Wallace struck his first blow for liberty in Dundee—let Scrymgeour strike his first blow for liberty on Wednesday." This slogan, with its historical reference to the incident in the 13th century when the young Scottish hero William Wallace stabbed to death the son of the first English Governor, Gallacher mocked mercilessly saying, "Scrymgeour is over sixty years of age—rather late in striking his first blow."

The other party workers quickly caught up, and walls, windows and hoardings were soon plastered with rival posters stridently acclaiming each candidate. Every polling station was picketed and early voters were plagued with pamphlet pushers.

With all the schools closed, gangs of children joined in the fun. Catchphrases such as "Morel, Morel, Morel's the man for me" and "Vote, Vote, Vote for Neddy Scrymgeour" were set to music and yelled lustily through the streets. Many youngsters carried banners, and their hurlies—wooden wheeled carts—were plastered with photographs, mostly of the left wing candidates.

The Downfielder's and the Prohibitionist's pipe bands were at one stage followed by a crowd of several hundred people marching down the Hilltown to the strains of "Bonnie Dundee". By late afternoon and into the evening voting activity increased and it was clear that this would be the heaviest poll ever. The transportation arranged by the candidates kept up the momentum and Gallacher's was the most conspicuous. As each load of supporters were seen off a huge red flag was handed in to the car with great ceremony and on reaching the polling booth the vehicle was met by an ardent party worker bawling through a makeshift megaphone consisting of a large gramophone horn "Vote, vote for Gallacher, the worker's friend." Gallacher himself toured the polling booths and paraded through the streets—with magnificent irony—in a horse drawn landau though it was observed by one humorist that it might have been more appropriate if Gallacher had exchanged conveyances with Winston, who was doing his rounds with Clementine in a motor car painted bright red.

Everyone was in high spirits and all of the ill-feeling which had undoubtedly been generated during the campaign seemed to be dissipated. All day long Winston, and especially Clementine, found themselves waving to cheering crowds. Only once was Winston observed to betray his characteristic "corrugated brow" and then, thought the observer, that was probably because of the pain from his operation. On the other hand if Winston had been superstitious the news that one of his cars had run over and killed a black cat might have caused him a moment's unease.

Between seven and eight o'clock in the evening activity increased and Winston recalled later how "great numbers of very poor women and mill girls streamed to the poll during the last two hours of voting, besieging the polling station in solid queues." Just before nine o'clock almost all activity died away. Instead the excitement now concentrated in the town centre as thousands of people thronged Bank Street outside D. C. Thomson's newspaper offices. A sea of upturned faces craned intently up at the illuminated screen on the wall of the Dundee "Advertiser" upon which, for the first time in the city, the nationwide election results were to be thrown by magic lantern from a window on the opposite side of the street immediately they were received by telegraph.

The first result coming from Wallesey in Cheshire—"Conservative majority, no change"—was screened at ten o'clock. As each result succeeded another, cheers and boos echoed through the crowd. The intervals of waiting between results were whiled away by showing humorous cartoons, views of the countryside and photographs of all the Dundee candidates and the national political leaders. Soon after midnight the results coming in flickered in quick succession and well into the small hours the excited crowd stood spellbound.

Dundee's result however would not be known until after the votes were counted in the morning, and although public speculation was rife the candidates' friends were prepared that evening only to express a cautious optimism on the outcome.

When asked at the Royal Hotel about Winston's prospects, Mr W. H. Buist, the retail house furnisher, said, "I think he is quite safe. It seems there was a tremendous poll, and Mr Churchill is quite sure that the heart of the country is sound and against Socialism, whatever may be the verdict in Dundee."

D. J. Macdonald's spokesman said, "A heavy poll is in our favour."

E. D. Morel said, "I cannot express a personal opinion, but my friends are very optimistic."

Pilkington's spokesman said, "Morel's in, but we are running strongly for second place."

A friend on Scrymgeour's behalf said, "We will be disappointed if we are not well on the top."

"Gallacher has polled well," said his supporters, knowing already he had not done well enough.

At nine o'clock the following morning the scene in the Marryat Hall, a large assembly room attached to the Caird Hall, was a hive of industry. Six long tables were surrounded on all sides by a hundred and twenty enumerators, and oblivious of restless onlookers and a hubbub of noise they tackled first the votes for the elections in the Forfarshire and Montrose Burghs, and after these had been declared, the greater task of counting the votes cast by Dundee.

Winston was the first candidate on the scene and accompanied by Clementine exchanged cheery good mornings with the groups of officials and pressmen standing round the hall doorways. While being filmed by one of the London movie news agencies he informed a prominent Liberal supporter, with a smile, "I am willing to bet 3 to 1 on my chances of success."

D. J. Macdonald, accompanied by his son, also arrived early and soon afterwards Gallacher; followed by Morel and his wife and daughter, Scrymgeour and his wife, and also Pilkington turned up. All of them took some interest in the proceedings and Winston in particular, taking a seat at the end of one of the tables, stayed for some time engrossed in the count.

The enumerators, working in pairs, sorted the voting papers into twenty one receptacles—fifteen for all the possible doubles and six for the "plumpers", or those who had voted for only one of the candidates, and, as the counting progressed, speculation increased as the double vote for Morel and Scrymgeour piled higher and higher.

The Churchill and Macdonald double rose slowly, only a good second.

Morel and Scrymgeour were naturally in great good spirits. Pilkington's poker face betrayed the extent of his expectations. Gallacher accepted the dramatic turn of events like a true philosopher and D. J. Macdonald remained cheerful.

Of them all Winston looked the most perturbed. His face was flushed with the suppressed excitement which was engendered by the possibility of defeat. Though Clementine continued to smile winsomely and did everything possible to keep him in good spirits he became suddenly forlorn.

Shortly after 2 p.m. the count was complete and a dense crowd collected by the waterfront in Dock Street waiting patiently in the dazzling sunshine for the result.

Then, when all seemed settled and the victors were to be declared the enumerators, who had risen to leave, were suddenly recalled to their seats. It had been found that there were apparently nearly one thousand voters too many. There was nothing for it but to examine all the tabulated sheets again when it was discovered that two of these had been entered up twice. That explained the discrepancy of the thousand votes, but at the same time it was found that one pair of enumerators who had received 500 papers had only counted 497! These too now had to be recounted.

Winston was agitated and ill at ease. After chatting briefly with D. J. Macdonald he left the Marryat Hall accompanied by Clementine and at the door leading towards the Caird Hall he left her abruptly to walk slowly down the marble floor of the corridor alone. Wanting for some reason to look into the Caird Hall Winston tried one of the doors, shook it violently, but found that it was locked. A chair was got for him, and puffing at a cigar, sat a solitary figure in the draughty corridor. Occasionally Winston rose restlessly walking over to one of the windows which overlooked the masts of the ships in Earl Grey Dock and to the broad shining waters of the Tay and the hills of Fife beyond. Winston had no eyes for the beauty of the scenery and after surveying briefly and solemnly the patient throng waiting in the street below turned back to his chair again. The recount took three hours and he talked briefly with the uniformed and bemedalled caretaker of the Hall enquiring interestedly about his war service. Clementine remained smiling and beautiful and stood in the corner conversing with friends, calmly awaiting developments.

Finally, at exactly ten minutes past five, after protracted discussions among the Returning Officers, the results were announced.

Winston had already been handed the list. After reading it he returned it without comment and immediately went over to shake hands and cordially congratulate Neddy Scrymgeour. D. J. Macdonald commented generously: "No man worthy of the name of a man will grudge Scrymgeour his victory." Now, as the figures were declared, Winston stood to attention his face flushed and excited yet utterly immobile.

All the candidates proceeded to the floor below, where from the open window the result was made public by Sheriff Malcolm.

Edwin Scrymgeour,   32,578
E. D. Morel,   30,292
D. J. Macdonald,   22,244
The Right Honourable Winston Spencer Churchill,   20,466
R. R. Pilkington,   6,681
William Gallacher,   5,906

Deafening cheers greeted the names Scrymgeour and Morel, and when the Sheriff uttered the words, "I accordingly declare these two duly elected" a full throated roar of approval sprang from the crowd.

Morel and Scrymgeour, accompanied by their wives, mounted the improvised platform as Winston and Clementine—she was weeping now—stood aside out of sight of the crowd along with the other unsuccessful candidates. The appearance of Dundee's new Members of Parliament was a signal for another vociferous outburst of cheering and when it had subsided Scrymgeour, speaking with considerable emotion, said:

"I want to offer my heartfelt thanks to Almighty God for this marvellous result. It is far and away beyond all I could have asked or thought. I want simply to tender to you my undertaking that with God's help it shall be my purpose to serve the masses in accordance with the obligations I have given . . .

Deafening cheers greeted Morel as he also said with emotion:

" . . . May I say how glad I am to think that the British people paid a tribute to Mr Scrymgeour, a man who sticks to his views. (Cheers) We have fought a clean fight, and we have fought a tremendous victory. (Cheers) We have not trimmed; we have put forward our programme honestly and straightforwardly and we have preached no class war. We have demanded justice for the workers . . . I find it impossible to put my feelings into words; my friends we have struck a great blow for honesty and morality in politics, we have struck a great blow—

A Voice—'At Churchill.'

at aggressive and restless imperialism. (Cheers) Once more my friends thank you for the honour you have done me." (Cheers)

As Morel stepped down from the dias he passed quite close to Winston and the two men exchanged neither a look nor a greeting. Sheriff Malcolm turned and asked: "Would you care to speak Mr Churchill?" Winston, his back to the Sheriff, his face drawn into a scowl and pulling at his underlip did not turn his head but just gave it a negative shake. The Sheriff coughed and repeated his question. Slowly Winston's head gave the same self-denying signal.

About to close the proceedings, the Returning Officer hesitated when Gallacher stepped forward boldly saying, "Hey mister, I'm going to say a word or two."

"It was," Gallacher recollected, "as though an electric current had gone through Churchill. He drew himself up, his eyes focused on his surroundings, his body half-turned though his feet never moved. Just for the moment my example almost nerved him to the effort. It was as if he was thinking: 'If that bastard can speak there can be nothing to keep me from doing the same.' But the current wasn't strong enough. He sank back, his scowl darker than before. His chance was gone."

As Gallacher commenced his short speech Winston strode from the room accompanied by Clementine and left the building. They were alone at first save for the presence of a friend who assisted Winston down the steps. Dead silence prevailed as the little party slowly made its way to the exit in Castle Street followed now at a respectful distance by an equally subdued crowd. A touch of pathos was added when a window in one of the houses in the tenements above "The Vault" was pushed up and a woman's voice called out: "Goodbye".

Winston paid no heed.

The spell broke, and to the accompaniment of cheering, hand-waving and booing he and Clementine took their seats in the car while a force of police held back the crowd.

'Neddy' Scrymgeour and his wife at the time of his victory send-off to Westminster in 1922. Dundee's Mr Greatheart, Scrymgeour on his programme of Christian Socialism and the prohibition of alcoholic drink had finally wrested the seat from Winston after six elections.

At the Liberal Club Rooms in Reform Street they were greeted warmly by friends and supporters where Winston told them:

"Fifteen years is a long time for our association to have endured. I would like at this moment to tell you how profoundly I will always feel in the debt of Dundee.

"My heart is devoid of the slightest sense of regret, resentment, or bitterness; on the contrary, looking back over these eventful years in which we have lived and fought through together, I feel I could have done nothing in these stormy times without your loyal and sustained support.

"All my life I will look back with feelings of the deepest regard for Dundee and for those in it who have stood faithfully by me . . .

"The great manifestation of the wish of the people of Dundee as such a figure now records must not be looked upon even by those who do not agree with it as any bad or evil thing. It is of the utmost importance that these great new electorates which have been enfranchised should have the feeling that the institutions of the country belong to them in the fullest sense, and that they can do what they like and choose by constitutional means and Parliamentary processes; that there is no need for violence and no need for silencing the voice of reason by clamour. The British Constitution provides the fullest method and opportunity by which popular wishes, however capricious, however passionate, however precipitate might be given full effect to. I have been all my life a sincere believer in democratic and parliamentary processes by representative government, and in the procedure of the British Constitution. I have often benefited by these processes and although on this particular occasion it may have gone against me, I have not one whit less regard and admiration for them . . .

"In Mr Scrymgeour's victory you see the victory of a man who stood for endurance and also for moral, orderly conceptions of democratic reform and action. You will find Mr Scrymgeour will have a useful part to play in representing Dundee, *where there is such fearful misery, distress and such awful contrast between one class and another. I do not in the least grudge Mr Scrymgeour his victory.* I hope you will forgive me if I do not address you longer, as I am far from well. I carry with me only the kindest thoughts of Dundee, and all my life you will find in me a sincere friend and wellwisher of the city and its inhabitants irrespective of class or party." (Applause)

Winston and Clementine returned to the Royal Hotel and prepared to leave to catch the 9.4 p.m. train to London. On leaving the Hotel and stepping into their car they were greeted by a party of red-gowned University undergraduates from the College a few hundred yards up the streets. Within a few minutes a large crowd had collected and amid noisy acclamations the car drove the short distance to Tay Bridge Station. The students ran after it and Winston and his party had barely arrived on the station platform when the noisy colourful crowd bore down and quickly surrounded him again.

For several minutes he stood in sight of what had now become a great concourse of people assembling on the bridge spanning the railway, and while the students lustily chanted "Churchill Begorrah", boos and cheers from the bridge mingled with the singing. Accompanied closely by his roistering retinue Winston walked up to the far end of the platform to the waiting train smoking a cigar and smiling broadly. As he moved along the platform, strains of "For He's A Jolly Good Fellow" and "Churchill Begorrah" followed, and before entering his private carriage Winston shook hands with the singing students. One Irish boy was so enthusiastic that his spectacles were knocked off to be trampled and broken under the feet of the crowd swaying round the carriage door and heedless of his loss he called again and again: "Cheers for Churchill", "Up Churchill, Up Collins", "Collins believed in you and we believe in you". Clementine too, smiling, shook hands with them all amid further cries of "Cheers for Mrs Churchill."

"Say a few words" they pleaded.

Leaning out of the compartment window Winston responded, his voice unable to conceal his emotion, "I appreciate from the very bottom of my heart you boys coming down to see me off. You are very kind."

Recalling all the happy associations which he had at Dundee during his fourteen years as M.P. he continued, "I have always been a democrat and have always believed in the right of the people to make their own institutions. I bow to that now even though I think that it is misguided. Accept my heartfelt gratitude, you boys, for the kindly thoughts which have caused you to come down here when others are away celebrating other things. (Loud cheers and laughter) Nothing has given me greater plesure than the fact that during the last year I represented Dundee I have been able to do something for Ireland."

This reference to Ireland sent the Irish students into further ecstacies, and renewed cries of "Good Old Churchill" resounded up and down the station.

The engine whistle shrieked the warning of departure. As the train moved off Winston called out "Goodbye boys", and leaning out of the window waved his hat until the lights of the station were swallowed up in the darkness of the night.

Dundee Election.
November. 15th 1922

Clementine? Churchill.

Josphoyl.
E. L. Speers J. J. Grall.

Winston S. Churchill.

A memento of the 1922 election from the autograph book of Miss Flora Scrymgeour
niece of Winston's long-standing opponent, signed by Winston, Clementine, General
Spiers, Lord Wodehouse and other members of the Churchill bandwaggon.

NOT THE END BUT THE END OF THE BEGINNING

Winston thought his world had come to an end. Not since the days of his lonely childhood, or even at the time he had lost the Admiralty, had he felt such a depression of spirit. His defeat in Dundee seemed to be as final a blow to his career as that of Napoleon at Waterloo.

What could he do? He had no base. Slaughtered at the polls by the Conservative landslide, his party, the Lloyd George Liberals, winning only 62 seats, had become insignificant.

His friends were sympathetic but baffled by the shock result. King George V considered the Scottish electorate "incomprehensible" while T. E. Lawrence, revealing common vulgarity behind his romantic image, thought that the people of Dundee "were bloody shits."

Winston himself tried to be more philosophic and replying to a letter of condolence from an ex-government colleague, H. L. Fisher, wrote: "If you saw the kind of lives the Dundee folk have to live, you would admit they have many excuses."

Those who knew politics realised that his career stood in ruins, his many achievements marred by over-enthusiasm and his blunders branding him as a bellicose incompetent. Lloyd George had always admired his many qualities yet at the same time had been apprehensive that his judgment might go haywire in a crisis. Once, at the time of the Ulster conflict in June 1922, fearful of being plunged into a civil war by Winston's belligerent statements, he had exclaimed in irritation, "The man is like a chauffeur, apparently sane, drives with great skill for months, then suddenly takes you over the precipice . . . there is," he added with studied exaggeration, "a strain of lunacy in him."

J. L. Garvin, editor of the Observer newspaper, who had hitherto nearly always been kind to Winston in his editorials, after the election listing his numerous mishaps was forced to conclude that Dundee might turn out to "be the best thing that ever happened to him."

Though he was far too courageous, resilient – and stubborn, ever to give up the fight before the battle was lost or won, he did brood constantly upon his defeat and filled with inner despair started work, as a distraction, on the second volume of his great history of World War I, 'The World Crisis' taking a long four month holiday abroad to recover his health, among other things playing tennis on the lawn of the British Embassy in Rome.

In the following two years, contesting and losing in two by-elections, he at last won his way back to the House of Commons as a Constitutional and Anti-Socialist independent. Dropping this over-elaborate though completely truthful label when the Prime Minister Stanley Baldwin surprisingly brought him into his Cabinet as Chancellor of the Exchequer, he then turned the political wheel full circle and became once more a Tory.

As Chancellor, he introduced many worthwhile reforms but no economist himself, and advised by the then financial experts to return to the Gold Standard, his period of office ushered in the Great Depression. Baldwin's Government, too, was in violent reaction against militant Trade Unionism and fully in sympathy with this policy, believing that workers were being led to Red revolution, Winston earned their undying hatred for his part in breaking the National Strike, though he did actually fight behind the scenes – albeit unsuccessfully – trying to force the grasping coal owners to make concessions to the starving miners.

On the fall of Baldwin's ministry Winston kept his seat in Parliament but was to be out of office for ten years, an old reactionary, alone and politically friendless, writing books, painting pictures, bricklaying in his garden, defending the right of Britain to keep the restless continent of India as a subject jewel of Empire and, fervently admiring Mussolini and that other new man in the rise of Fascism, Hitler. However, almost before anyone else, Winton was quick to realise the danger and urged rearmament on a massive scale. But, afraid of war and too feeble to fight for peace, the divided country, to its dire peril, ignored him almost until it was too late.

Only after war was reluctantly declared against Germany in 1939 was Winston brought back into harness as First Lord of the Admiralty. Then in 1940, with the resignation of Neville Chamberlain, he achieved the pinnacle of his career as Prime Minister of the British nation, united now under his leadership in standing alone against Nazi Germany's brutal subjection of Europe. Winston did not promise easy victories and, as in the 1st War, he made many blunders but his indomitable speeches in the face of a whole string of military disasters made articulate the stubborn resistance of the British people throughout the Empire. In the fourth year of the war the first sign that the flood had been stemmed came with news of the total rout of the Italians and Rommel's Afrika Corps in Egypt.

Speaking of this victory of El Alamein at the Mansion House on 10th November 1942, Winston, recognising at last the light at the end of the tunnel, said: "This is not the end. It is not even the beginning of the end. But it is, perhaps, the end of the beginning."

It was in the following year that the final postscript to his long association with Dundee was made.

He had never visited the city again, nor for that matter did he care much to hear it spoken of. There, though he would never have admitted it, he had experienced his darkest hour.

Once only had he been glimpsed, travelling south from Balmoral after an audience with the King, standing at his carriage window as the train pulled away from a brief halt at Tay Bridge Station. Scowling, he stared, out over the sidings, towards the black mass of spires and mill chimneys starkly silhouetted against the orange glow of the western sky.

Winston may well have thought he was finished with Dundee forever, but Dundee it proved was not finished with him.

In the autumn of 1943, while he drove himself ceaselessly co-ordinating the titanic struggle of Britain and her allies against Germany and Japan, a quaint and singularly irrelevent wrangle was taking place in Dundee City Chambers. There, while millions of men, women and children in occupied Europe and the Far East endured the horrors of total war, the Lord Provost's Committee met in earnest debate. Not, as might have been thought, in mobilising some action however small towards the goal of victory, but to discuss instead the question of whether or not to confer the freedom of the city on Winston "in recognition of his great and distinguished service to the Nation and the Empire."

To the nation at large that such an intention should have been contested at all might have been thought surprising, but although twenty years had passed since he had been Member of Parliament for Dundee, Labour voters there still bore him a deep resentment. The strength then of this undercurrent of feeling against him is testified to this day by the popular belief that his last words for Dundee, the city which had rejected him, were that with his going, *"the grass would grow green through its cobbled streets, and the vigour of its industry shrink and decay."* A myth incidentally which has not a shadow of foundation of truth; yet for all that, remains a stern prophecy which threatens still to be fulfilled.

Labour and Tory were almost evenly divided on the City Council itself but on the Lord Provost's Committee, the Progressives, as the Tories euphemistically called themselves, held the ascendency and naturally expected to get Winston enrolled as an honorary Burgess without any undue fuss from the opposition. After all the Lord Provost's Committee, dealing as it did with such uncontroversial subjects as the bestowal of Certificates and Medals on those of their fellow citizens who had distinguished themselves in some way, was supposed to be above politics. So, in support of the motion,

Councillor Robert Blackwood made much of Winston's fifteen years as representative for the city, concluding, perhaps a trife naively: "The Premier is an orator to whom the whole world listens."

Hearing this, Labour Councillor A. J. Bayne, all his working class prejudices outraged, promptly moved an opposing amendment demanding that no presentations of the freedom of the city should be considered "until the end of the war when our own sons and daughters are back from the various services."

This intervention caused an immediate stir, one of the Progressive Councillors protesting that if Bayne's unfortunate amendment appeared in the newspapers there were bound to be embarrasing consequences. What if Winston himself were to read of the disagreement? Anxiety on this head proved groundless for although reporters were present during the proceedings, not a word was printed either that evening or the following day in the Dundee papers, a discretion not infrequently exercised in such matters by D. C. Thomson. In any case these publications had long since ceased to be Winston's favourite reading material!

Bayne's amendment failed to get a seconder and Lord Provost Garnet Wilson accordingly declared that the proposal to offer the freedom of the city to Winston would be presented at the next full meeting of the Council.

A fortnight later therefore, on the evening of Thursday 7th October, 1943, with all thirty Councillors in attendance and Lord Provost Garnet Wilson again holding the Chair, the Minutes of the Committee of the 21st September were read.

Councillor Blackwood rose and moved approval of the Minutes. "It has been a tradition in Dundee," he said, speaking a trifle nervously realising full well the extent of the opposition against the proposal, "at least from the days of Asquith, that the reigning Prime Minister be invited to accept the honour of being admitted to the freedom of the city. If ever a man in politics deserves that approbation from his fellow countrymen it is Mr Churchill. We will do ourselves and the community great honour by making him a Burgess of the city." And, with splendid banality he concluded: "The Premier's wife is a native of the district, loves the district and he loves the district and his lady has a splendid record of service at this present juncture."

This time, backed by fourteen of his party colleagues, Labour Councillor Bayne, his ire unassuaged by this eulogy, again moved an amendment that no presentation be considered until the end of the war going on to complain that not a word of the proceedings of the previous meeting had been reported by either the evening or the morning newspapers. "That is," he said with pointed sarcasm, "a remarkable coincidence.

"Mr Blackwood," he continued, staring belligerently across the polished rectangle of floor formed between the parallel row of oaken tables at the Progressive Councillors seated on the opposite side, "has based a great deal of his argument on the Premier's representation of the city, but the last word written about Mr Churchill was his defeat in Dundee and that resulted in Mr Winston Churchill taking a long rest from statesmanship.

"This is not a time to waste the Corporation's money on ceremonies of this kind. The best course to adopt is to defer the matter until the end of the war, when the members of the 51st Division, nurses and men of the services will be home, and if it is so desired many of them can be offered the freedom along with the Premier."

Another Labour member, Miss Lilias Clunas, then rose to speak. Predicting that the whole affair would be a waste of money she declared: "There will be a casket, luncheon, people coming to the Caird Hall, and buses running." (Referring to fuel rationing) Then, discounting an alternative suggestion which had been mooted in private, that the freedom be given to Winston during the summer at an outdoor ceremony in Broughty Ferry's Orchar Park where the transport situation, it was hoped, might have been eased if local people were to come to the ceremony on bicycles, Miss Clunas could not resist a barb of humour:

"I don't think Mr Churchill will cycle from London to Dundee to get the freedom of the city."

Even the Progressives smiled.

"The Prime Minister will not travel light. He will probably bring Mrs Churchill, his son and daughters–*they* seem to get unlimited leave from the services–private detectives, secretaries, reporters and all that, and," she paused to add reproachfully, alluding to the ubiquitous slogan on war-time hoardings, "yet we are told 'Is Your Journey Really Necessary?' "

Harry Hird, Labour, put it even more bluntly: "I don't think the Prime Minister is worthy of the freedom of our Ancient Burgh. Mr Churchill has changed his political identifications no less than four times in a career that seems to be indicative of the fact that he cannot make up his mind which party is right or which policy is right. To claim that Mr Churchill as an individual has saved Britain and the British Empire is to castigate the Generals and the soldiers who did the fighting and the workers who made the munitions and gave

Britain today the finest army and well-equipped army. I am not forgetting," he added with inconsequential deference, "the Soviet Union.

"The position is, would it not be better to wait until the last round when the boys come home. The 51st Division and the Dundee lads in the Black Watch might have something to say. They might want Monty to get the freedom in preference to the Prime Minister. I believe that Monty is more popular with the troops than the Prime Minister. I regret that this man has been put forward. If I was asked who won the war I would say I don't know, but Montgomery and the 8th Army have had a lot to do with it."

These attacks put Progressive Councillor Caldwell, Dundee's Treasurer, completely on the defensive and he could only ask weakly: "Why rake up a man's past? Every one of us has surely made blunders. The man who never made a mistake never made anything . . . This will not only put Dundee on the map of Scotland, but the searchlight of the Empire will fall upon a city which is prepared to say to the Prime Minister, 'We know you are doing a good job, and we desire to honour you and honour you well for so doing.' "

This feeble defence encouraged Labour's Archibald Powrie, later Lord Provost, to a flight of unrestrained hyperbole:

"I told many people that the proudest day of my life politically was the day *I* threw Churchill out of Dundee."

Chirping in, his colleague, Peter Gillespie, referred ironically to the fact that the original suggestion to offer the freedom of the city had come from Garnet Wilson, now Lord Provost, the very man who had played such a significant part in unseating Winston in 1922 by introducing Pilkington the Independent Liberal:

"I think the Lord Provost said that too."

This untimely reminder of his past Garnet Wilson could not, under the circumstances, hope to ignore and sitting gravely upright on his high, carved, Provost's chair admitted shamefacedly:

"I have made my mistakes too."

Powrie, unabashed by the interruption, continued: "If we've to believe half we're told about our duties regarding the war effort then we have no business to stop it for a trivial affair by presenting the freedom of the city to anyone. There are some of us who claim that despite what is claimed for the Premier in the conduct of the war, his policy had a good deal to do with bringing it about."

Uncomfortably aware that the whole business had gone sour, Garnet Wilson cut short the debate, called for a vote and found that though the motion had been carried—it had only been by 16 votes to 15, the Council dividing cleanly along party lines.

Unwilling to let the matter rest Harry Hird, in supreme baa taste, and obviously provocative in his tone of voice, then suggested that Winston's invitation should also include the figures of the vote!

"That is out of order," Garnet Wilson retorted with asperity.

A Committee was then appointed to make the necessary arrangements for the freedom ceremony to be held in the Caird Hall on a date suitable to Winston, and those chosen included some of the Labour members who had opposed the amendment. As might have been expected, they ungracefully refused to serve.

A brief ten days later, on Tuesday, 19th October, 1943, a Special Meeting of Dundee Town Council was called. Opening the proceedings Garnet Wilson solemnly reported that he had received a letter of "some interest" from London. This he asked the Depute to read aloud.

Signed by T. H. Beck, Winston's Private Secretary, and addressed to the Town Clerk, it ran:—

> "10 Downing Street,
> October, 15th.
>
> Sir,
>
> I am desired by the Prime Minister to acknowledge your letter of October 8th, inviting him to accept the freedom of the City of Dundee, and to thank you for your courtesy. Mr Churchill regrets he is unable to accept the honour which you have proposed to confer upon him."

A pin might have been heard to drop in the stunned silence.

Neither from Winston's wellwishers or detractors was comment made to his massive rebuff.

Winston had had the last word after all.

End.